The Binding of Nations

The Binding of Nations
From European Union to World Union

Mark Corner

WITHDRAWN

© Mark Corner 2010

All rights reserved. No reproduction, copy or transmission of this publication may be made without written permission.

No portion of this publication may be reproduced, copied or transmitted save with written permission or in accordance with the provisions of the Copyright, Designs and Patents Act 1988, or under the terms of any licence permitting limited copying issued by the Copyright Licensing Agency, Saffron House, 6-10 Kirby Street, London EC1N 8TS.

Any person who does any unauthorized act in relation to this publication may be liable to criminal prosecution and civil claims for damages.

The author has asserted his right to be identified as the author of this work in accordance with the Copyright, Designs and Patents Act 1988.

First published 2010 by
PALGRAVE MACMILLAN

Palgrave Macmillan in the UK is an imprint of Macmillan Publishers Limited, registered in England, company number 785998, of Houndmills, Basingstoke, Hampshire RG21 6XS.

Palgrave Macmillan in the US is a division of St Martin's Press LLC, 175 Fifth Avenue, New York, NY 10010.

Palgrave Macmillan is the global academic imprint of the above companies and has companies and representatives throughout the world.

Palgrave® and Macmillan® are registered trademarks in the United States, the United Kingdom, Europe and other countries

ISBN 978-0-230-23086-6   hardback

This book is printed on paper suitable for recycling and made from fully managed and sustained forest sources. Logging, pulping and manufacturing processes are expected to conform to the environmental regulations of the country of origin.

A catalogue record for this book is available from the British Library.

Library of Congress Cataloging-in-Publication Data
Corner, Mark.
  The binding of nations : from European Union to world union / Mark Corner.
    p. cm.
  Includes bibliographical references and index.
  ISBN 978-0-230-23086-6 (hardback)
   1. International organization. 2. International cooperation. I. Title.
JZ1318.C686 2010
341.2–dc22   2009048416

Printed and bound in Great Britain by
CPI Antony Rowe, Chippenham and Eastbourne

To Jeremy

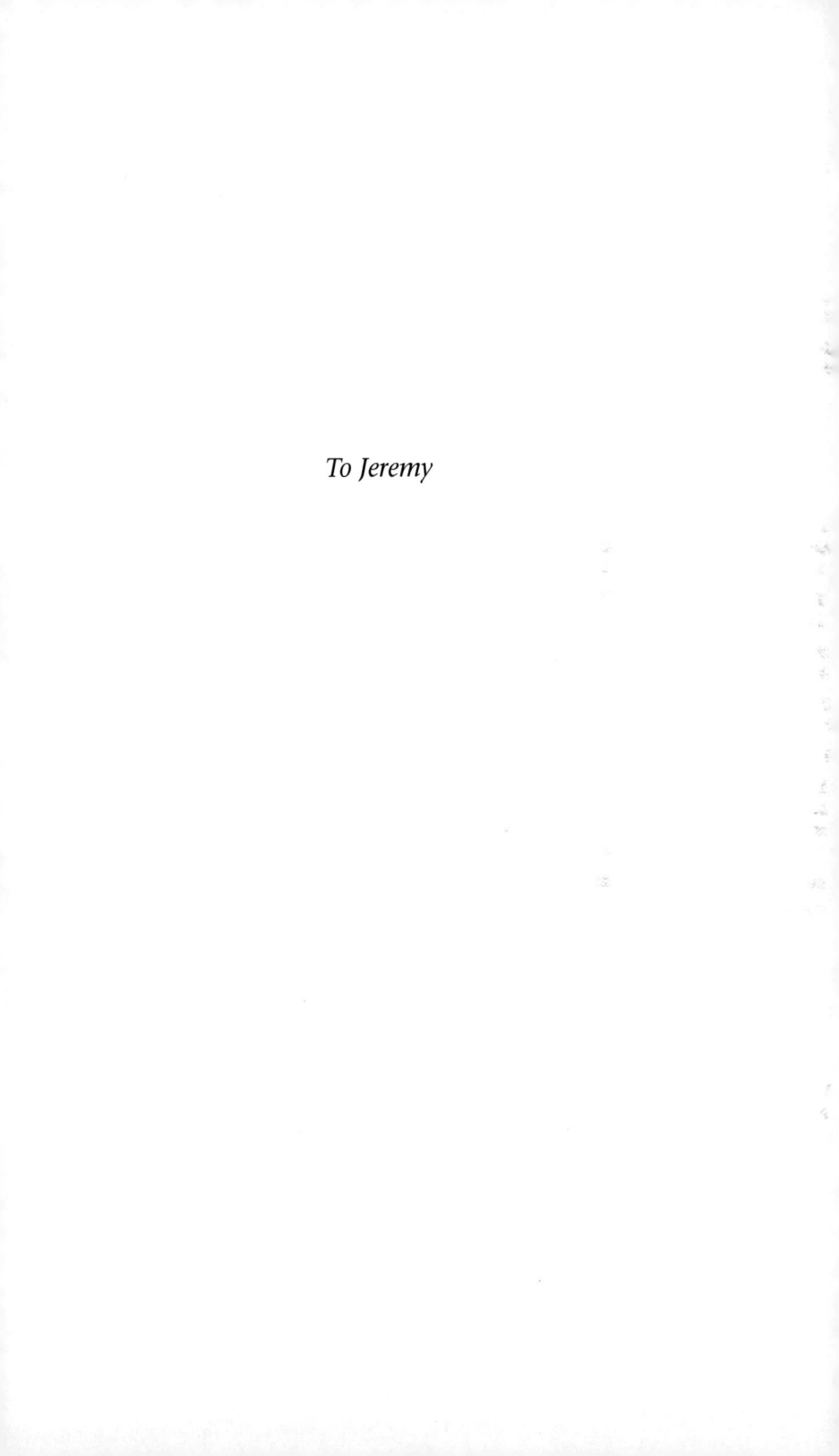

Contents

Preface	x

1	**Introduction**	**1**
	A proposal	1
	Patriotism is not enough	2
	The sharing of sovereignty	4
	The structure of the book	6
	A point about language	10
	Conclusion	13
Part I	**Towards European Union**	**15**
2	**The Rise of the Nation-State**	**17**
	The end of Christendom	17
	The nation becomes the nation-state	21
	The nation-state as a 'civilising force'	27
	Norbert Elias and the sociological perspective	29
	Conclusion	31
3	**From Nationalism to Supranationalism**	**34**
	The idea of 'supranationalism'	34
	'Supranationalism' finds its moment in history	36
	British and French approaches to supranationalism	40
	The British approach	40
	The French approach	42
	British and French approaches to the treaties of Rome	45
	Conclusion	52
4	**Managing Supranationalism**	**54**
	Introduction	54
	European law	54
	'Own resources'	59
	Supporting vulnerable economic sectors	62
	The later development of the European Union	65
	Conclusion	72
Part II	**Options for Global Governance**	**75**
5	**The United Nations**	**77**
	Introduction	77

The Security Council		78
Outside the Security Council – UN 'agencies'		83
The legal framework of the UN		88
Recent developments – The problem of intervention		91
The financial framework of the UN		94
Conclusion		97

6 Other Potential Global Authorities — 101
- Introduction — 101
- Financial and economic bodies — 102
  - The International Monetary Fund — 102
  - The World Bank — 105
  - The World Trade Organisation — 106
  - Organisation for Economic Cooperation and Development — 109
- G7, G8, G20 … G200? — 112
- The Commonwealth and the International Francophone Organisation — 114
- NATO and the OSCE — 116
- New organisations — 122
- Can the problem be bypassed? — 124
- Conclusion — 128

7 Other Regional Unions — 130
- Introduction — 130
- The African Union — 131
- ASEAN — 136
- MERCOSUR and UNASUR — 141
- Conclusion — 146

Part III   A Global Union — 149

8 Current EU Thinking — 151
- Introduction — 151
- 'Effective multilateralism' — 151
- 'Effective inter-regionalism' — 155
- Success and failure: Europe and its 'near abroad' — 157
  - The EU and the Southern Mediterranean — 158
  - The EU and Eastern/South-Eastern Europe — 161
    - The Balkans — 161
    - Europe's 'Far East' — 165
    - Turkey — 169
- Conclusion — 170

9	**A Global Sharing of Sovereignty**	**173**
	Moving beyond other organisations	173
	The McClintock system	176
	Food security	181
	Extending the sharing of sovereignty	187
	The EU as a member of a Global Union	189
	Conclusion	193
10	**The Copernican Revolution**	**195**
	Introduction	195
	A Union to serve the nation-state	199
	The sharing of sovereignty and the domestic analogy	201
	The EU and its malaise	205
	Can the EU manage a Copernican revolution?	207
	European 'presumption'	209
	The need for a trigger	211
	Conclusion	213

Notes	215
References	232
Index	237

Preface

Two experiences were crucial to the formation of this book.

One was that of attending the launch of a book on the relations between the EU and the UN. Academics, politicians and EU officials came together in Brussels to enthuse about a 'natural partnership' between the EU and the UN. I was reminded of the wedding service of Prince Charles and Lady Diana in 1981, when a somewhat over-enthusiastic Archbishop of Canterbury talked about a 'marriage made in heaven'. But the more the clichés flowed, the less convinced I was that these two organisations were really 'natural partners'. There was a smattering of 'Jean Monnet professors' present, but I couldn't help wondering whether some of them might have come away with the sort of misgivings that Jean Monnet himself had, when he perceived that the launch of the Council of Europe in London in 1948 was not the answer to the problem of post-war European cooperation.

The second important experience was that of reading John McClintock's *The Uniting of Nations: An Essay in Global Governance*. This was the first time that I had come across a sustained argument for a limited sharing of sovereignty, not simply as the foundation of a European Union but of a World or Global Union. The author was himself an official of the European Union, in the department concerned with Agriculture and Rural Affairs. It seemed to me that McClintock offered a much more plausible approach to global governance than that which I had witnessed earlier.

This book is an attempt to provide a systematic account of why I believe that 'the McClintock approach' is to be preferred. It could not have been written without the help I received from my university employer, formerly EHSAL and now going under the acronym HUB (Hogeschool-Universiteit Brussel). I want to thank them, among other things, for tolerating my presence under their noses at the computer in the staff room for the best part of a year. I would also like to express my deep gratitude to my wife and to a wide variety of EU officials and friends who encouraged me in this endeavour and did not think me entirely mad.

The book is dedicated to my two-year-old son in the hope that he, at least, may see the world advance beyond what Norbert Elias rightly identified as the present era of 'late barbarism'.

– Mark Corner

1
Introduction

A proposal

In its edition for 5th–11th July 2008, the front cover of *The Economist* pictured a broken Tower of Babel. The tower had various windows which were labelled 'UN', 'OPEC', 'WTO', 'NATO', 'IMF', 'EU' and so on. The headline was 'What a way to run the world', and the message was that the attempt to create a successful form of global governance – or global institutional oversight – had so far been a failure. Running the world, like building your way up to Heaven from below, was beyond the wit of men and women. Just as the original Babel turned the harmony of Eden into a 'babble' of mutually incomprehensible languages, so a world divided into about two hundred different nation-states was in danger of falling apart and failing to deal in a coordinated manner with the major problems of the day. Those problems were global ones, but the institutions which existed to respond at a global level were proving unable or unwilling to do so.

The leading article in *The Economist* ended with the following words:

> Faced with the need to reform international institutions, the rich world – and America in particular – has a choice. Cling to power, and China and India will form their own clubs, focused on their own interests and problems. Cede power and bind them in, and interests and problems are shared.

The summer of 2008 saw the debate about global governance reflected in the issue of *The Economist* achieve an unexpected prominence. Interest in the subject was generated in part by 2008 US Republican presidential candidate John McCain's championing of a so-called

'League of Democracies', drawing upon the ideas in a book by Robert Kagan.[1] Such ideas are not, of course, the exclusive preserve of the political right, as demonstrated by the alternative proposal of a 'Concert of Democracies'.[2] The language is often vague in these contemporary discussions about forms of global governance, but interest in the subject is intense, and is only growing thanks to the acknowledgement of urgent global problems such as climate change and financial collapse.

The aim of this book is to make use of this renewed interest in various forms of global governance. It presents a specific proposal for a type of world organisation that involves the sharing of sovereignty in specific areas. Whether this will be seen as a practical proposal, or another attempt to build another impossible tower up to heaven, is for the reader to decide.

Patriotism is not enough

There is a well-known memorial in Central London to Edith Cavell, the English nurse who was working in Brussels when the First World War broke out. In violation of military law she helped wounded allied soldiers to escape from German-occupied Belgium to the neutral Netherlands. The Germans arrested her and on 12th October 1915 she was executed by firing squad.

Her statue stands in St. Martin's Place near Trafalgar Square in the heart of the English capital. The inscription on the plinth beneath repeats her famous words to the Anglican Chaplain who was allowed to give her Holy Communion on the night before she was killed: *Patriotism Is Not Enough*.

The inscription does not say that patriotism is wrong or undesirable. It knows that love of country is almost as much of a basic instinct as love of family. But it adds the 'not enough'. Patriotism needs management. It needs a context. Otherwise it can lead to outbreaks of nationalist fervour that can produce violence and even mass killing.

It may seem common sense to say that two hundred nation-states require some sort of effective ordering of their relations with one another, just as two hundred people would. Most people agree with the idea of a voluntary limitation of individual rights in order to receive some sort of protection and security in a community – the 'social contract' that attracted many of the readers of Hobbes' *Leviathan*, who agreed with the 'nasty, brutish and short' character of their lives in a 'state of nature'. However, those readers also knew that Hobbes' work was partly a rationalisation of why the strong leadership of Oliver

Cromwell was preferable to that of an executed King who according to royalists had been placed on the throne by 'divine right'. Contemporary readers who think that the anarchic behaviour of nation-states needs to be controlled, just as the anarchic behaviour of individual citizens needs to be, might not be too keen on the idea of a 'global Leviathan' – let alone a global Cromwell.[3]

It is therefore extremely difficult to translate common sense into practical policy where the relationship between nation-states is concerned. A natural patriotism means that people feel genuinely attached to the states they live in and worry about sharing powers with other such states within international organisations. Although they may agree with Edith Cavell that, while desirable, 'patriotism is not enough', the idea of 'world government' or a 'world assembly' often seems hopelessly idealistic and impractical. Moreover, were it to become practical, they might well grow suspicious of it, fearing the emergence of 'world leaders' who rapidly turn into global despots.

The history of political thought reveals a number of attempts to make use of the so-called 'domestic analogy' in order to transfer to the realm of international relations the legal and political arrangements which maintain peace and security within states.[4] Such efforts have also raised the question of international law, and the extent to which it should be regarded as incomplete until it can be as binding upon the behaviour of individual states as national law is binding upon the individual members of a state. Immanuel Kant's famous philosophical sketch *Toward Perpetual Peace* puts the point clearly. Deeply aware of the moral failings of humanity, Kant observes that 'the maliciousness of human nature, although quite concealed by the coercion of government in the state of civil law, can be observed openly in the free relations between the peoples'.[5] The argument is stated as follows:

> It is understandable that a people would say: 'there shall be no war among us, for we desire to form ourselves into a state, that is, to establish a supreme legislative, executive and judicial authority over ourselves that will settle our disputes in a peaceful manner'. But when this state says: 'There shall be no war between myself and other states, even though I acknowledge no superior legislative authority that guarantees me my rights and to which I guarantee them theirs', then it is not at all clear what the confidence in my own rights is based on, if not on a surrogate for the compact of civil society, namely, a free federalism, which reason must necessarily

connect with the concept of international right, if the latter is to mean anything at all.[6]

As ever where this subject is concerned, language proves a minefield, since Kant does not mean by 'federalism' what others mean by 'federalism', namely a single state such as a federal republic (Kant's position in modern terminology would be more that of a believer in 'confederation' than 'federation', *Staatenbund* rather than *Bundestaat,* or in the words used by Kant himself a *Völkerbund* rather than a *Völkerstaat*). Kant makes clear that people do not want 'the positive idea of a world republic at all'[7]; however, they do want what he calls 'the negative surrogate of a lasting and continually expanding federation that prevents war'. They want some form of binding law at a level above that of the nation-state, in other words, but they do not want a single world state – a global Leviathan.

The book sets out to consider how the relation between these two hundred or so states might be ordered or managed without the creation of some kind of global despotism, or by providing a cure that is worse than the disease. It does so by focusing on Europe, partly because Europe was where the disease of unbridled nationalism was seen at its worst a century ago, and partly because Europe is the part of the world which since that time has arguably come closest to producing a cure.

The sharing of sovereignty

The dangers of unbridled nationalism were only too clear to Edith Cavell at the time of the First World War. She was working as a nurse a few miles from the trenches, the thin dividing-line between hundreds of thousands of young men who were daily engaged in killing each other. In other circumstances they might have been drinking or playing football together. For a period of weeks one Christmas they actually did so, in a No Man's Land between the trenches which hardly had room for a makeshift pitch. It was an episode their superiors later hushed up. Then they returned to the slaughter.

At the end of the conflict, with the dead and wounded running into millions, there was much talk of it as a 'war to end all wars'. Yet within twenty years Europe was back at war again, this time with even more killed and the rest of the world dragged into the fighting. Europeans learned from the first half of the twentieth century that they lived in a violent part of the world. A large number of nation-states, closely bunched together geographically but in other respects prone to fall apart, had yet again brought their own continent close to destruction. As they wandered among the ruins in 1945, the inhabitants of those states started planning another attempt to live together harmoniously.[8]

The humbling sense of belonging to a continent that has all too often been given to violence and atrocities is a feeling that some Europeans have lost sight of in the sixty-five years since the Second World War.[9] They have come to equate being 'European' with being civilised, and to suppose that bitter ethnic and national conflicts happen 'somewhere else'. Africans are 'tribal', Europeans respect 'diversity'. The conflict in the former Yugoslavia in the 1990s was another reminder that this was a distortion of the truth. Europe was perfectly capable of bitter 'tribal' conflicts. Indeed Europe in the 1990s was to some extent reverting to kind. The unusual period had been the relatively peaceful half century after the Second World War.

A sober reassessment of so-called 'European values' would have the advantage of enabling Europeans to value the institutions and political forces which have enabled them to remain at peace with one another after two world wars. The less one presumes that Europeans are somehow innately civilised, the more one values the institutions which have helped to prevent them from killing each other and to stop patriotism from spilling over into violent conflict. Whether or not Europeans have become more 'mature' since 1945, Europe has become better organised. It has embraced a system which has been uniquely effective at taming the nation-state without seeking to eliminate it.

The institutional architecture which this book will talk about as a model for managing relations between states is the sharing of sovereignty. The book argues that this has only been attempted by one significant international body, which is now called the European Union. Jean Monnet, the primary architect of what eventually became the EU, deliberately called for the creation of something that was not simply a treaty between states enjoying complete control of their own internal affairs. Monnet was disappointed in this respect both with the OEEC (Organisation for European Economic Cooperation), founded in 1948, and the Council of Europe, founded one year later. The former suffered from the 'intrinsic weakness' of a system that 'went no further than mere cooperation between governments', while the latter was 'going nowhere'.[10] He was backed by the French foreign minister Robert Schuman, who himself returned deeply disappointed from the launch of the Council of Europe in London in August 1949. Schuman believed that the Council would be little more than a talking shop. He recognised, in a very practical way, that states and their leaders could easily sit around tables making promises, declaring various targets and commitments, or even agreeing treaties. Realising those promises, however, required the states to face some real practical loss, including sanctions, if they did not adhere to their commitments. Such mechanisms simply didn't exist where treaties between independent sovereign states were concerned, or under the earlier proposals for some sort of European Union formulated by Aristide Briand and Edouard Herriot during the inter-war period.

Monnet offered sufficient sharing of sovereignty to make sure that individual nations avoid conflict with one another, together with sufficient national autonomy to enable people to remain attached to particular nations. He therefore appeared to avoid the problem which had bedevilled attempts to apply the 'domestic analogy' to international affairs, namely the belief that this could only be done in the context of creating a single world state. Monnet's approach represented what this book calls a 'binding' rather than an 'obliterating' of nations. It did not prevent nations leaving the group or breaking agreements, but the institutional architecture ensured that there was a practical cost to doing so. This is the sense in which patriotism is not enough rather than a bad thing. Monnet's system is one of patriotism and more.

The structure of the book

The book falls into three parts.

Part I explores the context and history of the European Union as a sovereignty-sharing body. Before examining the development of the EU itself, a chapter on nationalism provides important background to later institutional developments. Though nations have been around for centuries – and have been at war for centuries – there is case for saying that nationalism was a product of the nineteenth-century nation-state and contributed to the particularly brutal and destructive wars of the early twentieth century. Chapter 2 establishes the particular European context out of which a genuine alternative to competing, independent sovereign states emerged. That context was one of two extremely destructive world wars provoked by European powers.

Though it was in the continent of Europe after the devastation of two world wars that 'supranationalism' was born, it was by no means universally supported there. Chapter 3 examines the perspective of both France and the UK towards the sharing of sovereignty, and discovers a wide range of opinion in both countries. France may have had Monnet and Schuman to guide the Six towards the European Coal and

Steel Community, but it also had de Gaulle, who favoured a more inter-governmental arrangement but failed to create an EEC (European Economic Community) that matched his desires. There were similar differences in the UK, sometimes within a single individual. Harold Macmillan, British Prime Minister from 1957 to 1963, went through phases of ignoring the EEC, trying to dissolve it in EFTA (The European Free Trade Association) and then finally seeking to join it.

Much of this will be familiar to students of European Studies examining the formation of the European Union. It is therefore important to stress the particular perspective from which this book approaches the material and returns to some well-worn paths. Its intention is to explore the prospects of a global sharing of sovereignty. Therefore if, for instance, it traces the reluctance of Britain or (in a different way) France to opt for a supranational arrangement in Europe, it does so with the question in mind of how the leading world powers of today might be encouraged to join a Global Union.

Following on from discussions of early moves in the formation of what was then the European Economic Community, Chapter 4 looks at the later history of the European Union without simply repeating the many accounts of its development. The chapter explores the tension within the community itself, between areas of shared sovereignty and areas which are 'inter-governmental', together with some later developments which have added to the complexity of the EU. It also explores the development of binding and enforceable law above the level of the nation-state, which was an (perhaps the) essential feature of the new European Economic Community. Community law, enforceable and backed up by sanctions in those areas in which member-states chose to share sovereignty, was the *sine qua non* of the new organisation.

It is true that those areas were primarily economic; but it is also true that to create a single market out of several different national economies was a huge achievement and one that was politically sensitive all along the line. As Menon points out, those who sympathise with Fukuyama's famous comment about 'flabby, prosperous, inward-looking weak-willed states whose grandest project was nothing more heroic than the creation of the Common Market'[11] simply ignore the fact that creating such a market is an intensely difficult political undertaking. If nothing else can make this clear, the efforts to avoid financial and economic collapse in 2009 without a return to protectionist policies will. It is no mean achievement to devise a system whereby nation-states agree to be bound by Community law even when their own national economic self-interest is perceived to be at stake.

Having examined the nature of a system of shared sovereignty as applied within the EU, Part II goes on to examine other actual and potential models for global governance. Chapter 5 looks more closely at the United Nations (UN). Whilst there is some difficulty defining its precise nature as an organisation because of the different powers of the General Assembly and the Security Council, the UN appears to be another example of an inter-governmental organisation trading comprehensive coverage (a 'full house' of member-states) for effective action. There are a range of other organisations at world or regional level, such as the G8, the WTO, the IMF, which figure as windows in *The Economist's* Tower of Babel and need to be covered in a properly comprehensive survey. They are considered in Chapter 6. However, many of these organisations do not aspire to be more than treaty arrangements between independent states, and indeed do not always conclude anything as binding as a treaty.[12]

Having discussed a range of 'candidates' for global governance, Chapter 6 concludes by considering the argument that a more effective ordering of relations between states is unnecessary, because in a modern globalised world the nation-state is itself increasingly redundant. Those who see globalisation as a force which has effectively disempowered the nation-state don't emphasise world assemblies or regional groupings of nations like the EU. Instead they stress a networking strategy across borders including multinational corporations, non-governmental organisations (NGOs) and a range of civic associations. They talk of 'global issues networks'. When Anne-Marie Slaughter wrote *A New World Order*,[13] she focused not on world parliaments or assemblies, but on the 'networked world order' which she saw as already in the making and needing to be reinforced.

Though the 'globalisation context' of any discussion of new political arrangements must always be borne in mind,[14] it is argued in this book that the 'natural demise' of the nation-state can be exaggerated as much by some interpretations of globalisation as by those of supra-nationalism. States have certainly had to come to terms with the implications of new technology, but it must be borne in mind that this is often a double-edged sword. It may threaten to undermine the authority of the nation-state, but it may also be exploited by nation-states as a weapon with which to assert that authority. A globalised environment, in other words, may be precisely the context within which states take decisive action, either in terms of controlling what happens within their own borders or striking out against others outside those borders.

The European Union is not the only regional or sub-regional union in the world, and therefore a chapter needs to be set aside in order to compare it with the other major regional organisations grouping together different nation-states. Chapter 7 devotes its attention mainly to the African Union, ASEAN (The Association of South-East Asian Nations) and MERCOSUR (a grouping of South American nations). Its conclusion is that whilst these bodies sometimes talk of developing institutions similar to or even modelled upon the European Union, their arrangements do not involve to any significant extent the sharing of sovereignty. The chapter agrees with Menon that 'the institutions of the EU enjoy far more formal autonomy from them (the West European states) than is the case in any other international organisation'.[15]

Having examined both the development of the European Union and its claim to being a distinctive organisation through the sharing of sovereignty, the book moves on in Part III to outline in detail its proposal for the sharing of sovereignty at global rather than regional level.

The first chapter of this section is an appraisal of current EU efforts to develop a policy followed by an examination of its relations with its 'near abroad'. The problem is that some states in this area are actual or potential candidates for membership, while others have no prospect of membership (because they are not in Europe). Precisely because membership of a sovereignty-sharing organisation is a considerable incentive, the EU frets about what it can offer those neighbours who must be forever 'at the gates'. Grandiose-sounding phrases are developed making them 'strategic partners', for instance, inside a 'ring of friends', but such phrases are no substitute for the benefits offered by actual or potential membership. The concern is that the EU will either lose influence where it is vulnerable, at its borders, or will be forced to keep enlarging (or at least promising to enlarge) indefinitely.

This book offers a solution to the EU's dilemma of having to choose between boundless expansion and loss of influence. States deemed to be outside Europe would be invited to join a Global Union, one of whose other members would be the EU itself. The proposal draws on the arguments of John McClintock in *The Uniting of Nations: An Essay on Global Governance*[16] and is discussed in detail in Chapter 9. McClintock suggests a mechanism for developing regional unions and a global union *at the same time*. His proposal recognises the very limited degree to which other regional unions have so far agreed to share sovereignty, and at the same time avoids the danger of competitive regional blocs forming ahead of a Global Union. No one wants twenty-first century Great Power Blocs starting to threaten each other in the manner of nineteenth century Great Powers.

McClintock's Global Union would agree to share sovereignty *in certain agreed areas* – just as the EU did when, in the beginning (as the European Coal and Steel Community) it consented to do so in the management of coal and steel resources. The third edition of his book examines how a sovereignty-sharing body might operate in the area which McClintock chooses as a global equivalent to coal and steel, namely food security. In one sense this is a modest choice (though not if you are one of the millions of people directly affected by hikes in the price of food). However, it is best to establish the principle of shared sovereignty in a particular area and then (assuming that is successful, and without relying on any automatic effects of 'functionalist spill-over') encourage it to extend further. Having looked at the area McClintock has chosen in some detail, the final chapter then considers whether or not the EU might be prepared to act as a member of a Global Union.

A point about language

It is impossible to tackle the thorny subject of 'global governance' without encountering difficulties over language. Whereas nation-states have 'governments', those who talk about ways in which states might be prevented from getting out of control prefer to use the word 'governance'.[17] A cynic might define 'governance' as soft government. The point seems to be that whereas relations within states can be managed through an established institutional format providing an overarching political authority, the 'government', there is no such format available for organising the relations between states. They have therefore to be managed differently. However, this approach easily slides off into the sort of definition given by the former editor of *Global Governance*, Thomas G. Weiss and Thakur R., when they said that 'governance' refers to 'collective efforts to identify, understand, or address worldwide problems that go beyond the capacity of individual states to solve'.[18] A definition as broad as that means very little apart from the obvious point that states don't control everything.

People very easily let their language spin out of control in this field, perhaps because everybody is clear that something needs to be done but no one is clear how to do it. There is talk of 'multilevel governance', even though it isn't clear what 'governance' means on any one level, let alone several. There is mention of 'transformed states', without it being clear what they are being transformed into. The world is to be made into a 'cosmocracy', a 'post-national constellation' is to be established, 'soft power' is to replace 'hard power' (France is often mentioned as the champion of 'puissance tranquille', though French power is not always quite so 'tranquille'). There is 'Kantian multipolarity' (on the whole a good thing) and 'strategic multipolarity' (more questionable). Though the books and research papers on the issue don't always manage to come up with a new idea, they usually seem able to come up with a new phrase.

Difficulties over language make clear the need to specify exactly what kind of control or management above the level of the nation-state is being talked about. Clearly global governance means nothing without some 'institutional architecture',[19] and it is vital to demonstrate exactly what such a structure is. This book therefore believes that a close examination of political institutions and how they might be better or differently organised is an essential part of talking about 'global governance'.

It is just as difficult to delve far into the different interpretations of the development of the European Union without returning to the problem of definition. Terms are very often given different meanings from one writer to another, while translation obviously creates further problems. Nevertheless, at the risk of over-simplification there are arguably two main approaches. One approach thinks that the nation-state remained and remains the dominant actor in the history of the European Union. This can be called 'realist' or 'inter-governmental' (and has been more recently modified as 'neo-realist'). The other approach thinks that the nation-state has been subjected (how far is a matter of debate) to severe limitations within the post-war global environment. This approach is sometimes called 'liberal' and sometimes 'functionalist', but these terms are often misleading.

A 'liberal' viewpoint sees the modern world as one in which states are naturally limited in what they can do by the global environment and by the many networks of trans-national and sub-national organisations that proliferate in an age of mass movement and communications. It does not necessarily advocate the sharing of sovereignty which characterises the 'supranationalist' position.

The 'functionalist' viewpoint is the one most clearly identified with supranationalism. It is also associated with a process of spill-over, whereby integration in one area leads naturally (some would say inevitably) to integration in another. At its most extreme this becomes 'bicycle theory' of integration – unless you keep going you fall off. However, the 'momentum of a first achievement', to recall Monnet's own words about the Coal and Steel Community, does not have to apply exclusively to supranational arrangements. Momentum can be created in a number of different directions. Hence a school of thought that stresses the importance of 'interdependence' is said to 'borrow from functionalist logic, although it does not share its teleological conclusions',[20] which when translated means that you can build up momentum going in any direction you like.

The functionalist approach was later criticised for being too confident about nations being attached to a wider concept of the 'common good'. A more realistic approach, pioneered by Ernst Haas in the 1960s, was taken by the 'neo-functionalists' who stressed that integration came about from an 'institutionalised pattern of interest politics'.[21] In other words, integration worked when it had the support of the member-states. This approach, however, does not greatly differ from that of the supposedly opposing school of 'inter-governmentalists', who stress the fact that nation-states remain in the driving seat where integration is concerned. This was a very obvious point to make in the 1960s as the European Economic Community began to deliver (though it clearly wasn't the only cause of it) real progress in living standards throughout the Six. When in 1970 Leon Lindberg and Stuart Scheingold set out to examine the failure of the common transport policy in comparison to the common agricultural policy, they had a very straightforward point to make:

> In short, the Commission did not do as they had done in agriculture, namely shape their policy proposals so as to elicit the active support of the government (or governments) that perceived the greatest possible stake in integration.[22]

What the language more often obscures than reveals is the fact that the two sides to the debate do not necessarily have any real disagreements with one another. When a supposedly 'revisionist' academic like Alan Milward argues that the EU essentially exists to serve the interests of member-states and states that 'nation-states have played the dominant role in its formation and retained control over their new creation',[23] the supporter of 'supranational' (sovereignty-sharing) arrangements might well agree, depending on their understanding of 'retained control'. There is nothing controversial in Milward's notion of a European 'rescue' of the nation-state, so long as one does not interpret 'supranationalism' or sovereignty-sharing as a means towards creating a single world state. The problem comes when the dealings between members of the European Union are seen as nothing more than conventional statecraft between sovereign states, a position which has perhaps been adopted by some of the 'liberal inter-govenmentalists' associated with Andrew Moravcsik.[24] The key point, however, which is perfectly capable of being emphasised by both schools of thought, is that the European Union exists to further the interests of individual nation-states (here the 'inter-governmentalists' are right), but does so by leading them to share sovereignty in particular areas (here the 'supranationalists' are right). This point can be made at almost unimaginable levels of confusion and complexity. Jolyon Howorth, for instance, has coined the term 'inter-governmental supranationalism' for the perfectly valid point that even agencies and groups working in a realm where sovereignty has not been shared can move in the direction of common positions by virtue of the fact that they work together.[25]

Nevertheless, the two 'schools' do not have to be in conflict unless, to make the point once more, the 'supranationalist' starts to envisage an end to the nation-state. Unfortunately, some writers on supranationalism still present it in these terms, thus compounding the unnecessary confusion.[26]

Conclusion

This book is written from a perspective that presumes the nation-state to be a strong and enduring institution that will survive the global changes that are sometimes seen as likely to undermine it. People remain deeply attached to their country, precisely the reason why it seems desirable to devise a system, not for eliminating but for managing the relations between them. When there has been enthusiasm for an element of coercion in the international system it has tended to presume that it can only come from the creation of a world state. Hence the desire for this element of coercion has been perceived as a direct threat to the survival of the nation-state, towards which people remain on the whole fiercely loyal. The result has been the jettisoning of any element of coercion at all, despite the strong convergence of opinion after the First World War, for instance, that it was necessary. A means of binding states into a legal framework which they will not easily break, essential if states are not to continue destroying millions of lives through war, has been thought incompatible with the continued existence of the nation. The experience of the European Union, this book will argue, shows this not to be the case. It is trying to show a way of 'binding' or managing nation-states, not a way of eliminating them and certainly not a way of downgrading them to the status of regions within an overarching 'world state'.

It might seem from the foregoing that this is bound to be a book written from firmly within a 'europhile' stable. However, that is not quite the case. It is the sharing of sovereignty within a system of binding Community law that attracts this author, not the European Union as such. The EU often behaves as if it does not recognise the value of what it has developed. It operates like many other conservative organisations that feel themselves under siege, resisting new ideas and trying all the time to accommodate all its critics rather than to strike out with a definite vision of its own. It can sound grandiloquent, but this does not always mean that it is effective. In December 2008, at the end of the French Presidency, a report on the implementation of the European Security Strategy, *Providing Security in a Changing World*, declared that 'at a global level Europe must lead a renewal of the multilateral order'.[27] Yet it offered no practical suggestions of how to do so.

On 4th January 2007, The Guardian ran an article by Timothy Garton Ash entitled 'The European Union: 27 states in search of a story'. The EU has stumbled upon (this may be fairer as a description than 'discovered') a system to enable nation-states to cohabit on this planet, that of sharing sovereignty. If it is indeed 'in search of a story', then it might find that story, and even the solution to some of its (many) internal problems, through recognising how it can contribute to the development of the rest of the world, which often has a much more favourable view of its mechanisms than it does itself.

As the EU follows up on the ratification of the Treaty of Lisbon, it might take heart from finding that the mechanisms it struggles all the time to adapt and improve represent a discovery that could have global significance. After all, this is a time of global economic and environmental crisis when some radical thinking is necessary. It is also a time when global governance is high on everyone's agenda, even if they disagree about what precisely it means. As *Providing Security in a Changing World* recognised, 'we have a unique moment to renew multilateralism'.

The argument of this book is that the struggle of European nations to live together after centuries of conflict is not just a story for two or three dozen states but for a couple of hundred. The remaining chapters will attempt to outline in detail how this might be so.

Part I
Towards European Union

2
The Rise of the Nation-State

The end of Christendom

In the sixteenth century the different countries of Western Europe gave up their common religious bond and agreed to a policy of non-interference in each other's affairs, at least so far as religious belief (narrowly defined in terms of options, of course) was concerned. This is the principle of *cuius regio, eius religio* (let the ruler determine the religion) enshrined in the Peace of Augsburg of 1555. However it initially applied to only Catholics and Lutherans. Another century was necessary before thirty years of bloody conflict in Central Europe was ended in 1648 by a more general peace, the Treaty of Westphalia, which agreed to extend the *cuius regio, eius religio* principle of Augsburg to Calvinists.

By now hopes of a united Christendom had been dashed forever, a realisation that lay behind Pope Innocent X's outburst against a treaty which was 'null, void, invalid, iniquitous, unjust, damnable, reprobate, inane and devoid of meaning for all time,'[1] language which makes the remarks of a British eurosceptic commenting on the latest treaty emanating from Brussels seem positively benign. But did the Pope have a point, at least in the sense that the nation had finally been released from any participation, however notional, in a higher order which might have checked its activities? In John Osborne's play *Luther* the young monk Martin Luther confronts Cardinal Cajetan, who tries to convince him of the damage his opinions might do:

> You know, a time will come when a man will no longer be able to say, 'I speak Latin and am a Christian' and go his way in peace. There will come frontiers, frontiers of all kinds – between men – And there will be no end to them.[2]

Did Cajetan not anticipate future trends accurately when he warned the reformer of the consequences of his opposition to Rome? Did the frontiers spoken of not solidify into separate national blocs which were to spend much of the next four centuries at war, whilst the common language of Christendom dissolved into a Babel of different tongues? Cajetan has no very effective *theological* answer to Luther's complaints. He can offer no resistance to the barbs of the great reformer when he points out how odd it is that whereas there were only twelve apostles the remains of eighteen of them have apparently been buried in Germany. The corruption of the church and the irrationality of many of its beliefs is bypassed rather than defended. Cajetan's point is *political*. The irrationality and the corruption are part of a system, he claims, which nevertheless keeps the lid on some of the most undesirable human tendencies, including the tribalism that seeks enemies in order to reinforce confidence in its own identity. Catholicism, as its name implies (and as is retained in a notion like having 'catholic tastes') is universal. A universal church can never be 'national church'; it can never be hijacked, in the way that Russian Orthodoxy or Anglicanism have been, in order to represent the supposed 'soul' of a nation. Without it, Cajetan suggests, a patchwork Europe in which hostile nations rub up against one another in a constant state of friction might prove a worse arrangement.

The Thirty Years' War, which devastated much of central Europe during the early seventeenth century, was to bear out this prophecy; a far more horrific thirty years' war at the beginning of the twentieth century was to fulfil it.

After the Treaty of Westphalia in 1648 the genie of the nation was out of the bottle. Westphalia 'set the ground plan of the international order in Central Europe for the next century and more'.[3] From this point onwards it is characteristic to think of a number of independent sovereign nations vying for power, making and breaking treaties and engaging in various wars in pursuit of their own interests, while subject to no higher authority.

The Peace of Westphalia came just three years before the publication of Thomas Hobbes' masterpiece *Leviathan*,[4] a work composed while he was in exile in France. Here he observed the execution of a King across the Channel (Charles 1 was executed in January 1649), an act of regicide which for many people represented an act against God, whose chosen representative by 'Divine Right' was the monarch.

Though Hobbes does not directly challenge the theism of his day, *Leviathan* is an alternative *political* programme to that which sees monarchy as the only system of government, the only one instituted and blessed by God. He rejects the idea that because God supported the patriarchs and kings of ancient Israel, God clearly defined monarchy as the proper system of government for all nations at all times. Hobbes, in questioning the idea that the Bible contained a specific blueprint for a political order, is here one with the great astronomers who were beginning to question the idea that it contained the blueprint for a scientific order (Galileo had been ordered to account for himself before the Holy Office in Rome in 1632).

Instead, Hobbes argues that the state is a social construct, freely entered into by human beings who seek to overcome the endless conflict and vulnerability of living in a 'state of nature'. They therefore agree to create a commonwealth, a 'Leviathan' or artificial man, whose soul is sovereignty, whose reason is law, whose strength is wealth, whose rewards and punishments are its nerves, and whose important officials are its joints. Thus 'Leviathan' is not a monarch by blood or inheritance, a monarch put in place by the Deity just as God supported the patriarchs of old. Leviathan is a product of *human* design, man-made rather than instituted by God, a result of human need and voluntary agreement rather than divine fiat. Essentially, Leviathan was to be Oliver Cromwell rather than Charles I.

In chapter XXX Hobbes declares that 'the people are to be taught not to love any form of government they see in neighbouring nations. Such desire is like a breach of God's Commandment "Thou shalt not have the Gods of other nations"'. A prohibition of idolatry is thus secularised into a prohibition against any form of attachment to other states. 'Thou shalt not have any other Gods but me' is secularised into 'Thou shalt not have any other states'. Monotheism becomes 'monostatism'. Heresy becomes treason. The believer in Christendom becomes the secular equivalent of the polytheist, and attachment to the one true god becomes loyalty to a single state. The secular state, for its part, is not wanting in its demands for exclusive loyalty and devotion from each of its citizens.

Looking back on *Leviathan* some three and a half centuries later, we might well be struck by an obvious limitation in Hobbes' approach. His suggestion of recourse to a social contract in order to resolve conflicts between individuals in a 'state of nature' might well seem highly persuasive. But what if the nations that result from such an arrangement, receiving as they do the unswerving loyalty of their citizens, were *themselves* to become part of an anarchic tribal conflict between hundreds of states, a conflict that precisely mirrors that between individuals in a state of nature? What if all that Hobbes achieves is to transpose the state of nature to another level?

Hobbes tells us that in the 'natural state of mankind' (effectively a state lacking strong central government) we see the 'war of every man against every man'. In what was to become Hobbes' most memorable remark, the life of a human being under such a 'state of nature' was 'solitary, poor, nasty, brutish and short'. But where Hobbes had a strong sense of the destructive anarchy prevailing in a country without strong central government, he does not extend this to the relations between states. Hobbes himself was not enthusiastic about the so-called 'domestic analogy', feeling that whereas a 'state of nature' among individuals was absolutely intolerable, a state of nature among states might be bearable, since individual states could ensure the maintenance of internal peace.[5]

Someone with a much stronger sense of the possibility of destructive anarchy in the relations between states was Hugo Grotius, whose *De jure belli ac pacis* (*On the Law of War and Peace*) was published in 1625, a generation before *Leviathan*. Writing in the middle of the Thirty Years War (and at the same time the so-called Eighty Years' War between Spain and the Netherlands), Grotius had every opportunity to observe the problem of war between nations. The words from the Prologomenon to the *Law of War and Peace* have not lost their power:

> Throughout the Christian world I observed a lack of restraint in relation to war, such as even barbarous races should be ashamed of; I observed that men rush to arms for slight causes, or no cause at all, and that when arms have once been taken up there is no longer any respect for law, divine or human; it is as if, in accordance with a general decree, frenzy had openly been let loose for the committing of all crimes.[6]

Powerful as Grotius' words are, and highly influential on the formation of principles of international law ('a common law among nations', as Grotius called it), his book proposes no 'Leviathan' to enforce it. There is no social contract, no voluntary renunciation of power to a higher body. Whilst it advances a system of principles of natural law which are held to be binding, there are effectively no ropes to bind beyond those of conscience and self-interest.

It is true that Grotius recognised a parallel between municipal or domestic law, based on the consent of citizens to be bound by it, and international law based on consent. But he also recognises a key difference in terms of enforcement. Who is to enforce international law, or implement sanctions against those who break it? Some writers imply that Grotius did envisage such a body. May points out that 'Grotius envisages a 'Great Society of States' that is bound by certain laws 'between all states'.[7] This is true, but it is not clear that this 'Great Society' adds up to any sort of sovereign body which could impose penalties against offenders. The phrase 'great society of states' in Grotius, like similarly impressive titles in the *Law of War and Peace* such as 'common society of the human race', 'natural society of nations' or 'commonwealth of the world' is more a way of referring to (in today's language) the international community as such rather than a potential body with teeth. Grotius is a very important figure for emphasising the place of law at an international as well as national level. No single figure did more to establish the law of nations as a distinct body of doctrine. Moreover, he knew enough of war to recognise its vital significance. He wanted to devise rules for managing the conflicts that he knew all too well and made a significant contribution to a 'law of the seas' and to the 'just war' debate. But he did not explain how a law enforceable by sheriffs, magistrates and (later) policemen at home, with the authority to impose fines and imprison offenders, could be enforced in international relations.

The nation becomes the nation-state

The point made in the previous section can be simply stated. A reader of Hobbes may see the point that thousands of people subject to no restraint are liable to enter into perpetual conflict with one another. But that reader may also feel that hundreds of states subject to no restraint are likely to suffer the same fate. Yet while the individual who surrenders some control over his or her own life in order to receive the security of a rule-bound society is seen as acting wisely, the idea that states must surrender some of their sovereignty in order to receive the security of an international order and thereby gain freedom is usually seen as undesirable or (more often) hopelessly idealistic. It remains an idea ahead of its time although, as later chapters seek to point out, time is running out.

The three centuries after Hobbes produced few attempts to control the 'international anarchy' which at national level had been at least partially restrained. Occasionally, when one country or other threatened to dominate the others, there were calls for some kind of control over the perpetual rivalry and conflict which the Westphalian 'system' (or lack of system) had produced. The Napoleonic wars gave rise to the short-lived 'Congress' system in 1815, but barely a decade had gone by before the British Foreign Secretary George Canning was falling out with the other powers over intervention to suppress the revolution in Spain and made his famous remark: 'things are getting back into a wholesome state. Every nation for itself, and God for us all'.[8] Effectively Britain scuppered the system. In Thomson's words, 'First among the important victorious Powers, she broke with the system and thereby made it crumble'.[9] Arguably, it would have collapsed in any case. At all events, the Congress system proved ineffective and the nineteenth century progressed with increasingly dangerous rivalries between European nations threatening an even greater conflagration.

Compared with its successor, the nineteenth century was certainly a time of peace in Europe (though not outside Europe, where imperial ambitions and rivalries led to a series of wars and occasional massacres). The only 'serious' conflict between states was the Crimean War of 1854–6, and that was restricted to a relatively small theatre of war in South-East Europe. But at the same time the 'century of peace' was also a century of preparation for war, culminating in a massive arms race and an explosion of colonial expansion. As the title of one of the most well-known works on the years leading up to the First World War, *The Struggle for Mastery in Europe*,[10] makes clear, lack of general conflict or all-out war between European states proceeded alongside a state of perpetual friction and tension which expressed itself in number of ways, of which the most notable was the scramble for Africa at the end of the century as each state sought to outflank the others. It was a struggle which in the light of Darwin was frequently compared to that between species, an analogy which reinforced the idea that such conflicts were 'natural' and therefore inevitable. Though the Hague Peace Conferences of 1899 and 1907, with their many conventions and declarations (including the Geneva Convention of 1906 which sought to set out clearly the laws of war), continued to attempt to regulate the relations between states, they proved inadequate at preventing the slide into war (a third Hague Conference had been planned for 1915, by which time world war had intervened).

What made this vacuum in the enforcement of international law even more problematic was a development inside the nations themselves rather than in the relations between them. This development was the significant change that took place in the nineteenth century in the organisation of the nation into the 'nation-state'. It was a process that made the failure to control relations between nations even more serious, and threatened to produce precisely the sort of war which was to cost tens of millions of lives in the next century.

It is easy to read Shakespeare's words about 'this precious stone set in a silver sea' and imagine a sixteenth-century Englishman or woman watching a performance of *Richard II* and being as stirred by patriotic feeling as their counterparts today. But such stirrings of emotion would not affect the fact that people's lives were far less dominated by the particular nation they belonged to in Shakespeare's time than they were to become later. Whatever they felt if and when they went to *The Globe*, for the vast majority of English people the nation could never be the largest stage on which the activities determining their lives were played out. Their lives were dominated by their villages and by the local authority figures (priest, squire, magistrate) of their area. They had no national police force, no national service, no national education and curriculum, (in most cases they had no formal education at all) no national postal system or newspapers and they took no part in national elections. There were nations before the nineteenth century, but for most of the people within them, (even old-established ones like England and France) they were at the back of their lives rather than at the forefront.[11]

Because in the twenty-first century the particular nation people belong to is almost universally a major determinant of their lives, we easily forget the fact that before 1800 this was not the case. Because nations have been in existence for centuries, we think that they have played a major part in people's lives for centuries.

Hobsbawm describes this as a process whereby a 'nation' becomes a 'nation-state'. People talk naturally of 'the state' as something that affects their lives, while reserving for the 'nation' the more emotional attachment that has clearly been around for centuries. 'National feeling' could be stirred up easily enough by John of Gaunt, in Shakespeare's day as in our own. But national feeling has a very different effect in a nation which has been organised into a nation-state, one which has started to manage people's lives through 'state service', including in many cases military service, 'state administration' and 'state education', while providing them with various 'state benefits'.

Where Europe is concerned, the key changes took place in the nineteenth century.[12] Nationalism was something which initially appealed to the middle classes, to teachers, clergy, administrators, and some better-off artisans, rather than to the masses. This wasn't because the masses were all devotees of international socialism or some other trans-national ideal. It was because they weren't yet sufficiently drawn into the nation to feel nationalistic. In modern jargon, they didn't have enough of a stake in it.

The liberal state of the nineteenth century felt itself in a bind as it embarked upon this process of 'democratisation'. If it refused the vote to increasing numbers of articulate people, it would surely provoke revolution; yet if it granted these people voting rights, it was surely doomed to feed its own destruction by making it inevitable that its leaders would be voted out of office.

It didn't happen that way. As the franchise was extended it didn't bring revolutionary governments to power. At least part of the reason for this was the ability of governments, conceding that they were forced to absorb the masses into the developing structure of the nation-state, to turn this process into a means of encouraging nationalism. Once people felt able to identify with their country they could be drawn into an uncritical support of its aims and interests (and possibly be made to serve in its army through conscription). To the governments themselves nationalism was not a measure to keep people from communism, of which very few of them had much idea, but rather a way of managing their entry into mass politics and the life of the nation.

The masses made their entry in other ways too. Though secondary and tertiary education remained largely the preserve of an élite before 1900, primary education did not. By the end of the century it was universal (with some exemptions). This provided another opportunity to manage the growing significance of the masses in the state. Mass education, in an age before the existence of 'mass media' such as newspapers, (mass circulation newspapers were just beginning at the end of the century) radio and television, was the best means of instilling a sense of belonging to a state. Twenty-first century talk of a 'national curriculum' and 'citizenship' classes is simply the further refinement of a process which began in the nineteenth century with the first attempts at a national education system.

Education also raised the question of language, since this universal education would be in the single 'national language' of the country which people belonged to. A single language would also appear in the administration of the country, another area in which the masses were increasingly becoming involved as they started to encounter 'state officials' – the first policemen in their towns, the first postmen at their doors delivering forms concerning licences or tax payments. This was something new. At the time of the formation of Italy only 2% of the population actually spoke Italian and D'Azeglio reputedly remarked that having created Italy (following Italian Unification in 1860) it would now be necessary to make Italians. Eugen Weber made a similar remark about the need to turn peasants into Frenchmen.[13] When people's lives were largely determined by their local communities and business was conducted through oral transactions, there was little need for an 'official' language spoken in the same way throughout the country. Different dialects, in some cases as different from one another as separate languages, could happily coexist when there was no need to talk to people from other parts of the country or to exchange correspondence with them. But once the trappings of a modern state began to emerge, with mass involvement in national education and a national bureaucracy, things had to change. That 98% who did not speak Italian could no longer be tolerated in a 'modern Italy'.

It was in the nineteenth century that many of the 'trappings' of the nation-state as we know them today emerged. *The Invention of Tradition* examines many of the traditions which we often think of as centuries-old but which in fact go back only as far as the late nineteenth century when the 'socialisation process' was at its height. Public ceremonies flourished as (to many people's surprise) they had never flourished before. The first Bastille Day celebration in France was in 1880, nearly a century after the fall of the Bastille.[14] It was from the 1880s onwards that American schools began their daily ritual of honouring the flag.[15]

In Britain the institution of monarchy had seemed unlikely to survive the nineteenth century. Monarchs had lost any real power to determine, or at least interfere in, affairs of state, and this was bound to raise questions about the point of having them. Republican societies flourished in Britain in the early nineteenth century as they would find difficulty in doing today. After the death of George IV in 1830 *The Times* declared (on 15th July) that 'there never was an individual less regretted by his fellow-creatures than this deceased King', and caricatures of his obesity abounded. By the time Victoria came to the throne in 1837 many people seriously believed that she would be the last in the line.

Yet during the long reign of Victoria the monarchy was reinvigorated through the exchange of real power for symbolic power. The monarch became an indispensable emblem, like the flag or the national anthem, as head of the 'national' (or 'imperial') family. Through Disraeli's conjuring the 'Widow of Windsor' re-emerged as Empress of India and began to relish the role she had once abandoned, embarking on a Golden Jubilee in 1887 which was such a success that it had to be repeated in a 'Diamond' Jubilee ten years later. The Diamond Jubilee was celebrated as something akin to a Roman 'triumph', in which the 'barbarians' of the British Empire came to pay homage to their Queen in the 'grey eternal city' of London. Few listened to the aged Gladstone when he talked about 'false phantoms of glory' and recommended that Victoria abdicate.

To repeat, it is not suggested that these moves represented a conscious attempt to make the masses nationalists. It was more a measure taken to ensure that they could be successfully assimilated. But in the process it made the nation-state a more powerful force than the nation had ever been. In an age of mass education and, increasingly, mass communications, national passions could be encouraged in a way that was impossible a century earlier:

> In Spanish **patria** did not become coterminous with Spain until late in the nineteenth century. In the eighteenth it still meant simply the place or town where a person was born. **Paese** in Italian ('country') and **pueblo** in Spanish ('people') can and do still mean a village as well as the national territory and its inhabitants. Nationalism and the state took over the associations of kin, neighbours and populations of a size and scale which turned them into metaphors.[16]

The real communities to which people had been used – the village, parish or *barrio* – ceased to be, as they had once been, not just the focus of people's lives but the whole context of those lives, lives which very rarely involved a journey even to the next village or town (something which startles many of the characters in Thomas Hardy novels, for instance). Now something was reaching down to weld them into a larger entity – a state, a government, 'the authorities'. Sometimes this is expressed simply in terms of a 'nationalist' appeal against 'class' loyalties. That would be misleading. Even in relatively industrialised Britain there was very little 'class consciousness'. But there was a growing involvement in something larger than the local community, an induction into the affairs of state with both rights and responsibilities, and an encouragement to adopt nationalistic principles as the means by which a nervous élite could manage the transition to democracy. The point cannot be made in stronger terms than that, and yet even this shows what a potent brew was developing, a national consciousness that could permeate all levels of society and draw people together in pursuit of a common cause, such as that of imperialism (a word that emerged in the late nineteenth century, initially without the negative connotations it has now among most but by no means all historians).

This nineteenth century transformation was to make a difference to the point about 'individuals' and 'states' made earlier. There it was suggested that while Hobbes had a sense of the need for a state to manage relations between individuals and prevent the conflict that arose in a 'state of nature', he didn't see any reason for an international authority to govern the relation between 'Leviathans'. Part of the reason for this was that the 'Leviathans' had hardly developed into the closely-knit organisations that made up the modern nation-state. As mentioned when discussing *Leviathan*, Hobbes refers to the nation as an 'artificial man', with law as the mind or reason, rewards and punishments as the nerves, officials as the joints and so on. But in the seventeenth century these joints were hardly knit together in the way that they were by 1900. Individual monarchs squabbled and went to war, using professional armies and mercenaries to gain more territory or repel an attack. In the process they certainly caused many deaths, not least in the indirect consequences of armies crossing a continent and 'living off the land', effectively spreading disease and famine wherever they went. But they could not produce the consequences that the nation-state could, when huge populations could be mobilised for war and indeed willingly threw themselves into a conflict (Britain had no conscription before 1916) which the generals confidently told them would be over by Christmas. Few people anticipated the daily ritual of slaughter which was to follow the outbreak of war in 1914 and continue for four long years.

The nation-state as a 'civilising force'

Coupled with the rise of the nation-state in the nineteenth century was a confidence in its role as a vehicle of improvement. The forming of nation-states out of nations was seen as part of the evolution of human civilisation by nineteenth-century liberalism, often in a very naïve manner. From the perspective of this tradition:

> ...the development of nations was unquestionably a phase in human evolution or progress from the small group to the larger, from family to tribe to region, to nation and, in the last instance, to the unified world of the future in which, to quote the superficial and therefore typical G. Lowes Dickinson, 'the barriers of nationality which belong to the infancy of the race will melt and dissolve in the sunshine of science and art'.[17]

The First World War brought an end to such naïve optimism. It was recognised that an element of coercion had to be introduced into the international system. In particular, international law should become more analogous to municipal law by accommodating the idea of coercion. These ideas were taken up by groups like the League to Enforce Peace, some of whose members had unrealistic hopes of some kind of international military force, but the idea of a world court with binding powers was a widely-held opinion during the war years. Former President Taft wrote an article suggesting that the United States Supreme Court could serve as a model of a World Court.

However, despite such enthusiasm for an element of coercion in the international system, the League of Nations which emerged from the First World War had no compulsory jurisdiction by the Permanent Court of International Justice. There was a particular reason for this. Those who were most keen to advance the 'domestic analogy' (arguing that states should be bound by the sort of legally binding arrangements that apply to individuals within a state) felt hamstrung in their efforts because they believed this could only be done by creating a world state. They knew that an arrangement like that, even in the wake of a ruinous world conflict, was simply not acceptable to most people.[18]

Within 20 years Europe was back at war with even more killed and the rest of the world drawn into the fighting. The outcome of world war this time (closely examined in Chapter 5) was the United Nations, and this time the 'domestic analogy', unlike in the aftermath of the First World War, was rarely to be heard. However, it was to re-emerge during the Cold War in the context of calls for reform of the UN, for instance in Clark and Sohn's *World Peace through World Law*. Institutions, the authors stated in the preface to their work, need to be established 'corresponding in the world field to those which maintain law and order within local communities and nations'.[19] Other writers, such as Walter Schiffer and Frederick Schuman, both writing in 1954 after the Cold War had firmly settled in, were convinced that the necessary changes could not be realised within the parameters of the UN.[20] However, these writers make precisely the same presumption as did earlier writers who overtly or covertly wished to advance the 'domestic analogy', namely that it could only be properly realised within the context of a single world state. This is the clear conclusion of Schuman's work.[21]

But was there an alternative to a single superstate as the means of realising the 'domestic analogy'? Was there another way of creating a system of binding and enforceable law above the level of the nation-state, something that might offer a genuine chance of international peace and security? Arguably one possible alternative was being developed on the European mainland. It will be closely examined in the course of the next two chapters.

Norbert Elias and the sociological perspective

The idea of a 'civilising' process within the developing nation-states of the nineteenth century has been famously explored by the sociologist Norbert Elias.[22] In *The Civilising Process* Elias noted a growing revulsion in modern Western European societies against public acts of cruelty such as executions (which with hanging, drawing and quartering could amount to public displays of people being tortured to death). There was evidence of increasing concern about violence against both children and animals (infanticide became illegal, together with the placing of children in factories or brothels). The violent aspects of sport, both where humans and animals were concerned, showed signs of decreasing. In Britain, for instance, bull and bear-baiting disappeared and cock-fighting was outlawed, though fox hunting remained. Forms of boxing and wrestling became less violent too, with new rules introduced to control them. These developments were seen as evidence of changing sensibilities towards violence.

The changing sensibilities, however, required a particular institutional context. For Elias a stable central organisation and firmer monopolisation of physical force is inseparable from acquiring civilisation. Like Hobbes, he thinks in terms of overcoming the anarchy of a state of nature. Like Freud, acquiring the 'apparatus of psychological self-restraint' is seen as essential to becoming civilised:

> The monopolisation of physical violence, the concentration of arms and armed troops under one authority, makes the use of violence more or less calculable, and forces unarmed people in the pacified social spaces to restrain their own violence through foresight or reflection; in other words it imposes on people a greater or lesser degree of self-control.[23]

In a 'warrior society' people had less control of their passions. Later, however, people learned to control these passions and even to sublimate them (it is always wrong to see sublimation as a negative thing in Freudian thinking). The battlefield, as Elias puts it, is 'moved within':

> The more peaceful constraints exerted on people by their relations to others are mirrored within; an individualised pattern of

near-automatic habits is established and consolidated, a specific "super-ego"...[24]

However, a state might do the precise opposite of what Elias envisages. Rather than be a part of the 'civilising process', it might encourage or even insist upon the use of violence by these unarmed people in their 'pacified social spaces'. It might, as much of Nazi ideology was doing at the very time when *The Civilising Process* was first published in 1936, entrench the violent 'warrior society' it was meant to supersede. Rather than making courtiers of warriors, it might glorify the warrior spirit and compel the rest of society into vulnerable subordination to it. It might compel people to fight and die in large numbers. Rather than restrain violent feelings and actions, it might encourage violence and brutality and prevent legal measures against those who acted in such a manner. Elias tells us that a strong central authority will reduce the fear and terror one person must have for another: yet the totalitarian systems of the twentieth century illustrate very well just how such fear and terror could be enhanced and even institutionalised by the state. Elias emphasises that the nation-state represents an essential stage in the development of the 'civilising process', but takes too little account of the fact that it might be the agent of a new barbarism. He insists that 'as long as the instruments of physical violence – weapons and troops – is not very highly centralised, social tensions lead again and again to warlike actions'.[25] But strong central governments with complete control over those instruments may deliberately use them to provoke wars or repress their own populations.

Towards the end of his long life (born in 1897, he lived through both world wars and the cold war that followed them, dying in 1990) Elias became more aware of this question in his writing. He began to consider how the 'civilising process' might be extended into the international arena. He hints at this in the concluding words to *The Civilising Process* itself, where he talks about seeing:

> The first outlines of a worldwide system of tensions composed by alliances and supra-state units of various kinds, the prelude of struggles embracing the whole globe, which are the precondition for a worldwide monopoly of physical force, for a central political institution and thus for the pacification of the earth.[26]

Later he returned to this theme. 'We may be entering an era', he wrote, 'in which it will no longer be individual states but unions of states which will serve mankind as the dominant social unit'.[27] Note that whereas the comment at the end of *The Civilising Process* might be seen as implying a single 'superstate', in the later work he talked of 'unions of states', not of a single world state.

The fact that we had not learned how to curb wars convinced Elias that 'modern times' represented less a late stage of human development than the era of 'late barbarianism'. Human beings had made much progress in eliminating violence, but until they found a way of sweeping away cruel and violent behaviour in the one area where it was still permitted (and even encouraged and glorified) they were still living in a 'pre-civilised' world order, however enlightened their domestic arrangements were.

Conclusion

Since nations have been around for hundreds of years, it is easy to conclude that forming oneself into a national group is somehow part of the human condition. The nation acquires some of the natural authenticity accorded to the family. Patriotism becomes as natural as the love of mother for daughter or daughter for mother (hence we talk of a 'motherland' or 'fatherland'). Our country is our 'national home' or 'homeland', and other countries are 'neighbours'.

If this is so, then it is important to emphasise where the analogy breaks down. In countries subject to the rule of law families in a street are bound to abide by various rules or face penalties. If they behave badly even inside their own homes (for instance if children are abused), the families can be split up and their children taken away. If necessary the police can break into their homes and arrest their occupants. There is no such sanction for a breakdown that occurs within a nation (although the UN has recently talked about something called a 'responsibility to protect', sometimes written as R2P, which is discussed in Chapter 5). The case for regulating national behaviour is hardly weakened by pointing out how natural it is to love one's country, since even the love of mother or father for child is not seen as a reason for complete non-interference in the affairs of individual families.

But applying such restraint to nations has always been considered much too difficult to try, as the seventeenth century thinkers who originated much of what we now call 'international law' realised. 200 Leviathans (of varying size and power, of course) are hard to manage. Moreover, as the nation evolved into the nation-state during the nineteenth century, it became a much more powerful and integrated unit which could unleash (quite apart from technological developments) terrible atrocities against others.

The progress of 'civilisation' in the nineteenth and twentieth centuries is therefore easier to make sense of in terms of behaviour *within* states rather than relations *between* them. What use were the improvements noted by sociologists like Elias when states still went to war with one another and when technology took their violent behaviour, when they were at war, to new limits of destructiveness? The children who could no longer be exposed on hillsides or sold into slavery faced and still face cluster or phosphorus bombs which would tear off their limbs or skin instead, while the people who were no longer being executed in large numbers at home could and can be slaughtered in their thousands by their 'enemies' abroad.

In 1648 the Treaty of Westphalia brought to an end the Thirty Years' War in Europe by enshrining the principle of non-interference in the internal religious life of states, at least insofar as they chose from an acceptable list of Christian options (it added Calvinism to the Catholic and Lutheran options permitted by the Peace of Augsburg a century earlier). In modern writing there is a tendency to use the term 'Westphalian' of any approach which rules out interference in any domestic affairs of another country, thus extending what was originally applied to religious interference to all kinds of interference. Hence Robert Cooper talks of 'the old Westphalian concept of state sovereignty in which others do not interfere'.[28] No one tells you what to do within your own borders, and when it comes to other nations you do what you can to get the better of them in a constant diplomatic and, where necessary, military game.

This chapter suggests that such non-interference should no longer be acceptable in a twenty-first century environment which can recognise the horrific consequences of war in the last century (not to mention the first decade of this one). As nations coalesced into nation-states in the nineteenth century, the potential for organised aggression against other states grew. The 'nasty, brutish and short' lives, from which people managed to move away in their domestic affairs, failed to become any less nasty, brutish and short where external relations were concerned. Yet the sort of 'social contract' which had brought people out of a state of nature and into states could not, it seemed, be applied to the state of nature that existed between states themselves. Instead the state was viewed in a positive light as the bringer of civilisation within nations (through law and a monopoly over armaments), ignoring its capacity to unleash all the horrors of war against citizens of other states and encourage (or brainwash) its own citizens into helping it to do so. Interference in the domestic lives of families was accepted, despite the basic ties of blood, whilst it was ruled out of court in the domestic lives of nations.

This curious split within western civilisation has been studied by writers like Suganami who have explored the 'domestic analogy' in detail. Suganami shows that whenever – for instance in the aftermath of World War One – there was a general consensus that some form of coercion at international level was needed, the presumption that it would entail the creation of some form of all-powerful superstate stopped progress towards some kind of binding international arrangements in its tracks. Before long the world had returned to the unsatisfactory system of treaties (and entreaties).

There is, however, a form of international arrangement which introduces a system of binding law without the creation of a 'world state'. This book will argue that such an arrangement involves the limited sharing of sovereignty, and that it has so far been realised in only one institution with worldwide significance, the European Union. In this sense Jean Monnet's biographer François Duchêne was justified in seeing the EU as a new stage in political civilisation, which 'stressed the virtues of rules and institutions in unifying peoples and not as new forms of the old game of coalitions of states'.[29] That a relatively successful sovereignty-sharing system has emerged in Europe is not necessarily a great tribute to Europeans; they adopted it in circumstances of unparalleled destruction and under considerable outside pressure. Nevertheless, the characteristics of the post war arrangements into which much of Europe was pushed (and partially embraced) proved hugely significant. They make it possible to claim that '… it is meaningful to regard the EU as evidence of a civilising process "beyond the nation-state"'.[30]

Before examining such a claim about the value of a sovereignty-sharing organisation at global level, it will be necessary to examine more closely the emergence of such a body in Europe itself in the aftermath of World War Two. The next chapter will turn to that development.

3
From Nationalism to Supranationalism

The idea of 'supranationalism'

Sometimes a new idea is thought out in advance and then applied to situations as they arise. At other times a situation arises, appears intractable and a new idea is squeezed out of it through pressure of circumstances.

In the latter case the idea begins to take hold not so much because people know it to be good but because there is no alternative. It has a *faute de mieux* validity, for which it wins a grudging acceptance. But even in conditions like that, an idea can be strong. It can be as strong as Churchill recognised democracy to be, when he described it as the worst form of government excepting all the others.

The idea struggles to survive. Its opponents try to smother it even as its supporters try to spread it. In the end it appears to have taken root in some places even as it has been stamped out in others. But still, in however attenuated a form, it lives.

Such an idea was Jean Monnet's proposal of 'supranationalism'. The main reason why it took centre stage in 1950 was not because people accepted that a new way of ordering relations between states was necessary. Rather, it stole into prominence as a way out of an awkward situation in Franco-German relations. It had its advocates and its critics in even measure – and whether it prevailed was often a matter of political alliances and convenience. The French foreign minister Robert Schuman could trail its merits in a grandiose way when making speeches. He could talk about putting an end to war and guaranteeing eternal peace. He could say that this was the 'supreme attempt to save our continent and preserve the world from suicide', words he used in St. James's Palace in London in May 1949. But he knew perfectly well that he could begin to succeed only by showing that 'supranationalism' was the answer to the immediate problems of France.

What is this idea of 'supranationalism'? It is essentially a sharing of sovereignty between nations, as opposed to a treaty or agreement between nations.

It is limited to particular areas – initially, in the case of Europe, it was limited to coal and steel. In practical terms, it means that the nations agree to vest authority in a 'High Authority' of some kind – a body that is above the level of the nation-state (hence the appropriateness of the term 'supranationalism'). This authority then takes the decisions in those areas where the pooling of sovereignty has been agreed upon.

Unlike a treaty, an agreement which does not carry the force of law, the sharing of sovereignty is legally binding and legally enforceable. The decisions of the High Authority are binding – legally binding – upon the nations concerned. Thus when the high authority set up in 1951 decided upon a particular arrangement concerning coal and steel, the French, German, Italian and Benelux countries (Belgium, Netherlands, Luxembourg) were each individually obliged to implement it. The law of the Six overrode national law in these particular areas.[1] The development of 'Community' or 'EU' law will be examined in more detail in the next chapter.

The arrangements put into place through the formation of the European Coal and Steel Community required not only a supranational legal authority but also a range of other institutions, in order to provide the checks and balances essential to any sovereignty-sharing arrangement between nation-states. These institutions would come to be known by some as the 'Brussels bureaucracy', though not all of them are located in Brussels. First there would be the High Authority itself (forerunner of the modern-day European Commission). Then, as discussed in the previous section, there would be a Court of Justice to ensure that the legally binding decisions of the High Authority were respected. Further, once the High Authority was created it was inevitable that there would be questions about monitoring and overseeing its work. Some would argue that this monitoring and oversight should be the responsibility of a powerful inter-governmental body, like a Council of Ministers, representing the individual member-states. Others would favour some kind of assembly or parliament, which might be made up of delegates from national parliaments or might be popularly elected. Both these bodies, in one form or another, were to emerge over time. They would not only monitor the activity of the High Authority but also one another, in a complicated system of mutual appraisal. Yet it is not unreasonable to say that all these developments, complicated though they may seem, were implicit in the initial decision to share sovereignty.[2]

The 'institutional architecture' which emerged in the European Union has enabled it to distinguish itself from two other forms of international cooperation. The first of these, sometimes called 'intergovernmentalism', is a treaty or agreement between states, or a forum for discussion between individual sovereign states like the Council of Europe or the General Assembly of the United Nations. The second is one in which the member nations are parts (perhaps regions) of a single nation-state, sometimes called a 'superstate'.

A supranationalist mechanism allows sufficient sharing of sovereignty to make sure that individual nations avoid conflict with one another, together with sufficient national autonomy to enable people to remain attached to particular nations. It represents a 'binding' rather than an 'obliterating' of nations. It does not prevent nations leaving the group or breaking agreements, but the institutional architecture ensures that there is a practical cost of doing so. This is the appropriate way of saying that patriotism is not enough rather than saying that it is a bad thing. It is patriotism and more. It may be a 'messy' arrangement, and it is frequently accused of being bureaucratic, although 20,000 'fonctionnaires' is hardly excessive for a population of close to half a billion people. But it arguably works more effectively than some of the 'tidier' alternatives.[3]

'Supranationalism' finds its moment in history

For all his talk about putting an end to war and guaranteeing eternal peace, French foreign minister Robert Schuman knew that 'supranationalism' could only begin to succeed if it appeared to be a practical answer to the immediate problems of France.

He had already seen one post-war attempt to bring together the countries of Europe, when the Council of Europe was formed in 1949. The Council was set up by ten Western European countries, including the UK, in 1949. It set out to promote cooperation in such fields as human rights, culture and protection of the environment. In time many other European states joined it – it currently has nearly 50 members, including both Russia and Georgia, recently involved in a bitter conflict. It has what look like pale reflections of many of the institutions which nowadays make up the EU. For instance, it has a Consultative Assembly, although one nominated by member governments. It has a Commission and a Council of Ministers (Council of Foreign Ministers). It established a Court of Human Rights at its headquarters in Strasbourg in 1959, which examines breaches of the European Convention on Human Rights signed in 1950. It has, in Alex May's words, 'continued to work steadily, but unspectacularly, producing conventions and agreements on such subjects as terrorism, human rights and the environment'.[4]

Unlike the EU (which took over its flag in the 1950s), it is limited by being inter-governmental. Article 1 talks grandly of its aim being 'to achieve a greater unity between its Members', but goes on to say that this aim will be pursued 'through the organs of the Council by discussion of questions of common concern...' In other words, the organs which were set up in order to implement this 'greater unity' are only able to operate through debate and persuasion rather than through binding law. When the British foreign secretary, Ernest Bevin, remarked in 1949 that the Council of Europe had to be supported because Europe must have its 'talking shop', the condescension contained more than a grain of truth.

No one knew this better than Schuman himself. On 16th May, 1949, just 11 days after the signing of the statutes of the Council of Europe in St. James's Palace, London, Schuman made a speech in the Festival Hall, Strasbourg. He confessed that the Council of Europe was characterised by 'a timorousness that many people will find disappointing'. States, he noted, 'have not yet consented to renouncing any part of their sovereignty'. The debates of the new assembly set up by the Council could have a moral and psychological effect, he claimed, and he hoped that they would. But that was all. 'They can influence governments and parliaments,' he went on to say, 'but they can create by themselves neither rights not obligations'. He remained absolutely determined, even just a few days after what was supposed to be the momentous signing into existence of the Council of Europe, to pursue his supranational alternative.

In a climate where support for supranationalism was by no means universal (even in France itself) Schuman knew that it could only succeed if it supplied a practical answer to an immediate problem. Fortunately, such a problem was at hand – Germany.

The nature of that problem, and the way in which it affected French policy in the late 1940s, is easily stated. There were three options, all of which appeared bad. Keep Germany weak, and this would make it more difficult for the whole of Europe to recover economically. That had been the experience after World War One, when reparations had kept the German economy down. Despite the benefit to their economies in terms of reparations payments, the UK and France found themselves losing much more than they gained, because Germany could not afford to buy their exports. A weakened Germany undoubtedly contributed to the slump and high unemployment that followed, with all the political troubles that came in the wake of economic depression.

Allow Germany to grow strong again, however, and there was the risk of a new military threat. In the late 1940s that was a danger taken seriously by Britain, France and the US, and at first even eclipsed the threat from the Soviet Union in a growing atmosphere of Cold War. After all, there were measures taken after World War One to prevent such a threat, and within twenty years they had failed.

There was a third option – that of dismemberment – which was certainly considered during the war. De Gaulle thought of detaching the Rhineland from Germany; Monnet at first thought of removing the Ruhr and Lorraine from both France and Germany, creating a new 'Lotharingia', the middle kingdom once ruled by Lothar, grandson of Charlemagne.[5] Such ideas were eventually deemed unworkable, though the dismemberment option was pursued in terms of the separation of the Federal Republic from the German Democratic Republic in 1949. This, however, was a product of the Cold War and the particular problems of Berlin rather than a deliberate measure to keep post-war Germany weak.

The problem with the 'dismemberment option' was that it ran the risk of the first option, namely a Germany too weak to act as the engine of European economic recovery. This was why the idea of separating the Ruhr from Germany (and perhaps joining it to France), was firmly opposed by the United States. The American priority was to revitalise Europe economically (not just for reasons of philanthropy, but also in order to prevent the spread of communism to Western Europe and to provide markets for American exports), and that could not be done by following the sort of line advocated with heavy irony by François Mauriac when he said that he loved Germany so well he preferred two of them.

Hence the dilemma was that a weak or dismembered Germany might repeat the economic chaos of the 1920s, while a strong Germany might repeat the military rearmament of the 1930s. An alternative to both had to be found for the 1940s. The arrangement proposed through the European Coal and Steel Community was that alternative. It did not arrive riding on a wave of enthusiasm for supranationalism; it emerged as a way of allowing Germany to recover under European auspices.

On 9th May, 1950, the day that is the real beginning of the development that was to lead to the European Union (the day which is now celebrated as 'Europe Day'), Robert Schuman's plan providing the basis for the establishment of the European Coal and Steel Community was published. 'The French Government proposes that Franco-German production of coal and steel be placed under a common "high authority", within an organisation open to the participation of the other European nations', it began. Later it made clear the new structure that was being introduced:

> By pooling basic production and by creating a new high authority whose decisions will be binding on France, Germany and the other countries that may subsequently join, these proposals will lay the first concrete foundation for a European Federation which is so indispensable to the preservation of peace.[6]

Though he talks of a 'European Federation', Schuman had learned something from the failure of the earlier Hague congress, held in 1948, to translate its ideas into reality. He had learned the advantage of 'beginning small', taking a particular area in which to pool sovereignty and then trying to extend it to other areas. This approach is sometimes termed 'functionalism', a form of supranationalism that seeks to introduce itself gradually, hoping for a 'spill-over' effect from one function to others that might be considered appropriate.

In April 1951 the Treaty of Paris was signed, establishing the European Coal and Steel Community. Jean Monnet, who had long advocated a gradualist approach to European federation as head of the post-war French Planning Commission, became the first president of the High Authority in 1952. Though limited to one particular area (coal and steel), there was a crucial difference between what was done here and what was done in the case of the Council of Europe. What was agreed at Paris involved a sharing of sovereignty by creating a 'High Authority' whose decisions were binding on the individual countries.

The history of what became the EU was to be (and remains) one of constant arguments over the relative weight to be given to the various institutions involved. There have been very different assessments, for instance, of this High Authority (and of the European Commission into which it later mutated).[7] As the next chapter will examine, the later history of the EU has made it difficult to assess the relative strength of the various institutions (and new ones that have been created). As John Gillingham wrote:

> The European integration process has indeed been a history of zigs and zags, of false starts, delays and even backsliding as well as of solid long-term accomplishment.[8]

However, is possible to recognise these 'zigs and zags' whilst at the same time recognising the distinct nature of the 'integration process' itself. The creation of the High Authority heralded a new form of regional (and potentially, as this book will argue, global) organisation, whatever the later wrangles over its powers and over the mechanisms for overseeing the way it used them.

British and French approaches to supranationalism

The British approach

It is a commonplace to identify Britain as one of the most 'eurosceptic' members of the European Union today. However, British concerns about efforts at European integration go right back to the earliest stages of post-war development. Britain chose not to become part of the European Coal and Steel Community, launched in 1951 and described in the previous section. There was undoubtedly an economic aspect to this decision. The British economy appeared healthier than that of its neighbours, and it was also more diversified. Britain had trading links that were worldwide and focused at least as much on the Commonwealth and the sterling bloc as on the rest of Europe. Finding a workable framework for European coal and steel was less of an imperative to a country that felt it had its own coal and steel industries under control and was producing much more than its continental counterparts.

Herbert Morrison's remark to the British cabinet when he reported on Schuman's plans for the European Coal and Steel Community – 'It's no good, we can't do it, the Durham Miners won't wear it' – is commonly quoted as an off-the-cuff remark, but it had a significant point behind it. Coal had been nationalised in Britain and steel was in the pipeline for the same treatment. The Schuman Plan (announced in 1950) appeared to involve a different system of management and could therefore be presented as a threat to the new government's domestic policies. It has to be remembered that the UK had just elected its first-ever Labour government with an overall (in fact a landslide) majority. Previous Labour governments, in 1924 and 1929–31, had been minority governments, forced to share power in coalitions that could easily bring them down. After its victory in 1945 Labour felt that, at last, it could introduce the measures it wanted – such as nationalisation – and it was relatively enthusiastic (at that time) about the task. Sharing sovereignty with other countries sounded like a way of making Labour a minority government all over again and forcing it to trim on economic measures it was determined to enact.

But there was also a political dimension to British reluctance to get involved, an almost instinctive feeling that whatever the 'continentals' were thinking up it must be an unacceptable challenge to national sovereignty. Ernest Bevin, foreign secretary under the Attlee government of 1945–51, expressed it colourfully if not very clearly when he voiced concerns about the proposal for a European Assembly put forward by France and Belgium in 1948 with the words: 'If you open that Pandora's box, you never know what Trojan 'horses will jump out'.[9]

The idea that sovereignty shared is sovereignty lost rather than gained was reinforced by some of Britain's recent wartime experience. The country emerged from having fought and won a long six-year war, including a year in which it had to 'go it alone'. 'Very well, alone!', the famous Low cartoon published in June 1940 of a man on the south coast shaking a defiant fist at the Nazi enemy, now embedded just across the Channel after the fall of France, represented a strong national feeling of at last being able to conduct the battle without troublesome allies. As the war proceeded, of course, it brought new and even more troublesome allies into the picture, as being part of the Big Three (effectively a big Two-and-a-half) forced Churchill to adapt his policies to the demands of Stalin and Roosevelt. There was a sense that the 'glory times', from the Battle of Britain through the Blitz to the moment when Hitler turned away eastwards to attack the Soviet Union, came when Britain fought alone (although material support from the United States was in fact vital during this period). Now, a few years after the war was over, here was another proposal for 'working with allies' when the national preference was for 'going it alone'.

It is sometimes suggested that Britain was concerned about a European bloc developing that would undermine the Atlantic alliance and attempt to plough a different furrow to America. In fact this is a case of reading back concerns that were to arise much later in the century; the evidence from the immediate post-war period is precisely the opposite. As Judt remarks, 'The Americans were frustrated by the UK's reluctance to merge its fate with Europe'.[10] The US was keen for Western Europe to coordinate its response to post-war problems by cooperating both in economic renewal (such cooperation was made a condition of aid through the Marshall Plan) and in defending itself against the growing Soviet threat. The US was also acutely conscious of the rivalries and economic protectionism into which European states had fallen in the 1930s as a reaction to the Depression. It was not worried about facing a rival European bloc; it was worried about a Europe that didn't pull its weight in the world and left its neighbour across the Atlantic to carry the can. As American concerns about the Soviet Union grew, its concerns about the failure of the Europeans to develop a coordinated response to it rose also. If anything, British suspicions about the European Coal and Steel Community irritated the Americans.[11]

The British approach to post-war organisation was therefore driven by a clear principle. If it's inter-governmental, support it; if there's anything supranational about it, keep out of it, ignore it and if possible squash it. The British welcomed the Council of Europe, and were indeed one of the ten founder members of the organisation, launched in St. James's Palace, London to great fanfare in 1949. They campaigned for the formation of NATO (North Atlantic Treaty Organisation) in the same year, another inter-governmental body whose members included Turkey, Canada and the United States. They also accepted the OEEC, the Organisation for European Economic Cooperation, a body set up in 1948 to coordinate national responses to the American Marshall Plan, once again an inter-governmental body and forerunner of the OECD (the Organisation for Economic Cooperation and Development).

However, the British government stayed outside the negotiations which led to the European Coal and Steel Initiative and talked instead of negotiating some sort of association with it if it came to life (it was not clear at the time that it would). Benelux attempts to entice Britain into the fold as a counterweight to French and German influence within the European Coal and Steel Community (ECSC) were a complete failure. Arguments that this would provide an opportunity for Britain to play a leading role in Europe went nowhere. Whether or not one agrees with Hugo Young's judgement that 'visceral hostility' was able to trump 'cool calculation',[12] it is clear that the British stayed aloof from anything smacking of supranationalism. Sovereignty shared was viewed as sovereignty lost rather than gained.

It is noteworthy that the Dutch, despite severe misgivings about supranationalism, plunged into the ECSC negotiations to good effect. By championing the cause of a Council of Ministers, for instance, they managed to ensure important safeguards against the overweening power of the proposed High Authority. The British attitude, however, was not to get involved – although when the Schuman Declaration was made on 9th May 1950 without consulting London, the British were naturally infuriated.

The French approach

To describe the French approach as the precise opposite of the British one would be an over-simplification. However, what the French managed to see and the British arguably didn't was that a sovereignty-sharing arrangement could be in the interest of individual nation-states, especially if they played a leading role in it. The French view was never simply that a supranational arrangement was the only effective way of controlling German recovery under a European umbrella; it was that such an arrangement helped France. Even though French concerns to protect their national interests were (and are) as great as those of Britain, the notion that a sovereignty-sharing system was nothing but a threat to such interests was seen as too simplistic. They might seek to modify it and to change the balance between 'supranational' and 'inter-governmental' in its complex structures, but they saw no reason to stand aloof from it. To this extent recent 'revisionist' writing by Alan Milward and others, associating the development of the EU with the recovery rather than the undermining of the nation-state,[13] may be seen as bearing out the French as opposed to the British view.

Within a year or two of the establishment of the European Coal and Steel Community in 1952, it seemed for a while as though the 'British view', that is to say a belief in purely inter-governmental arrangements, would prevail. This was because of the failed attempt to share sovereignty in the area of defence through a European Defence Community (EDC). Once again French fears of a resurgent Germany were a key factor in the equation. The outbreak of the Korean War, and the subsequent invasion of a divided Korea from the North, led to many parallels being drawn in Europe. The fear of a 'Korea-like' push westwards through a divided Germany led to United States insistence upon West German rearmament. France baulked at the idea of any German remilitarisation, fearing a repeat of the 1930s. Yet France had to accept that some form of defence against a 'Soviet push' was essential. The answer seemed to lie in putting German resources under wider European management once again – in this case German military resources as opposed to the industrial resources of coal and steel.

In May 1952 the Pleven Plan (named after French premier René Pleven) was formalised into the European Defence Community treaty, which then had to be ratified by the individual member-states (the Six who had originally created the ECSC and were eventually to sign the Treaty of Rome). It was soon ratified by the Benelux countries, Italy and Germany, which left France as the only one left to sign up – and of course this was the country from which the original proposal had come.

Under the plan Western European military forces were to be managed by a nine-member commission. A European parliament and defence ministry would already be in place by the time a European army was established. It would be under a common military and political authority, although participating states, apart from Germany, would be able to maintain existing defence ministries, general staffs and armed forces kept separate from the European army. Germany alone would be permitted no armed forces at 'national' level and no more than one third of the troops in any European force.

By the time of ratification, however, France was not enthusiastic. Robert Schuman, the foreign secretary, faced opposition at home, not only from the Gaullists but also from his own party and the socialists – indeed divisions over the issue cut right across party lines, as they were to do twenty years later during Britain's tortuous process of joining the European Economic Community. In 1953 Schuman was replaced as foreign minister by George Bidault, a Christian Democrat ally of Schuman's but an opponent on the question of the European Defence Community.

To some extent the Pleven Plan ran into trouble because of political circumstances beyond its control. Agreed in 1952, it finally went before the French assembly in 1954, by which time Stalin had died and there was a ceasefire in Korea. At the same time, it was clearly more controversial to apply supranational ideas to such a sensitive area as national defence. De Gaulle, at the time in opposition, railed against a 'stateless hotchpotch' replacing the army of Turenne and Napoleon – precisely the sort of language which would be familiar to British concerns about the dilution of national identity within some bland and ineffective 'euromix'.

In August 1954 the French national assembly rejected the European Defence Community in a close but decisive vote (technically a vote not to discuss the matter rather than to reject it as such). Gaullist and communist opposition was solid but the other parties were divided too: the socialists, for instance, split 50 for and 53 against. When the French delegates finally rejected the proposals, the delegates burst into an impromptu rendering of the *Marseillaise*. France had its own way of providing a 'nationalist backlash' against supranationalism. The British Prime Minister, Winston Churchill, (the Conservatives had returned to power in the 1951 election) wryly observed to Eisenhower: 'I do not blame the French for rejecting the EDC, only for inventing it.'[14]

To add insult to injury, it was a British proposal that finally resolved the matter. Within a few months an alternative inter-governmental solution had been found, based on a conference in London a month after the French vote and to a large extent masterminded by the British foreign secretary, Anthony Eden. Eden suggested that Germany (alongside Italy) be allowed to accede to the Treaty of Brussels, signed in 1948 between Britain, France and the Benelux countries, essentially as a defensive alliance against the very country that was now being invited to join it. A new Western European Union would be formed which included both Germany and Italy. The participation of the two former axis powers was specifically recognised as a step towards full NATO membership. German rearmament was plainly envisaged, but it would be controlled by NATO and explicit American and British guarantees, not by a supranational body. French fears of German resurgence would be allayed by the clear manner in which the new union was integrated closely into the NATO alliance.

Had France only been motivated to support supranationalism as a way of overcoming its fears of German resurgence, this would surely have meant no further supranational initiatives after 1952. Once the fear of Germany had abated (as it began to do in the 1950s) the French would have no more interest in the sharing of sovereignty than the British, particularly if de Gaulle returned to power (as indeed he did just four years later, in 1958). Monnet's approach would by then have had its day. In retrospect, it is clear why Craig Parsons could remark: 'In August 1954, almost everyone thought the community adventure was over.'[15]

But it was not over.

That this was so is testimony to the more sophisticated attitude that the French had (and perhaps still have) towards supranationalism than the British. The British, as the first part of this section tried to bring out, saw it as a 'zero-sum' game or even worse; it was giving away powers and getting nothing back in return. The French view was more subtle. It recognised that certain things would be managed at a level above the nation, and that this might make them no longer exclusively French. However, it also recognised that the resulting arrangement could be beneficial to each member of the community. It was never simply a question of 'giving powers away'; it was more a question of receiving them back in another form. It was the recognition of this that led, against all expectations, to the Treaty of Rome being signed within three years of the collapse of the Pleven Plan, and (more surprisingly, perhaps) to the survival of the European Economic Community during the eleven long years of the de Gaulle presidency (1958–69).

British and French approaches to the treaties of Rome

Following the rejection of the European Defence Community, those who were enthusiastic about supranationalism turned to other areas in which they believed it could be introduced. Top of the list was atomic energy. On the one hand, German expertise was essential to the process of developing an atomic programme; on the other hand, allowing a separate German atomic programme to develop was unthinkable. As in the case of coal and steel or German rearmament, the supranationalist route beckoned as a way of controlling German development; once again, as with defence, an inter-governmental alternative was available, in the form of cooperation with the more advanced British and American atomic programmes. This was certainly the preference of some members of the ECSC, and as with German rearmament it looked as if the inter-governmental approach might once again trump the supranational.

To try to prevent this happening, Monnet linked a supranational atomic energy body (Euratom) to a supranational European economic community under a liberalised trading regime. In other words, in order to get Germany, for instance, to sign up to supranationalism in the area of atomic energy, which it was reluctant to do, Monnet linked this area to another in which Germany much more enthusiastic about sharing sovereignty. However, he made it clear that the choice was between accepting both or none at all.

The fact that even Monnet, the champion of supranationalism, was reluctant to introduce it in too many areas at once is yet another indication that there was considerable hesitancy in France about the principle of supranationalism, even outside the sensitive area of defence. Trade liberalisation was also a sensitive area. To have trade relations managed by a supranational authority was a frightening prospect for many sectors of the French economy, including its farmers, later seen as champions of the EEC. The prospect of abolishing quotas and subsidies under supranational management appeared to be a means of kicking away the props from beneath many French businesses. The 'business class' was inclined to oppose it.

The complexity of the political situation when the famous Messina Conference of June 1955 set out to re-launch the supranational approach meant that no one could be sure of the outcome. An inter-governmental committee was set up under the Belgian foreign minister Paul-Henri Spaak, which was to work out proposals for a common market. In the discussions it was often the smaller countries of the Six, and in particular Belgium and the Netherlands, which took a lead role. This was partly because of the failure of Benelux (Belgium, the Netherlands and Luxembourg) to bring about significant economic progress by inter-governmental means. These three countries had been in a customs union since January 1948, but it had brought limited benefits. Beyen, the

Dutch foreign minister, wrote a memorandum to Spaak in April 1955 claiming that:

> ...it is vital that a feeling of joint responsibility of the European states for the common welfare should be embodied in an organisation which follows the common interest, with an executive which is answerable not to the national governments but before a supranational parliament.[16]

It was a clear enunciation of Monnet's supranationalist approach. Beyen explained to the British ambassador in 1955 that the OEEC 'does not offer the degree of control western European countries need to make sure their economies are not at loggerheads'.

Britain had sent a low-level observer, an official at the Board of Trade, to the Messina talks, who had been instructed to pursue a line of 'cooperation without commitment'. Appeals to the British to send a cabinet minister had fallen on deaf ears. Once proposals started to be formulated, the official (Russell Bretherton) was instructed to explain that Britain had no interest in any new institutions. Instead the proposals should be discussed within the looser (i.e. purely inter-governmental) framework of the OEEC, precisely the organisation that Beyen had attacked as failing to offer a sufficient degree of control. Bretherton left the conference and did not return. Meanwhile Britain was accused of trying to use its influence with America and Germany in order to undermine the negotiations.

Between the Messina conference and the final signing of the Treaty of Rome came the Suez Crisis of 1956. The debacle of the Anglo-French invasion of Egypt's Canal Zone brought home to both countries that they were not the 'global powers' that they once were and led to recriminations and soul-searching. In the French case, however, wounded national pride did not lead to withdrawal from the EEC negotiations but increased the country's willingness to bring about a successful conclusion. For one thing Suez had demonstrated the limits to Anglo-French cooperation; for another, it underlined the advantages of a wider European organisation which could wield the power France lacked when acting alone.

In the next year significant progress in a supranationalist direction was made. On the basis of a report by the Belgian Foreign minister Paul-Henri Spaak, the famous Rome Treaties were signed in March 1957, establishing the EEC and Euratom (in addition to the ECSC, so that there were now strictly speaking three communities, each one of them an expression of supranationalist principles). The complication of having three communities was partly to make sure that the 'High Authorities' for the two new organisations (they were now called 'Commissions', a less exalted term) had less power than the one for the ECSC (the three eventually merged a decade later). Once again this illustrates how the tension over the relative power of supranational and intergovernmental elements within what was to become the European Union was inherent from its inception.

The Treaties of Rome meant that a range of economic policies were to be decided by the Six within a framework that was supranational. The progressive integration of policies in areas such as agriculture, transport and trade was impossible without an active role for the supranational Commission in initiating and implementing legislation (as the High Authority did within the ECSC). Other bodies, such as the Council of Ministers, might be there to oversee its activities and occasionally reject its proposals, but it would never be able to abolish the Commission or the Court of Justice and turn the clock back to a treaty between independent sovereign states.

It is therefore to these treaties above all others that the European Union today looks back as its foundation documents, despite the fact that supranational arrangements went back to the Coal and Steel Community of 1951. *50 years together*, as the slogan ran in 2007. Not fifty-seven years since the Schuman Plan of 1950, not fifteen since the Treaty of Maastricht. Rome is seen as the point of no return. For all the talk in the Treaties – later to inspire some and haunt others – of 'ever closer union' among member-states, its real significance lies in the institutional arrangements which, though they were now some six years old, became firmly embedded in the life of Western Europe at this point.

Once it was clear that the European Economic Community was going ahead without their participation, the British set about developing an alternative to the six-member EEC purged of supranational elements. It finally emerged as the European Free Trade Area (EFTA). This body of seven members, signed into being in Stockholm in 1960, produced the jibe that Europe was now 'at sixes and sevens'. In the early stages the idea was not to set up a rival organisation but to draw the EEC into the OEEC, in which it would eventually be dissolved like sugar in tea. This soon proved impossible when the US developed a plan to broaden the OEEC into a worldwide organisation including itself, Canada and possibly Japan (this was the genesis of the OECD, the Organisation for Economic Cooperation and Development). The last thing the US wanted was rival trade blocs within Europe, and it tended to regard the British, despite the fiction in Britain itself that it was committed above all to its 'special relationship' with the US, as obstinate and uncooperative. The US embassy in London sent a telegram to the State Department complaining about Prime Minister Harold Macmillan's 'exaggerated and emotional statements' concerning the EEC, EFTA and NATO.[17]

EFTA was never likely to entice 'the Six' away from their separate arrangement. The Six were committed to a common external tariff, while Britain was arguing for free trade between countries but a right of each country to set its own import tariff. Behind this position was British concern over imports from the Commonwealth, a subject of emotional as well as economic importance as settlers in New Zealand and elsewhere started talking of betrayal by the 'mother country'.[18] Either the common tariff would have to be given up, or New Zealand butter and a host of other commonwealth imports would have to be exempted from it. Neither option was acceptable to the Six.

Meanwhile British concern about a 'hostile bloc across the Channel' (the words of a cabinet minister, David Eccles) grew. It occasionally descended into hyperbole, even at the highest level. Harold Macmillan (who became Prime Minister when Eden resigned over Suez in 1957) talked of leaving NATO and of how 'we should not allow ourselves to be destroyed little by little. We should fight back with every weapon in our armoury.'[19] It seemed to be 'Very well, alone!' all over again.

Yet within two years of these words Macmillan had decided to negotiate British entry to the EEC, a remarkable conversion. Macmillan managed with great skill to change his party's position on membership of the EEC, without inducing a single resignation. Monnet, who became a great champion of British entry, always held firm to the view that the British would enter when they were convinced that there was no practical alternative, whatever their dislike for supranationalism. The approach to take was always to insinuate the practical advantages rather than try to commend the theory. Monnet was confirmed in this opinion when a month before Britain's application he and Harold Macmillan had walked side-by-side to the Senate House in Cambridge in order to receive honorary degrees.

There were, of course, economic reasons for Britain's shift. The country's trade with the Commonwealth was declining, while its trade with the EEC was growing. But there was a political element too. The Commonwealth was little more than a shadow of the former Empire, and events in South Africa and later Rhodesia, where former colonies were allowed to become apartheid regimes, were making Britain highly unpopular within it. Macmillan's famous 'wind of change' speech in February 1960 is seen as acknowledgement of the fact that the days of Empire were over, but that wind blew through Europe too. The dynamic new US President, John Kennedy, with whom Macmillan liked to think of himself as on especially good terms, was also making clear that he supported an expanded EEC. Britain could not hide behind the notion that its lack of enthusiasm for the EEC was connected with its loyalty to the US.

Where the EEC was concerned Britain had moved in record time from denial through anger to acceptance. What this did not mean was any ideological conversion to the merits of a supranational arrangement. Indeed, Macmillan felt that one of the reasons why de Gaulle, who had come to power in France in 1958, might not veto British entry, was that the two countries would be able to work together in order to diminish or even eliminate the supranational elements of the EEC. This time British entry would itself be the tea in which to dissolve the supranationalist sugar. While the Labour leader, Hugh Gaitskell, treated his party conference in 1962 to dire warnings of 'the end of a thousand years of history' and Britain ceasing to be 'the mother country of a series of independent nations',[20] Macmillan's government went ahead with its application for membership.

But de Gaulle did not welcome Britain as an 'inter-governmental ally' against supranationalism. He twice vetoed Britain's entry, first under a Conservative government in 1963 and then under a Labour government (Gaitskell having died and been replaced by Harold Wilson) in 1967. There were various reasons for this, but a certain perception of French national interests was clearly crucial. De Gaulle wanted an EEC large enough to dominate Europe, but small enough to be dominated by France. As Vanke comments, de Gaulle was 'a Realpolitiker in European affairs, certain about the value of French independence, less certain and more flexible about the best means to enhance it'.[21] Yet precisely that flexibility permitted him to work within the EEC when he came to power a year after the Treaty of Rome was signed, rather than seek to undermine it. He had condemned the proposed European Defence Community as 'a Frankenstein' in 1954, and was clear that Europe did not command the congenital loyalty of its subjects. It was possible to be *mort pour la patrie*, but not to give your life for Europe. De Gaulle's language was as strongly imbued with nationalist rhetoric as that of anyone on the other side of the Channel. Europe was 'composed of indestructible nations, forged at the fires of history', and it was 'derisory puerility' to want to smelt any of them together. At the time of signing of the Rome Treaty, he attacked that too as an unacceptable surrender of French sovereignty. Yet when he came to power a year later, he accepted it.[22]

Quite simply, he could see how the sharing of sovereignty might be made to serve France's interests. He might have been an intergovernmentalist, but he attacked the Council of Europe as ineffectual. The EEC was *not* ineffectual, and France was in a position to play a pivotal role in it. Even in the delicate area of foreign policy, where the European 'Frankenstein army' had been swept away only four years earlier, there was an opportunity to leverage French power globally, 'the means for France to recover what she ceased to be after Waterloo; first in the world'.[23]

There was a great deal of *folie de grandeur* in such remarks. De Gaulle did not have everything his own way within the EEC. He successfully kept the UK out (though it was to enter four years after he left office in 1969) and he successfully pushed through the common funding of Community agriculture. Through the so-called Empty Chair crisis of 1965–6 he also managed to prevent the introduction of Qualified Majority Voting (QMV) in the Community. The original idea had been that after a few years during which voting had to be unanimous, the Six would be in a position to accept QMV – but de Gaulle refused to let this happen. Any member-state could continue to block progress in the Council of Ministers on anything that opposed its 'very important interests', and each state was left to decided what those interests were. Vanke talks of the Luxembourg Compromise as having 'encaged supranationalism before it could fly and strongly influenced the history of European integration for the next two decades'.[24] It is noteworthy that this is the year in which Jouve's *Le Général de Gaulle et la Construction de l'Europe* comes to an end. De Gaulle had stayed inside the EEC, but he had striven mightily to rein in its supranational 'tendencies'.

Yet De Gaulle could only cage the bird; he couldn't kill it off. The Fouchet Plan, which would really have destroyed it through an intergovernmental European Union, was successfully resisted by the smaller countries of the Six and Commission President Walter Hallstein. When de Gaulle tried twice again to act unilaterally, he was rebuffed on both occasions. In the end he settled for a bilateral Treaty of Franco-German Friendship, but even this had to have a preamble endorsing the EEC. De Gaulle was learning the hard way that even the 'leader' of the EEC had to accept certain constraints. The sharing of sovereignty could no more be a zero-sum game of winning than of losing. Possibly de Gaulle was never reconciled to this, as suggested by his last desperate overtures to the British in 1969 at a lunch in the Elysée Palace for the British ambassador, in which a joint move towards an inter-governmental union of the EEC and UK was discussed.

A reasonable assessment of de Gaulle's position would be that he was always determined to realise French interests within the EEC and occasionally an arm or a leg would appear outside the tent when his efforts grew too intense. Yet throughout his period in office he remained inside it, using it to further French interests, for instance by ensuring that French farmers were supported by the Community rather than by the French state. That was hardly what had been expected when he came to power in 1958. The reasonable expectation then might have been that France would seek to join the UK outside the EEC, rather than that the UK would seek to join France inside it.

Conclusion

There are endless studies of EU institutions which make it clear that it is very hard to define the body adequately. This chapter has not looked at these in depth. It has simply focused upon the efforts of two countries, Britain and France, to come to terms with an organisation containing elements of supranationalism.

In the 1950s and 1960s the two most powerful European nations both faced the prospect of participation in a sovereignty-sharing organisation. Both contained powerful forces opposed to supranationalism. In the UK aloofness from the ECSC and subsequent EEC moved to outright hostility and an attempt to set up an alternative organisation. However, within a very short time of the successful creation of the EEC the UK was applying to join it.

In France the mood was different. The country could claim to have pioneered the European Coal and Steel Community, and though it rejected the European Defence Community it returned to the supranational fold with the talks at Messina in 1955 and the Treaty of Rome two years later. French enthusiasm survived de Gaulle precisely because he could recognise its value in serving French interests, even though he balked at the reciprocal way in which France would have to serve Community interests. Yet he did not withdraw. He may have tried and failed to push the Community in a more inter-governmental direction, but he couldn't destroy the fundamental principles of supranationalism or the balance of forces represented by the Community's major institutions, the Commission, the Court of Justice, the Assembly (later Parliament) and the Council of Ministers.

Later in this book it will be argued that a Global Union might be expected to face its global equivalents of France and the UK, the really powerful nations that are likely to be the most resistant to any sharing of sovereignty. However, it should not be presumed that such 'big fish' are never going to take the bait of supranationalism. On the one hand they might see, like France, how joining such a body could effectively serve their own interests, leading them to influence and even lead such an organisation from within. On the other hand, they might, like Britain, reject the idea of supranationalism entirely, and yet be drawn into the organisation anyway by a recognition of its practical value, precisely the way in which the United Kingdom was eventually brought to the point of applying to join the EEC.

In January 1963 de Gaulle signed the Elysée Treaty of Franco-German friendship with the German Chancellor Adenauer, only to find that it had been effectively scuppered by a preamble insisted upon by the German *Bundestag*, which demanded a clear endorsement of NATO and the EEC. The disappointment was shrugged off by de Gaulle in a famous remark which said that 'Treaties are like roses and young girls – they last while they last'. The remark was interesting in that it expressed a certain attitude towards treaties, which came and went like a passing love affair and could be broken without too much damage being incurred by whoever chose to ignore their stipulations.

What the supranational elements in the Treaty of Rome managed to do was devise a practical method, through binding legislation, of making the initial enthusiasm of countries towards working together sustainable. It was to be more than the 'passing fling' of a treaty. It was a method as practical as marriage itself in curbing the 'here today, gone tomorrow' character of romantic attachment. No one could say that divorce was impossible, but it had to be made difficult. The supranational ECSC, EEC and (after 1992) EU remain organisations which a member-state may leave but only at the cost of unravelling a great deal of legislation that is as vital to the functioning of the state that leaves as it is to the functioning of the Union as a whole.

The essential test of this 'marriage' in the 1960s was as much the way in which France was kept inside the Community under de Gaulle as the way in which the UK was encouraged to make three attempts, the last one successful, to join it. For all his flirtation with other systems, the French leader kept his country married to a 'difficult wife' during eleven long years in which he was tempted, but never determined, to seek an annulment.

4
Managing Supranationalism

Introduction

The history of the EU in the forty years since de Gaulle's fall from power has been exhaustively covered by many historians. There is no need to repeat such coverage here. Instead, what will be useful for the purposes of this book is to look at the methods used in order to establish and manage a supranational body. It will then be possible to consider later in the book which of these methods, if any, might prove useful in the context of a wider Global Union.

The development of the EU put in place, sometimes as much by accident as by design and usually in the context of some pressing political necessity, a set of arrangements which have significance beyond Europe. As a series of legal acts, they make it possible for decisions made by the union to be binding and enforceable. They also establish systems which make it possible to provide practical assistance to member-states in a number of ways. There is thus both a carrot and a stick element to the EU's ability to make member-states carry out decisions which they may individually be opposed to.

This chapter will begin with the precondition for anything supranational to work, namely a binding legal system. It will then examine two important ingredients of the European Union in particular – namely 'own resources' (essentially an independent Community budget) and support for vulnerable economic sectors. A later chapter will consider whether any of these systems could be carried over into the operations of a Global Union.

European law

The previous chapter mentioned the legal basis of supranationalism and argued that the development of Community law was crucial to the success of any sovereignty-sharing arrangements. There was no point in a decision being taken by a 'High Authority' if it could be ignored by individual member-states. This section will examine that legal basis in more detail.

It is generally recognised that 'the European Communities are subject to the rule of law to an extent unparalleled in the history of relations between sovereign states'.[1] Hence the importance of the European Court of Justice within the institutional structures of the EU. As the previous chapter made clear, the Court of Justice was established as long ago as 1952, when it was the Court of Justice of the European Coal and Steel Community. Subsequent treaties have added to it – a Court of First Instance at the time of the Single European Act and judicial panels at the Treaty of Nice – but the essential role of the Court has remained unchanged. It has one judge per member-state, and decisions are made in chambers containing an odd number of judges, usually three or five but occasionally more in difficult cases. The Court adopts a single judgement and does not publish the views of any dissenting judges. Deliberations take place without officials present and confidentiality is preserved.

Of course the system applies only in areas to which it has been agreed that Community law should apply (areas in which nation-states have agreed to share sovereignty). Whenever the European Commission uses its exclusive power to initiate legislation, it knows that any proposal must be framed under a particular article of the Treaties of Rome, as amended by later treaties (only the unanimous agreement of the European Council can secure any changes to these). The so-called 'eurocrats' do not have carte blanche to initiate new legislation in any area they like. Though they may make nothing stronger than recommendations, they also have the power to frame binding legislation – either a 'directive', which offers a choice to member-states over how they implement the legislation, or a 'regulation', which prescribes the method of implementation in addition to the result to be achieved.

So far as the rulings of the Court are concerned, individual states agree to be bound by judgements that their individual appointees to that court may not have supported (which is not to suggest that they are appointed merely to represent their own countries' interests). Apart from adjudicating in disputes between different Community institutions, for instance the Council and the Commission, the Court reviews the application of Community law by member-states.

When, under an inter-governmental arrangement, states assume obligations by concluding a treaty, they are free to determine for themselves how they fulfil those obligations. Within the EU, on the other hand, any Treaty lays down legal obligations which the member-states must fulfil, if necessary by overriding their own national laws in the process.

One of the most important moments in the history of what was to become (after 1992) the European Union came in 1962, five years after the Treaty of Rome, when a Dutch importer of a chemical called ureaformaldehyde alleged in a Dutch court that tariff arrangements for the chemical were illegal under the Treaty setting up the European Economic Community (the product, imported from Germany, had been reclassified by Dutch customs so that the duty rose from 3% to 8%). Effectively, the Dutch importer was demanding that his own government respect the Treaty. He was treating Community law as if it was akin to the law within his own country, and using it to challenge the action of his own government. The European Court of Justice responded by supporting him. The words used by the Court in this, the *Van Gend en Loos* case, were to be quoted many times in the future:

> The Treaty is more than an agreement which merely creates mutual obligations between the contracting states...The Community constitutes a new legal order in international law, for whose benefit the states have limited their sovereign rights.[2]

In a case the following year (*Costa v. ENEL*, involving Italy's national electricity supplier) the Court made clear that to challenge the idea that Community law overrode national law was to call into question the whole legal basis of the Community:

> By creating a Community of unlimited duration, having its own institutions, its own personality, its own legal capacity of representation on the international plane and, more particularly, real powers stemming from limitation of sovereignty or a transfer of powers from the states to the Community, the Member States have limited their sovereign rights, albeit within limited fields, and have thus created a body of law which binds both their individuals and themselves.[3]

National governments could therefore clearly be overruled when it came to regulating their own markets if these regulations came into conflict with Community law. Nowhere was this more important, as the EEC sought to improve the workings of the single market, than in the matter of non-tariff barriers, a major impediment to free trade between member-states. A non-tariff barrier was in effect a way of protecting domestic companies from competition – though it might present itself as an innocent piece of health and safety legislation, for instance.[4] Commission attempts to remove such barriers by harmonising rules over product standards got nowhere. This was largely the fault of the Council of Ministers, in which representatives of national governments succumbed to the pressure towards protectionism of their domestic industries. In the end the logjam was broken by the ruling of the Court of Justice in the *Cassis de Dijon* case, which declared that Germany had been acting illegally in banning the sale in Germany of a French liqueur whose alcohol content did not 'meet German standards'. The Court ruled that if a product was safe for sale in one member-state it must be safe for sale in all, provided that basic health and safety standards were met. A later attempt by Germany to protect its brewers by arguing that their beer was 'pure' and that of others contained 'additives' that might be dangerous on health grounds was also rejected. In a similar way the Court ruled against an Italian prohibition against the sale in Italy of pasta products made from the 'wrong sort' of wheat.

The implications of this for the functioning of a common, and eventually a single, market were considerable. They established the principle of 'mutual recognition', ensuring that products from one country were recognised in another. The alternative would be an EU 'standard' product available everywhere; the EU thus managed to avoid the sort of system which British tabloids are forever parading as its attempts to make bananas straight, apples red or turn British beer into 'eurofizz'.

As pointed out in Chapter 1, it was naïve of Francis Fukuyama, in his famous essay 'The End of History?', to talk of 'those flabby, prosperous, self-satisfied, inward-looking, weak-willed states whose grandest project was nothing more heroic than the creation of the Common Market'.[5] For the creation of such a market was highly demanding *politically* – states are naturally very possessive where their economic 'national champions' are concerned – as recent attempts to apply what came to be called the 'Community method' to liberalising services and 'unbundling' energy provision make clear.

Of course an effective Community legal order is one thing; the power to enforce its decisions through an infringement process is another. Should a state be found to have breached Community law, it is pursued by the European Commission, which then asks the European Court to bring it back into line. In order to do this, however, it needs to have the power to sanction. The Maastricht Treaty, which came into force in 1993, for the first time gave the Court the power to impose penalties on member-states. The procedure was applied for the first time in July 2000, when Greece was ordered to pay 20,000 euros per day until it complied with certain environmental protection directives.

The penalties are hardly slight. In July 2005 France was fined twenty million euros for permitting its fishermen to catch and sell fish that were smaller than permitted under EU legislation. A further sixty million had to be paid every six months until France complied with the rules. Precisely because such sums are not negligible, such sanctions rarely have to be applied.

There are regular disagreements between the Commission and the member-states which are bound to implement legislation. As this section has made clear, in such circumstances it is the Court, and not the member-states themselves, which determines whether they have complied with community legislation. The only way of avoiding what a particular state considers to be an undesirable law is to win a change to the Treaties, ensuring that the article under which the legislation was framed no longer applies. This must, however, be done through the European Council – by unanimous vote of Heads of Government. Otherwise there is no way out for a member-state short of leaving the European Union.

The European Court is a clear expression of supranationalist principle. No member-state can veto its decisions, either directly or through the particular judge which it nominates for the Court. No member-state can refuse to implement its decisions. As has been made clear above, sanctions may be – and have been – imposed upon a member-state which is seen to be ignoring or failing to implement its decisions.

It seems reasonable to conclude that the development of Community law and its implementation through the European Court of Justice (ECJ) is one of the most crucial developments in European Integration:

> one of the surprising features of the EU has been the emergence of the ECJ as one of its most important institutions. Although the court was originally viewed as a means of settling rather technical disputes, it eventually emerged as an institution which actually 'constitutionalised' the Treaty of Rome. The role of European law is now so important that it is difficult to talk about European integration without incorporating a discussion of the European legal system.[6]

Should a global sovereignty-sharing body emerge, then a global equivalent to the European Court of Justice could be expected to have similar powers in acting against member-states that failed, for instance, to take action in those areas where states had agreed to share sovereignty. For instance, if climate change was one of those areas, it could take action by imposing sanctions for non-compliance against states which did not cut their carbon emissions. It would take measures similar to those taken by the European Court against Greece for its failure to meet environmental standards in the 1990s. Its law would be binding upon member-states in those areas in which the member-states of a Global Union had agreed to share sovereignty, overriding national laws if necessary. Part III, which examines McClintock's plans for a Global Food Security Community, the area of 'small beginnings' (though significant for millions of under-nourished people) which he proposes as the global equivalent to Europe's Coal and Steel Community, demonstrates in a similar manner that the organisation releasing the food would have to be a supranational one, having a measure of political authority and a legal right to oblige its member countries to take particular actions.

'Own resources'

If the precondition of an effective supranational body is law, a crucial ingredient of its successful operation is money. This too is something for which developments in the EU provide a useful model.

The Commission hoped that it would have its own resources by 1970, following full transition of the six to a customs union. Community financing would come from agricultural and industrial duties, rather than being dependent upon national contributions, which was the previous arrangement. This would be vital to the capacity of the Commission to take important financial initiatives, including those that supported less well-off member-states, and develop a medium-term planning cycle. Alongside the receipt of 'own resources' (effectively tax-raising powers, though with strict limits as to what might be raised) would come a duty to inspect the use of them, a requirement which would be devolved from member-states to the Parliament.

Undoubtedly the politics of the Common Agricultural Policy (CAP) played an important part in the decision concerning the community budget. The first President of the Commission, Walter Hallstein, relied on this assumption when he tried to persuade de Gaulle to support the creation of 'own resources' during the 1960s. From a French perspective, the agricultural issue had to be resolved before any future British entry made the future of the CAP even less secure, and France hoped for a resolution which would see a substantial slice of Community funds used for agriculture. Therefore it could be expected to welcome the 'own resources' move. As for the other five, a budget largely devoted to bolstering the Common Agricultural Policy was easier to wear politically if it was seen to be coming from the European Community in general, rather than from the national contributions of their own states, which might be receiving little benefit from the policy. Hence they could be expected to support 'own resources' too.

Hallstein's gamble, when he introduced his budgetary proposals in April 1965, was that 'de Gaulle would trade a desirable financial outcome for an undesirable political one'.[7] It failed. The so-called Empty Chair crisis followed, in which de Gaulle prevented any of his ministers from going to Council meetings, and before the issue was resolved Wallstein had left office. However, Hallstein's perception of the political issues at stake was vindicated in the long run. De Gaulle stepped down in 1969 without the funding of the CAP having been adequately settled; his successor, Georges Pompidou, proceeded to 'relaunch' the Community through a special meeting at The Hague at the end of 1969. Settling the funding of the CAP issue would be connected to granting the Community its own resources, as Hallstein had seen it would be. It was also tied to an agreement that the Community should enlarge.

Thus the creation of 'own resources' was agreed. Funding was to be achieved through charges on products imported from countries outside the Community and a maximum 1% of each state's VAT (Value Added Tax) revenue. Candidate countries were not consulted on this funding method, and the UK, as a large importer of foodstuffs, was to be particularly resentful of its implications. When a truce was finally called over the 'British Budgetary Question', at the Fontainebleau Summit in 1984, the money to finance the settlement reached was partly financed by raising the VAT revenue to 1.4%, thus illustrating nicely the principle that budgetary disagreements were best solved by creating a bigger cake rather than slicing the existing one differently. The particular case of the UK in regard to the budget will be touched on again later in this chapter.

In the late 1980s the management of 'own resources' was improved by the development of the first multi-annual financial framework, covering the period 1988–1992 and intended to coincide with the completion of the internal market by 1st January 1993. At the same time a new 'own resource' was added to the budget, based on a proportion of each state's GNP (Gross National Product). This could be used in order to make up any budget shortfall to a desired level, thereby ensuring financial stability and providing a 'budget cap' (1.2% in 1992, raised to 1.27% in 1999 and kept at roughly the same amount in 2006 at 1.24% of GNI – Gross National Income).

It is true that barely 1% of the national income of each member-state (and about 3% of its public expenditure) is going into the EC budget. Taken together, however, these contributions still add up to a sizeable amount of money. Moreover, the multi-annual financial framework allows for a high degree of forward planning. From 1993 the EU moved into seven-year budgets, so that the beneficiary of a project decided upon in 1992 would have a clear idea of what they would be receiving for the rest of the twentieth century. In a similar way the budget agreements made in 2006 determined funding levels until 2013. This degree of forward planning is something that no individual national government could be confident of achieving.

The year 2008 is the first ever in which EU spending on economic growth and greater cohesion (about 45% of the budget) exceeded that spent on agriculture (about 40%). Such statistics can mislead, because there is an element of 'cohesion policy' in the CAP itself. Nevertheless, the growing importance of 'cohesion' should not be under-estimated. The purpose of such spending is described as a policy of 'convergence' – that is to say of narrowing the gap between the richest and poorest regions of the Community. 'Convergence' essentially represents redistribution, though redistribution in the name of economic efficiency as much as social justice. Beneficiaries from cohesion spending are assessed in terms of their relation to average GNI, and if they fall below a certain percentage they receive assistance.

The point to stress is that within a seven-year cycle the sort of large infrastructural projects that need to be developed become affordable, and they are deliberately targeted towards areas where there is a particular need to generate new investment. The latest estimates (2008) are that cohesion policy, representing about 36% of the EU budget, can command resources of some three hundred and fifty billion euros over a seven-year period. This is a not an insignificant amount of money.

A Global Union would also have to be in a position to allocate resources, and to allocate them knowing that they will be available for some time ahead. The resources need not amount to a huge percentage of GNI (it should be noted that a number of countries already spend close to 1% of their national income on 'aid' – i.e. poverty alleviation). But a substantial part of them should be directed towards investment in long-term projects that, for instance, develop the infrastructure of countries and allow them to move out of poverty rather than be constantly drip-fed aid. Though there may be a case for direct income payments on a short-term basis in addition, the long-term perspective is the one that matters for ensuring that countries are not only helped in a crisis but empowered to cope with a crisis themselves in future.

Once again Part III, which examines McClintock's plans for a Global Food Security Community, demonstrates how vital it is for any such organisation to have own resources. His proposal involves the development of a system of strategic reserves, kept for release in an emergency, whereas at present most current stocks are operating stocks. Clearly this strategic reserve will involve an outlay of expenditure.

Supporting vulnerable economic sectors

A second crucial ingredient of an effective supranational body is an element of support for vulnerable economic sectors. Such an idea has to be handled carefully. It does not mean what its critics would call 'interfering' in every area but in some – if the circumstances warrant it. It means that a particular economic sector within a supranational union of states may have to be protected or assisted in a certain way.

Such support suggests a 'third way' between socialist planning and a total market free-for-all. Once again, however, it is not being suggested that such an approach be applied in every area of the economy. Indeed it may not prove necessary in *any* area. But there may be circumstances where it *is* appropriate.

This 'third way' has its detractors in Europe, both since the emergence of Thatcherism in Britain and in the reaction of post-communist states to the policies of the Soviet-controlled regimes that preceded their liberation. Yet it is still well represented in the mainstream of political thinking, both right and left, throughout the continent.[8] It is not 'anti-capitalist'. The essence of the approach is to set parameters within which capitalist business can flourish. The rest of this section will attempt to define it further and explore its operation in the crucial and controversial area of agriculture within the European Union.

In the early part of the twentieth century, large swathes of Europe were dominated by an impoverished peasantry producing enough food for the market and receiving enough to live on in return. Occasionally a precarious situation became even worse and extreme poverty or emigration resulted. After World War Two there were chronic food shortages and a widespread fear that the same situation of barely adequate levels of production, generated by large numbers of rural workers who could barely make ends meet, would return. The lure of fascism for impoverished rural communities in the pre-war period was seen as an added spur for taking measures to improve their condition after 1945.

The discussions after the war turned to the question of assisting domestic farmers in order to avoid solving the food problem by importing from abroad. For Europe always had an alternative to increased domestic production – it could import food from places like Canada and the US, while running down its own agricultural sector.

However, governments feared more than the possibility of famine. They feared a return of the mass unemployment before the war, not to mention an exodus from the countryside to the towns at the very moment when demobilised soldiers were being reintegrated into the community.

The first measures to help agriculture, which were taken in the 1950s, enabled the European farming industry to increase production very rapidly. In 1950, for instance, France was a net importer of food. But in the next decade its agricultural production soared.[9] The Rome Treaties of 1957 enabled it to find a market for its agricultural exports. Just as France opened up its home market to (largely) German industrial exports, so Germany opened itself up to French agricultural exports. Tariffs would only apply to countries outside the Six, and the Six would set a common tariff on imports from non-EEC countries.

Furthermore, the Rome Treaties guaranteed a minimum price for farm products. This was the move which later led to the development of the CAP as a means of carrying an ever-increasing share of cost arising from this guarantee (and from setting the guaranteed price at a high level). Once farmers had been guaranteed a market and a price, their livelihood was largely assured in the absence of natural disasters like drought.

The Common Agricultural Policy (CAP), introduced in the early 1960s and then further developed before its final arrangements were formalised in 1970 ahead of British entry (and partly through the creation of 'own resources' discussed in the previous section), soon became controversial within the EU. High fixed prices meant that Europe's food production became too expensive to compete on the world market. High external tariffs could keep out cheaper food from abroad, but what was going to happen with the surplus created at home, once the immediate post-war fear of under-production had transformed itself by the end of the 1960s into a growing problem of *over*-production? Various attempts to deal with this fed into the media headlines of the next four decades. There was a plan to keep the food in storage ('butter mountains' and 'wine lakes') or to give it away ('free

EEC butter for pensioners'). It could be sold cheaply outside Europe (the so-called 'dumping' controversy, which critics saw as the 'dumping' of unwanted produce on third world countries at the expense of their own indigenous farmers). A quota system could be introduced (a system of milk quotas was introduced in 1984, but it was difficult to introduce quotas across the board). At the end of the century measures were taken to decouple subsidies from production levels. That, of course, generated its own unfavourable headlines ('farmers paid not to produce'), although the emphasis upon animal welfare, healthy eating and reviving the countryside did at last inject some favourable publicity into the CAP's subsidy regime.

In retrospect, it seems clear that prices were set at too high a level, which in turn ensured that the CAP would be an enormous drain upon the Community budget, at one point touching 75% – in a Community of some of the world's most advanced industrialised states – before falling to its present more 'modest' level of about 40%. It was also a policy designed to benefit some forms of agricultural production (cereal and livestock, the stock-in-trade of French agri-business) rather than other forms (for instance the olive trade of Southern Italy or the sheep farmers of Wales and Scotland). However, it is one thing to say that the CAP is an example of managing trade badly; it is quite another to say it illustrates that trade should not be managed at all.

Ironically, it is precisely the argument used against 'dumping' that can be marshalled in support of the initial moves that led to the CAP. The argument is that by dumping food (in this case EU surpluses) on poor countries at knock-down prices, you may help the urban poor in those countries with lower prices but you also put their own domestic farmers out of business by under-cutting them. Precisely the same could have been said in favour of support for Europe's farmers after World War II. By importing from abroad, the European population could have been fed (subject to dollar availability, since the food would have come largely from Canada and the US). But in the process its own agricultural sector would have been diminished beyond repair. What became the CAP was a system of support for a vulnerable industry ensuring that farmers survived. It may have been selective in the producers it chose to support, it may have (by simply rewarding raised production levels) have done little at first for environmental or health concerns and for supporting the small farmer as opposed to 'agri-business', and it may have given too much support overall. But the attempt to protect domestic agriculture through price guarantees and a guaranteed market did enable an important sector of the economy to survive and helped the entire countryside to stay alive.

Though the specific proposal of a Global Food Security Community outlined in Part III is concerned with action to prevent prices rising too high rather than (as in the case of the CAP) ensuring that they do not go below a minimum (though that may be an issue it should address too), a clear implication of rising food prices is that not enough is being done to support farmers at home. A Global Union focused upon Food Security would be likely to find itself addressing wider questions of poverty in the countries threatened by rising food prices. It would take the view that supporting the domestic industries of poor countries so that they can produce more is a far better way of helping them than the provision of aid. Without presuming any 'functionalist inevitability' in such a development, it is more than possible that addressing the way in which poor countries are buffeted by price shocks in the food market will lead to an examination of how they may be helped to sustain higher levels of domestic production.

The later development of the European Union

The first three sections of this chapter examined a legal framework, own resources and support for a vulnerable but vital section of the economy as the precondition and instruments of economic and social progress within what became the European Union. The rest of this chapter looks more closely at the later history of the Community in order to examine how the instruments discussed above (legal framework, own resources, support for vulnerable economic sectors) were used in order to hold together and enlarge the Community once they were in place (by 1970).

At a number of points in its history the Community has faced strong opposition from one or more states about the impact of proposed policies. It has responded by offering them financial and other forms of assistance. Though such an approach might be dismissed as bribery, such a view would be too simplistic. Member-states often opposed developments leading to the single market because they felt that they were too economically weak to be able to handle them. Forms of regional assistance were intended to provide them with the means of doing so.

The European Regional Development Fund, the first example of sustained assistance to poorer parts of the Community, emerged within a particular political context. That context was the attempt to retain the UK as a new member of the Nine (as the original Six had become). The UK had finally joined the European Community in 1973, but a year later the Conservatives fell from office and a Labour government returned to power eager to 'renegotiate' the terms of entry and committed to holding a referendum on the results of those negotiations.

No one wanted the first phase of enlargement to run into any further difficulties (Norway had already voted in a referendum against entry), especially in the case of by far the largest new member (the other two, Ireland and Denmark, amounted to less than ten million people). The UK was already taking a line which was to become familiar during Mrs. Thatcher's premiership in the early 1980s. The line was that the UK was effectively being short-changed by the Community, contributing far more than it received back.

Whatever the truth of this complaint, the historical circumstances of UK entry made it almost inevitable that it would be voiced. The country had the misfortune to join the Community at precisely the time when the post-war boom was coming to a close. Oil prices skyrocketed in 1973, the year of the UK's entry to the EEC, which was also the year of the Yom Kippur war. Whereas the original Six were able to feel that the Community had helped them through the period of high growth in the late fifties and sixties, the UK could easily see entry as the time when its economic troubles really began (which it was) and therefore as the cause of those troubles (which it wasn't). There was a *post hoc ergo propter hoc* confusion in this, as there was in the tendency of the Six to trace their economic recovery solely to the Treaty of Rome. In any case, there was a danger that by 1975 enough people in the UK would be willing to blame the EEC for its economic woes that the country would withdraw from the Community a mere two years after entering it.

Furthermore, the UK had a case when it claimed that it would end up being a large net contributor to the EEC budget. In May 1974 a treasury report claimed that by 1980 the UK would be responsible for 24% of the EC budget, despite accounting for only 14% of its GDP. The Community had only just been granted its 'own resources'. With independent control of its budget the Commission was all too likely to be accused of unfair allocation of resources. The increasing strain of the CAP on that budget, together with the fact that Britain had a relatively small and 'efficient' farming sector, fanned British complaints. The feeling was that having been kept out of the Community in the sixties, they were being 'charged a rip-off entrance fee' in the seventies.

For this reason most other member-states felt that the renegotiation had to offer the UK something extra, (the alternative was to reduce the costs of the CAP, but this was anathema to a number of countries, particularly France). The European Regional Development Fund was that additional something. It would provide assistance to regions in difficulty, particularly (where the UK was concerned) those parts of the country affected by post-industrial blight as it came to terms with rapid manufacturing decline. Britain would receive 28% of the regional development fund's budget, thereby supposedly offsetting the costs of its contribution to the CAP.

The intervention of the oil crisis in the negotiations meant that the size of the Regional Development Fund was kept low.[10] In the event it never amounted to more than 8% of the EEC budget, and the UK's sense of being required to finance the budget disproportionately remained throughout the 1970s, culminating in Margaret Thatcher's attempt, after she became Prime Minister in 1979, to 'get my money back', as she put it. Though a settlement was reached at Fontainebleau in 1984, the issue has continued to smoulder and occasionally blazes up (it was re-ignited in 2005–6 over the setting of the 2007–13 budget).

Nevertheless, the principle of the fund was more important for later developments in the EU than its size. It established the idea of providing assistance to depressed regions, and paved the way for much larger and more effective funding later on through instruments like the Structural and Cohesion funds.

Such assistance might often be politically motivated, but it also represented a perception that poorer countries were entitled to help in meeting the economic challenges of integration. As Loukas Tsoukalis puts it, 'economic and social cohesion is Community jargon for redistribution'.[11] Elsewhere he writes:

> Regional integration has served as an instrument of economic development, a catalyst for modernisation and in many ways a kind of convergence machine for the benefit of the less developed countries of the European continent.[12]

This became clear in the 1980s, at the time of the Single European Act (SEA) of 1986 (the most significant piece of community legislation after the Treaty of Rome, and sensible enough to slip through under a veil of modesty by calling itself an 'Act' rather than a 'Treaty'). The SEA was a pill of economic liberalisation that was sugar-coated with a range of social and environmental measures. In the UK the Thatcher government was keen to promote a 'proper' single market that would allow the EEC to compete with technological rivals like Japan. To this end it was even persuaded to end the veto power of member-states in certain areas in the Council of Ministers, allowing QMV (Qualified Majority

Voting) to arrive just twenty years after de Gaulle effectively vetoed it though the Empty Chair Crisis and Luxemburg Compromise of 1965–6. Thatcher saw the Single European Act as a step forward. In her memoirs, *The Downing Street Years*, she declared that 'At last, I felt, we were going to get the Community back on course, concentrating on its role as a huge market....' What she had not anticipated, she claimed, was that 'the new powers the Commission received only seemed to whet its appetite.'[13]

Removing the barriers to a functioning market was a desirable end that every member of the European Community agreed to; the real sticking-point was what could reasonably count as a means to achieving that end. For most members of the European Community, including a number of right-wing political parties like Chancellor Helmut Kohl's Christian Democratic Union (CDU) in Germany, a successful market was one in which the state set out certain parameters within which the economy could grow and society could prosper. Arguably the same tradition was present in the British Conservative Party too, though it had been eclipsed by the arrival of Thatcher. In any case what the British Prime Minister viewed as interference, the German Chancellor viewed as preparing the ground.

On the whole it was the Chancellor's view of capitalism which prevailed within the supranational institutions, in the form of a strengthened Commission and Parliament, charged with preparing the way for market liberalisation. Where Thatcher saw a Commission entrusted with market liberalisation having its 'appetite whetted' for poking its nose into other areas, from the perspective of Commission President Jacques Delors these 'other areas' were merely ones in which anyone serious about market liberalisation *had* to 'poke their nose', simply in order to prepare for that liberalisation in a proper manner.

From Delors' perspective the economic liberalisation that was part of the SEA could not happen in a vacuum. In particular, it had to be acceptable to the new member-states. Greece (joined in 1981), Spain and Portugal (who both joined in 1986) represented over sixty million people from the poorer South of Europe, roughly the same percentage of the wider Community as the ex-communist countries which joined in 2004. Like the Eastern enlargement of 2004, the Southern enlargement of the 1980s meant accepting countries that had been through a period of dictatorship which they had successfully put behind them. Both groups of states were relatively poor, with an impact on the EU budget that existing member-states feared, just as they were to fear (and exaggerate) the movement of unskilled job seekers northwards and westwards. Both in 1986 and in 2004 countries were being brought into an environment of economic liberalisation that was bound to challenge them and cause temporary difficulties which their domestic populations would resent. To win acceptance of a demanding economic environment, measures to help those areas which were likely to find the burden of adjustment particularly difficult were regarded as crucial to making the consolidation and expansion of the Community *as a functioning single market* possible.

For Delors, the success of the SEA depended upon sharing the wealth of the Single Market programme and therefore reducing the disparities between richer and poorer member-states. The term used for the measures used to support this view – 'Cohesion Policy' – illustrates the presumption behind it, namely that such measures provide a way of binding member-states together in pursuit of an economic goal. The view was that a measure of wealth redistribution would ensure that they remained committed to the economic liberalisation process about which he was as enthusiastic as Margaret Thatcher.

A 'cohesion policy' clearly required financial support – hence the 'structural funds'. In early 1987 Delors called for a doubling of these, with aid directed in particular at regions with per capita income below three-quarters of the EC average (mostly Greece, Ireland, Portugal and Spain). Finance was to come from a new funding mechanism for the Community budget, to be based on member-states' GDP.

When it came to justifying such 'largesse', Delors repeated the end envisaged by both Margaret Thatcher and himself – liberalised markets. Referring to an influential report by Tommaso Padoa-Schoppa,[14] Delors quoted its concerns about 'the serious risks of aggravated regional imbalances in the course of market liberalisation'. It has to be remembered that Delors was initially supported by Thatcher for the post of Commission President, precisely because she knew he had played an important role in reversing the policies of the Mitterand government when the socialists came to power in France in 1981. But though not a socialist committed to high levels of public expenditure in a controlled protectionist environment, he was certainly committed to the view that the right conditions must be created for capitalism to work in. At the same time these would be the right conditions for the Community to maintain its cohesion after a substantial increase in membership from poorer countries.

Other controversial matters, like the free movement of people within the EC, were proposed in the 1980s on similar grounds. Markets work better when people can move to where the jobs are. Scrapping frontier formalities (customs and immigration controls) was therefore a further measure, expressed in the Schengen Agreement of 1985, which could be justified as a move towards allowing an effective single market.[15]

The 'Delors package' succeeded thanks to the preparedness of Chancellor Kohl to finance it by raising the size of Germany's contribution to the EC budget. By 1992 structural funds had doubled in size and cohesion had become accepted as an instrument of economic integration. Even the British government, which benefited from the new 'objective 2' funds supporting economic conversion in declining industrial regions, was able to reconcile itself to the policy, while continuing to baulk at the 'social policy' which stressed the harmonisation of working conditions and other 'social' factors as another crucial condition of successful liberalisation (eventually the new British Prime Minister, John Major, secured an opt-out from these provisions in the Maastricht Treaty).

The Maastricht Treaty, ratified in 1993, put in place a three-stage route towards monetary union, declaring that a single currency would be in place by 1999 at the latest. Strict requirements – 'convergence criteria' – were established to make sure that member-states did not have deficits or inflation rates that might threaten the stability of the new currency. After Maastricht, precisely the same argument about support for the less well-off member-states was generated by the now clear prospect of a single currency.

Once again the poorer countries, led by Spanish leader Felipe González, emphasised that the demands of European Monetary Union necessitated further Cohesion spending. Plans were drawn up for a Cohesion Fund which would support environmental and transport projects in states with a per capita level below 90% of the community average. There was even a programme specifically designed to achieve convergence. Just as the poorer countries had required assistance in order to maintain their commitment to economic liberalisation in the 1980s, so they required it in order to maintain their commitment to the single currency in the 1990s.

By now the British had withdrawn from the project to achieve European Monetary Union – indeed the single currency issue was to dog British politics for a decade and may well do so again as the country looks for ways out of its economic woes. Yet it was perfectly arguable that a single currency was a natural – some would say an obvious – corollary of a single market, the very thing the British had championed in the 1980s. If the French were not permitted to pamper their pet firms, the British should not be allowed to pamper their pet currency.

At the end of the century the same approach was taken towards the projected enlargement of the EU to take in the post-communist states of Central and Eastern Europe. If countries like Spain had needed help in meeting the 'convergence' criteria demanded by the implementation of a single currency, countries like the Czech Republic and Poland needed help in meeting the 'Copenhagen criteria' which set down the conditions for membership of the EU – democracy and the rule of law, a functioning market economy and the adoption of EU rules and regulations. 'Agenda 2000', the proposed budgetary package for the seven-year period 2000–6, therefore included a large amount of cohesion money for candidate countries, both before and after they joined the EU.

The years after 1969 have seen several stages of expansion and consolidation, during which the number of member-states has more than quadrupled. As a later chapter will explore further, what became the EU did not begin with a ready-made regional block of nations and then decide what the members of that block could do together. It began with a small number of states who gradually absorbed additional members as and when they showed themselves able and willing to abide by the main rules and regulations of what was to become the European Union. That not only meant a functioning market economy, but also the sort of political freedoms that involved throwing off the regimes of the Greek Colonels, General Franco, Portugal's Salazar and the Soviet-imposed dictators of Central and Eastern Europe.

There is no doubt that the process of absorption and enlargement would have been much more difficult, if not impossible, without a willingness to support the new members of the Community. Even the UK, which arguably had the most to lose, both in terms of perception of its own status and in financial terms, was partially reconciled through the support for Regional Development agreed in the 1970s. In the 1980s it was agreed that the new accession countries from the Mediterranean area would need support in meeting the demands of market liberalisation. In the 1990s this support was extended to help them meet the convergence criteria for monetary union. In the 2000–6 budget, Cohesion Funding moved its focus towards the economically weaker states of Central and Eastern Europe recovering from communism. Though the provision was not as generous as some wanted, no one denied its importance, least of all the new member-states themselves. Their leaders noted the fact that they were formally welcomed into the Community in May 2004 in Dublin, capital of the one country that had most obviously benefited from regional funding, Ireland, though the factors that transformed a once very poor country into the 'Celtic Tiger' of the 1990s are certainly not all attributable to the EU and perhaps look less attractive in the context of the current world financial crisis.

Throughout the forty years of expansion between 1973 (the first wave of enlargement) and 2007 (the last to date), it was accepted that new member-states, even the weaker ones, would have to show that they could withstand the rigours of a market economy. At the same time, it was thought to be in everyone's interest to help them do so. Such help was not thought of as interfering in the market, but as making sure that it worked effectively. It enabled the Community to grow from one of six members into one of twenty-seven representing half a billion people. Whatever the problems along the way – and there were many – it is difficult to deny that this was an achievement.

Conclusion

This chapter has avoided going into the development of the EU in detail – many excellent books have already done so. It has instead looked at a number of instruments used to facilitate that development. Its intention is to prepare the ground for a discussion of ways in which a Global Union might act to deal with the problems in those areas in which it chooses to share sovereignty. As with the European Union, it will be argued that an approach which offers practical assistance to countries that find it difficult to meet the financial and social costs of changing policy is much more likely to be successful than one that can go no further than exhortation or non-binding obligations.

As the last section has sought to illustrate, it is an approach that has some chance of binding new members even when they are invited to develop policies that are not in their immediate national interest. Recent conflicts over the Treaty of Lisbon notwithstanding, such an approach has been able to maintain the Community through a phenomenal period of rapid expansion.

The European Union developed a structure within which real incentives could be offered to member-states to remain in the Community. Expansion was therefore able to proceed, with new members signed up to the *acquis communautaire* and prepared to accept their obligations under European law. As the UK found in the 1970s, the Mediterranean countries in the 1980s, the potential members of a single currency in the 1990s and the post-communist countries in the new century, the demands of membership go hand-in-hand with practical assistance towards their accomplishment. The economic demands of membership, and in particular the creation of a dynamic, liberalised market, require such assistance to make the system workable. Measures on the protection of working conditions and infrastructural investment in poorer regions of the Community do not represent a retreat from capitalism to socialism, but a way of oiling the wheels of capitalism. They are crucial both to successful market liberalisation and to the willingness of member-states to embrace it.

This is the context within which Part III will consider the approach that might be employed by a proposed Global Union. It will be fleshed out in detail there. What this initial chapter has sought to do is to establish the groundwork for that approach, by suggesting that it is based upon methods already operative within the EU – a common budget, practical assistance to poorer regions of the Community and support for vulnerable sectors of the economy – applied in ways that are binding upon member-states. The use of these methods within the EU shows how much can already be achieved by operating within a world where binding laws apply and there are real sanctions for non-compliance. As the next chapters will begin to explore, it is a far more effective arrangement between nations than those which have been developed elsewhere.

Part II
Options for Global Governance

5
The United Nations

Introduction

The previous chapters have set out to examine the sharing of sovereignty in the context of the European Union. Later in the book there will be a closer discussion of what it might mean to share sovereignty at the global level. Before that is done, however, it will be useful to focus upon global bodies that already exist and upon regional unions apart from the EU that have grown in importance in recent years. Just what are the available options for global governance?

Chapter 7 will examine how far other regional unions, as much as their European counterpart, might be the basis for a Global Union. Chapter 6 will examine a range of existing global or potentially global institutions, but there is arguably one that deserves particular attention, the United Nations, and that will be the single subject of discussion in this chapter.

It is clearly the United Nations that people look to as the most significant global 'player' in the modern world. It is the one international body that can claim a general remit. It is involved not only in managing conflict and peacekeeping, but also (if its 'agencies' and other associated bodies are thrown into the equation) in promoting a range of important initiatives from education to climate change. Whatever its failings, it was not set up to be simply a forum for states to air their differences. It was to be an international actor in its own right, with a legal capacity and certain legal privileges and immunities which would enable it to operate in detachment from its member-states.

Given this fact, why should a book like this argue for the creation of another global body? The UN has been around for over sixty years – why not use that institution, possibly reforming it in some way, in order to manage global affairs better, perhaps even introducing an element of shared sovereignty?

One point needs to be made clear. While this chapter sets out what is arguably a critical view of the UN, it is not in any way suggesting *replacing* it with a proposed Global Union. The argument will be that the Global Union is a supplement to the UN. There is some comparison with the EU in its relation to the Council of Europe. Monnet and Schuman were certainly dissatisfied with the latter as falling short of the sovereignty-sharing organisation they desired. However, the emergence of the European Coal and Steel Community as an alternative organisation, which eventually developed into the European Community and finally the European Union, was never envisaged as making the Council superfluous. The Council of Europe remains an important European body, and even has some advantages over the European Union (above all comprehensiveness – the fact that its fifty-odd members include all those who might be considered wholly or even partly European). Similarly, this book's advocacy of a Global Union is not intended either to replace or to make redundant the UN.

However, despite its aspiration to an effective world role there is a systemic weakness in the UN system, one that is likely to make it a constant prey to the interests of certain powerful nation-states. By examining that weakness this chapter will identify ways in which a body based upon the structures of the European Union could establish a different and in some (but not all) ways stronger global institution.

The Security Council

The governmental structure of the UN, Frederick Lister points out, 'is an amalgam of two disparate branches'. He goes on to spell out what these are:

> Its collective security branch was designed to be run by the Security Council, whose members are empowered by the Charter to take decisions of sovereign import that are legally binding on all of the UN's members. In the other branch of its mandate, the UN operates in the traditional way of IGOs, that is by adopting widely supported resolutions that are not usually binding upon its member states.[1]

On the one hand there is the collective security system which will be considered in this section. Such a system was considered vitally important to those who framed the UN Charter while the world was still at war, and at a time when states were deeply conscious of the failure of the League of Nations to end conflict on a global scale, barely twenty years after the conclusion of the supposed 'war to end all wars' in 1918.

The League of Nations intended to prevent anything like the First World War ever happening again. Its Covenant (constitution) was given pride of place as the first part of the Treaty of Versailles, and both Covenant and Treaty came into force on the same day, 10th January 1920. It was going to be the first international authority, its supporters hoped, that was not an empire. It was going to settle disputes through arbitration and consent, and it was going to use collective force against aggressors. There would be an annual General Assembly in which every member-state had an equal vote (the first General Assembly met in November 1920 and meetings continued until 1941, in the thick of the Second World War), an Executive Council and a permanent secretariat. On the face of it, the arrangements sound similar to those made for the United Nations, with its General Assembly and Security Council.

The League's Executive Council had four permanent (five were intended, but the US did not take part) and four non-permanent members, a similar pattern to the UN Security Council today. Indeed after a number of changes bringing the total number up to fifteen, including the admission of Germany as a fifth permanent member in 1926, the closeness to the modern-day UN Security Council became even more pronounced.

But there was a crucial difference. When a state was attacked, the Executive Council of the League could only advise members on how to fulfil their obligations to support it. Under Article 16 of the Covenant, it would '...recommend to the several governments concerned what effective military, naval or air force the Members of the League shall severally contribute to the armed forces to be used to protect the covenants of the League.' In other words, the Executive Council had no powers to impose any binding obligations on Members of the League. It could only make recommendations.

Moreover, the two most powerful states in the world after 1918, the United States and the Soviet Union, were not members of the League. The US Senate voted not to join the League in November 1919 and refused to ratify the Treaty of Versailles in March 1920. Meanwhile the Soviet Union turned in on itself when the communist revolution failed to spread westwards, leaving the European powers and Japan to manage the League.[2] Effectively, responsibility for a new world order was placed in the hands of European powers at precisely the moment when Europe ceased to have the power to exercise that responsibility. Moreover, there were understandable reasons why Britain and France would be very reluctant enforcers of world peace. They had been severely weakened by four years of conflict fought on an unprecedented scale, leading to huge economic and military losses.

The weakness of the Executive Council therefore reflected the unwillingness of the Great Powers to play a major role in enforcing collective security. Either like the US they refused to join the League at all, or like Britain and France they were reluctant to use their military weight in order to protect members who were attacked.

The collective security system of the UN was designed to be different. All the Great Powers would be involved. Ideological and other differences between the US and the Soviet Union were already clear during the Second World War, but adopting the Charter while they were still allies against Germany and Japan made it possible to bring both into the United Nations. By giving a veto power to each one of the victorious Great Powers in World War Two (they remain the only veto-wielding powers to this day, even though there are now other members of the 'nuclear club'), the UN was framed in such a way as to make sure that they were all comfortable as members. The US, as the most powerful country in the world, was likely to be the most difficult to tempt into the UN organisation (it had refused to take part in the League of Nations). However, in the words of Senator Vandenberg as he sought to overcome isolationist sentiment among Republicans and secure ratification of the Charter, 'the US retains every basic attribute of its sovereignty'. The Charter, he continued, 'gives us a veto on war and on any steps leading to war'.[3]

The price of this was that each veto-wielding nation-state could prevent action being taken against an aggressor if it believed that its own national interests would not be served. But the veto at least meant that the UN and the Security Council would not be hampered by the absence of the most powerful states in the world – the situation which had so severely weakened the League.

A further way in which the collective security system of the UN would be different from that of the League was that the Security Council would have binding powers – what White calls 'supranational powers to prevent and control war'.[4] It was to achieve this purpose that the Security Council was deliberately set apart from the UN's other principal organs. It could issue orders binding upon member-states. In this area – but in this area only – the UN would deal not in recommendations but in binding obligations. The Security Council would determine whether an act of aggression had taken place, what sanctions should be imposed as a result and what measures should be taken to enforce them. Member-states were required to support and assist in these measures. If the Security Council decided that force was to be used, this decision would override all considerations of the rights of member-states to have exclusive authority within their own domestic jurisdictions. Such a right to intervene, together with a right to bind all member-states to the consequences of its own decisions, gave and continues to give the Security Council considerable powers.

The Security Council is a block of only fifteen countries, with five permanent members and a rotating block of ten others out of the hundred and eighty-seven. It therefore represents less than 10% of the world's nation-states and (depending on who makes up the 'rotating' members) perhaps a third of its population. This clearly raises a problem of democratic legitimacy, (a question raised still further by the Security Council's habit of referring to itself as 'the international community'), but as this section has suggested such a system might be defended on the grounds that it ensures that the most powerful states in the world are all willing to remain members.

Security Council reform is a constant item on the UN agenda and a series of proposals have been put forward, including one by the Secretary-General of the time, Kofi Annan, in March 2005, proposing to lift the number of Security Council members to twenty-four. A counter-proposal later in the same year proposed twenty members. Other permutations have been bandied about over the last three years without agreement being reached, but it may be that there will eventually be a decision to increase the size of the Security Council and the number of permanent representatives (perhaps without veto powers). This will not remove the issue of democratic legitimacy, but it may help to make it less pressing.

Conflict also arises from the fact that the veto power of the Five extends not only to decisions authorising the use of force but to other areas too, such as the appointment of the Secretary-General, amendments to the Charter, the enforcement of decisions by the ICJ (International Court of Justice) and decisions on applications for membership of the UN. This effectively means that they can make sure certain matters are not dealt with at all by the Security Council – which passed no resolutions, for instance, on the Soviet invasion of Czechoslovakia or the Vietnam War. Hence Security Council reform, when it is not talking about removing the veto power of the 'Big Five' altogether, turns to ways of restricting its range.

To sum up, the Security Council has considerable power when it exercises it, but it will only be able to exercise it when every single one of the five veto-wielding powers can agree. This may be a necessary condition of the system working at all, but it limits the number of occasions when the Council will be able to sanction the use of force against aggressor nations. Some have argued in the post-Cold War environment cooperation between 'the Five' will prove easier, but this is not as obvious at the end of the first decade of the new century as it might have appeared in the early 1990s during the initial euphoria over the collapse of communism.[5]

Attempts have been made during the last sixty years to transfer some of the Security Council's enforcement authority to the General Assembly. The most important was the establishment of a procedure for the General Assembly of the United Nations to meet in 'Emergency Special Session' if there was no unanimity among the permanent members of the Security Council. The so-called 'Uniting for Peace' procedure was agreed in 1950 and requires a two-thirds majority among General Assembly members. It talks grandly of instances where the Security Council 'fails to exercise proper responsibility for international peace and security'. In such circumstances the General Assembly may take 'collective measures', which may include 'in the case of a breach of the peace or act of aggression the use of armed force where necessary'.

In reality there has been no leakage of power out of the hands of the Security Council. The distinction drawn by Lister remains valid. In the first place there is the collective security branch of the UN run by the Security Council through decisions that are legally binding on all members, and in the second there is the other branch of its mandate, in which the UN adopts resolutions that may be widely supported but are not binding upon its member-states. Therefore in practice an overwhelming vote of the General Assembly meeting in Emergency Special Session means very little. Its recommendations, unlike the decisions of the Security Council, are not legally binding, and are therefore frequently ignored. The General Assembly's most recent special session (its tenth) was a series of meetings between 1997 and 2003 following a ruling of the International Court of Justice on the legality of the Israeli-built security barrier in the West Bank. The eventual resolution of the assembly, calling for an end to the construction of the barrier and the demolition of those parts of it which were on Palestinian land, was passed by an overwhelming one hundred and fifty votes to six, with ten abstentions. Yet despite being passed so overwhelmingly, the resolution has made little or no difference to the situation on the ground in the Middle East. Emergency Special Sessions of the General Assembly do nothing to ensure practical measures to deal with the problems they highlight, even when such measures are supported overwhelmingly.

It seems reasonable to conclude that the Security Council will remain, and will guard its right to remain, the sole body which can make decisions that are binding upon all member-states. The Security Council may be willing to concede certain changes, growing in size or revising the area within which a veto is applied, but it is determined to remain the sole arbiter of when disputes endanger international peace and security and the only body which may make decisions concerning the use of sanctions, including military force, that are binding.

The ability of the Security Council to make decisions that are binding upon member-states might seem to provide a parallel to the EU in those areas in which it has agreed to share sovereignty. However, it needs to be stressed that even binding decisions require some sort of legal framework, as the EU recognised when it established the European Court of Justice (ECJ). This is not the case with the Security Council. The obvious parallel to the ECJ would be the International Court of Justice – but neither the Security Council nor individual member-states are bound by the ICJ in the way that member-states of the European Union are bound by decisions of the ECJ. The implications of this are extremely important. They are examined later in this chapter.

Outside the Security Council – UN 'agencies'

If the problem faced by the Security Council is that of democratic legitimacy, the problem where other parts of the UN organisation are concerned is that of effectiveness. In the other branch of its mandate, according to Lister's definition, the UN operates in the traditional way of IGOs (Inter-Governmental Organisations), adopting resolutions that are not binding upon its member-states. This includes the promotion of international cooperation in the political, economic, social and human rights fields. Here the UN 'in IGO fashion serves as a vehicle or convenience that governments have created to help them carry out certain functions that are best handled transnationally'.[6]

When a number of 'specialised agencies' were established in the economic and social spheres at the end of the Second World War, the assumption was that they would be coordinated. Planners looked to the Bruce report of August 1939, which proposed a Central Committee for Economic and Social Questions for the League of Nations, as the model for the Economic and Social Council which was to be one of the 'principal organs' of the United Nations. In this way they hoped that the new organisation would realise the aspirations of the Bruce Report for effective international action to achieve social and economic goals like full employment and higher living standards.

In the event, the Economic and Social Council (ECOSOC) never achieved the controlling or even coordinating role intended for it. Effective management through ECOSOC as the principal executive organ of the UN became, instead, the recommendation of those who were still hoping for fundamental reform of the institution a generation later.[7] Despite Evan Luard's quip that the agencies emerged, as the British Empire was supposed to have done, 'in a fit of absence of mind',[8] their free-floating, uncoordinated nature was arguably built into the UN system from the beginning, where outside the Security Council there was no effective control mechanism.

A number of well-known organisations dedicated to managing international relations are linked in one way or another to the UN, including the IMF (frequently spoken of in 2008–9 as a means of reviving a world economy falling into recession), the World Bank and the WTO (World Trade Organisation). These three in particular could be considered 'candidates' in any consideration of alternative global institutions that might play an important role in global governance (for precisely this reason some will be examined in closer detail in the next chapter).

However, when their connection to the UN is examined further, it is found to be a very loose one. What are frequently referred to as 'UN agencies', such as the World Health Organisation (WHO) based in Geneva or the IMF (International Monetary Fund) based in Washington, are in reality separate legal persons with their own councils, secretariats, headquarters and budgets. In theory Articles 63 and 64 of the United Nations Charter require the agencies to make regular reports to the Economic and Social Council of the UN (ECOSOC), and allow this Council to coordinate their activities. In practice there is little coordination. The Council is hamstrung by Article 62's ruling that it can do no more than 'make recommendations'. Though called an 'organ' of the UN, the equivalent of ECOSOC in the EU would not be one of its key institutions like the Parliament, Commission, Council or Court of Justice, but something like the Economic and Social Committee or the Committee of the Regions, though even these have more powers to force issues onto the agenda of the main EU bodies than does the Economic and Social Council of the

UN. White argues that 'historically, there has been very little control by ECOSOC' in trying to coordinate a 'huge and unwieldy system'. His conclusion is that 'in theory and practice, then, the specialised UN agencies are not the "agents" of that body in the full sense of that word'.[9]

The UN would certainly not be the first organisation to contain an alphabet soup of agencies all jockeying for power and insufficiently coordinated from the centre. But it has particular problems in this regard. On the one hand, as already mentioned, there are the quasi-independent 'agencies' like the IMF and the WHO. Beyond the 'agencies' there are certain other organisations associated with the UN, such as the IAEA (International Atomic Energy Authority) and (since 1995, and only very loosely associated) the WTO (World Trade Organisation). These are global bodies which are well known on the world stage, but they are only in a very limited sense 'UN bodies'. They are independent organisations rather than UN 'agencies' and simply have the right to coordinate their activities with the UN through a 'relationship agreement' if they so choose (the WTO talks of a responsibility to 'liaise' with the UN). They have no institutional links with the UN, even though they support cooperation.

The problem is not simply that as part of an unwieldy and bureaucratic system the 'agencies' and related bodies have been able to stray from the centrally managed leash. It is that they have been able to break the leash and set off in an entirely different direction. They have been able to pursue policies at variance with the principles of their foundation. The World Bank and the IMF, for instance, two UN 'agencies' based in Washington, were created in 1944 as part of a determination to prevent a repeat of the mistakes that led to the rise of fascism. They were intended to prevent the sort of economic shocks and crashes that destabilised and ultimately destroyed Weimar Germany. To do so they focused on long-term investment in development in order to pull countries out of poverty, using Keynesian methods (Keynes himself was part of the UK delegation at Bretton Woods where the institutions were set up).

Within a generation a very different economic philosophy had come to dominate both organisations. States seeking loans were required to cut government spending (rather than spend their way out of trouble by deficit financing) and remove all barriers to foreign investment by a combination of privatisation and deregulation (making it difficult to protect domestic industry during its fragile infancy). Such a transformation led one chief economist at the World Bank to remark that

'Keynes would be rolling in his grave were he to see what had happened to his child'.[10]

By the 1980s the 'agencies' were imposing these 'structural adjustment' conditions upon any candidate for loans. The same conditions which South America faced in the 1980s were imposed on South Africa, parts of Asia and Russia in the 1990s. The result was often precisely the sort of economic crisis – huge levels of unemployment and currency collapse – that had brought Weimar Germany to collapse. By now, however, they were portrayed as the sort of brutal measures which could effect much-needed shock therapy to 'ailing economies'.[11]

This is not the place to discuss the relative merits of 'developmental' and 'free market' economics. What can be said, however, is that within the course of a generation the IMF and World Bank – whether for good or ill – managed to transform the criteria upon which they gave loans to countries in need of loans out of all recognition. Out went the Keynesian approach of the 1940s, expanding welfare provision and public sector investment, and in came values of the Chicago School of Economics, whose alumni packed the boards of these two bodies and sought to apply the ideas not of Keynes but of Milton Friedman and Friedrich von Hayek. The process was helped, of course, by the weighted voting system in these two bodies, which reflects levels of contributions and therefore provides the US, Japan and the wealthier European countries with about half the voting strength on the two bodies.

Once again, this is neither the place to debate these very different forms of 'economic architecture' nor to bemoan the shift from Keynes to Friedman – many economists would welcome it. The point being made is that the transformation did not reflect any change of economic opinion within the UN itself or among members of ECOSOC. Indeed, if anything the 'development economics' of the 1960s remained the dominant ideology there. While the boards of the IMF and the World Bank were packed with economists from the so-called Chicago School (both Friedman and Hayek taught at the University of Chicago), the UN remained oblivious to, or at least unable to influence, such profound changes of policy on the part of its two 'agencies'. In all likelihood it was a situation which the 'agencies' themselves welcomed: on the one hand they could benefit from the respectability conveyed by their connection with the UN, while on the other they could relish the lack of UN control over their actions.

This is the point of the remark by Taylor that the UN system was one lacking 'any central brain',[12] in the sense of lacking any effective central management. It may be the case that the metaphor became less appropriate in the years after his book was published in 1993. Although bodies like the IMF and the World Bank continued to pursue the sort of economic philosophy that would have had Keynes turning in his grave and many members of ECOSOC squirming in their seats, a change of thinking began to be discernible by the end of the millennium, for instance in the World Bank's report *Development and Human Rights: The Role of the World Bank*, published in 1998. Nevertheless, Taylor's metaphor represents an important insight into the nature of UN governance. In the same passage he writes that the loose organisation of the UN 'allowed the member-states to avoid the problems which would arise if the instruments of collectivity were to be strengthened'. In other words, the more the various 'agencies' and organisations became part of an effectively coordinated programme of action to deal with problems, the more individual member-states would be forced into accountability, and this was the last thing that a number of them wanted. The loose and unwieldy UN structures had come to suit the purposes of some countries. The last thing that they would be willing to concede would be a tightening-up of those structures.

Indeed a kind of unholy alliance arises. The UN, in order to demonstrate the range of its activities, likes to call bodies like the World Bank and the IMF its 'agencies'. At the same time the 'agencies' like to be able to shield under the UN umbrella, though in practice retaining a free hand in the policies they pursue. The last thing an unholy alliance of this sort achieves is effective governance.

By way of comparison, the community agencies established by the European Union, beginning from the 1970s but expanding considerably in the 1990s, are governed by European Community law and managed by agency boards which contain representatives from member-states, the Commission and in some cases the Parliament. They receive (partial or total) funding from the community budget and their own budgets are examined by the Court of Auditors. They reflect both the desire to establish EU bodies in more member-states of an enlarging European Union and recognition of the growing complexity of certain scientific and technical tasks that require separate attention. However, they remain firmly bound to carry out EU policy within a tightly controlled legal, financial and managerial framework. The twenty or so agencies dotted around the Union concentrate on particular tasks such as improving living and working conditions (Dublin since 1975), harmonising the internal market (Alicante since 1994) and developing vocational training (Turin since 1995). But in each case the agency is not given any discretionary powers and the Commission retains oversight over the 'delegated competence'. They cannot set off on an entirely different course to that desired at the centre. Indeed, this is surely what one would normally expect of any body that could be designated an 'agency' of another.

The legal framework of the UN

The legal capacity of the UN rests upon the International Court of Justice (ICJ), a body of fifteen judges (no two may be from one particular state) to whose statute all member-states are party. Like the Security Council, which it mimics in terms of size, the five countries that are permanent veto-wielding members of the Council are also guaranteed that one of their nationals will be a member of the Court.

The Court has a theoretically broad range of jurisdiction, which includes interpreting treaties, applying international law, determining breaches of international obligations and fixing upon the reparations to be made for such breaches. Each member of the UN has undertaken to comply with decisions of the ICJ in any case to which it is a party. If a state fails to honour a judgement of the Court, the aggrieved party may bring the case before the Security Council.

In practice, however, the Court's jurisdiction is limited to cases over which it is specifically given jurisdiction by treaties. Beyond that, states may voluntarily declare themselves prepared to be bound by the Court's rulings throughout the areas described in the last paragraph – but less than half have done so, and often with conditions attached. Moreover, even if a state fails to honour a judgement of the Court, and the matter is taken by the aggrieved party to the Security Council, Article 94 merely says that the Council 'may, if it deems necessary, make recommendations or decide upon measures to be taken to give effect to the judgment'. In other words, the Security Council puts member-states under no stronger obligation than the Executive Council of the League of Nations did when it made recommendations to member-states. As a result, ICJ rulings can be ignored, as happened when Nicaragua filed a suit against the US government. The US refused to appear before the Court, to accept its ruling as binding or to pay the damages awarded against it.

It is not even clear that the ICJ can require the UN itself to act legally, at least so far as the Security Council is concerned. Regarding the Lockerbie case in 1998, one of the judges argued that though a decision of the Security Council must be in accordance with the UN

Charter, 'it does not follow...that the Court is empowered to ensure that the Council's decisions do accord with the Charter'.[13] Judge Schwebel's ruling is interesting because it effectively sees any sort of judicial review of the Council's actions as an undue limitation of its authority; the implication is that the only arbiter of whether the Security Council has acted constitutionally is the Security Council!

For this reason it is difficult to see how the International Court of Justice can be effective as the principal legal organ of the UN, or how there could ever be a systematic review of Security Council decisions or a challenge to their legality. As Suganami points out, the UN Security Council makes binding decisions on what enforcement measures should be taken when it determines that there is a 'threat to the peace, breach of the peace or act of aggression', but it does *not* have to determine whether this follows any breach of international law. In the League of Nations, on the other hand, sanctions were to be directed under the Covenant only against nations that resorted to war *unlawfully*.[14] The danger is that *de facto* the Security Council, rather than the ICJ, becomes the judicial organ of the UN, prompting obvious criticism concerning the separation of powers in that body.

Compounding this concern about the Security Council is its creation of its own judicial organs, such as the International Criminal Tribunals reviewing cases in the former Yugoslavia and Rwanda. This system was naturally challenged by defendants brought to trial, and the answer given was that it was all part of the Council's task in maintaining peace and security. However, the idea that its authority in this area allows the Security Council to create its own judicial organs remains unconvincing, once again raising concerns that it is acting as the *de facto* judicial organ of the UN. It seems that if it has to make use of legal bodies, the Security Council prefers to create its own rather than be subject to a body (the ICJ) which might not always endorse its decisions or the positions of its most powerful members.

In fact we find in the judicial area a similar case of the proliferation of agencies and quasi-agencies, or in this case a proliferation of courts and quasi-courts. Indeed the quasi-agencies themselves may create quasi-legal bodies, as when the WTO creates a Dispute Resolution Panel, which then deals with issues with which the ICJ might well be involved. Then there are all the bodies spawned by treaties, dealing with everything from the law of the sea to torture and degrading treatment. Given that the Law of the Sea Convention of 1982 created a Law of the Sea Tribunal, and given that this tribunal might well reach a different view to the ICJ which has jurisprudence in the area of the law of the sea, then precisely the same sort of muddle is created in the area of law as is created in the area of practical policy initiatives when overlapping agencies fail to be coordinated.

Clearly there is the need for a legal equivalent (despite their poor record) of ECOSOC or the ACC (Administrative Council on Coordination), and clearly the ICJ is the only body which can play that role. But once again the fears of some member-states that their own interests might be compromised by too strongly centralised a system, in this case that of law, means that they prefer a loose muddle with all sorts of hidden exits through which they can escape responsibility. Hence the UN remains as 'loosely' or inefficiently structured in the legal area as it does where its agencies are concerned.

The slow progress towards the development of the ICC (International Criminal Court), which despite its formal inauguration in 2002 suffers from the refusal of a number of countries, including the US and China,[15] to support it, illustrates the point further. As opposed to *ad hoc* tribunals like those specifically created to deal with crimes in the former Yugoslavia or Rwanda, the ICC would represent the *universal* application of international criminal law (though probably not in a comprehensive range of areas – the ICC has jurisdiction over only a small part of international criminal law). But this is precisely why the US and China are reluctant to endorse it. Once again the preference for specific organs or instruments controlled by the Security Council trumps the development of a powerful controlling mechanism at the centre of the UN.

Is there an opening for the UN to develop a legal system that is both comprehensive and binding? In time more member-states may be willing to accept a broader remit of the ICJ's functions. But crucial to such a development would be for the Security Council to use the authority it already possesses in order to bind member-states to accept rulings of the International Court of Justice. As yet there is little sign of this.

The related area of human rights is another in which the preference on the part of individual nation-states for UN muddle over a degree of central control which might threaten their autonomy has spawned a range of 'norms', 'processes' and 'organs', described by White as 'chaotic and lacking rational coherence'.[16] Yet again an increasingly elaborate structure of institutions emerges, in this case addressing human rights, while new initiatives, like the Vienna declaration of 1993, concentrate on updating and refining the standards to be achieved rather than addressing the chaotic structures or the question of how to realise those standards in practice.

What this section is suggesting is that there is a discernible pattern in the UN structure whereby a potentially powerful legal body like the ICJ, or a potentially powerful economic and social body like ECOSOC, are effectively denied the power to carry out their remit. Whether it is the proliferation of 'alternative courts' like the ICC and the ad hoc tribunals, or the effectively autonomous bodies like the World Bank and the IMF, heavily packed with controlling board members who take a very different view to that of ECOSOC, the policy is the same. Create – and even celebrate – a host of new 'initiatives' and the bodies that go with them, but use them in order to block rather than facilitate effective control on the part of the bodies which ought to be managing affairs from the centre. A lack of legal enforceability bedevils rulings of the ICJ (when it is able to make them), while the economic and social arrangements called for by ECOSOC are largely ignored by those who run the UN agencies and quasi-agencies themselves.

Recent developments – The problem of intervention

In 2004, a high-level panel set up by Kofi Annan endorsed the emerging norm of a Responsibility to Protect (R2P), stating that use of force by the international community was a possible step as a last resort. The panel proposed some basic criteria that would legitimise the use of force by the Security Council 'in the event of genocide and other large-scale killing, ethnic cleansing and serious violations of humanitarian law which sovereign governments have proved powerless or unwilling to prevent'. In September 2005, at the United Nations World Summit, Member-states accepted the responsibility of each state to protect its population from genocide, war crimes, ethnic cleansing and crimes against humanity. Moreover, world leaders also agreed that when any state fails to meet that responsibility, all states ('the international community') are responsible for helping to protect peoples threatened with such crimes. 'All states' – but once again acting through the Security Council. Diplomatic, humanitarian and other peaceful methods should be used first, but if these failed then states should act 'collectively' through the UN Security Council by using force in a 'decisive and timely manner'. This was hailed as an historic decision at the UN's 60th Anniversary World Summit.

The intervention envisaged under 'R2P' would be pursued for humanitarian reasons, on the grounds that the state in question is deliberately making life unbearable for at least some of its citizens. This was certainly offered as a reason for intervening in Kosovo in 1999, though the intervention did not receive UN authorisation. But there is another kind of intervention that has become increasingly obvious.

This is a form of intervention based on Article 51 (in Chapter VII) of the United Nations Charter, which talks of 'the inherent right of individual or collective self-defence if an armed attack occurs against a member of the United Nations'. Evan Luard pointed out some of the undesirable implications of Article 51 nearly thirty years ago. He wrote that it brought a 'significant alteration in the emphasis of the Charter as a whole' and went on to suggest that the United Nations....

> ...might now become a system in which breaches of the peace were met in the first place by action taken by individual states or groups of states, while only at some subsequent stage would the Security Council be called on to take action if necessary. In other words, it made it...substantially more likely that conflict situations would be dealt with in the traditional way, as for hundreds of years before.[17]

The problem was that even though the acts of self-defence were meant to be provisional until the Security Council stepped in, the Security Council might well be paralysed by one or more of the Five wielding its veto. Instead of a new system of collective security under a powerful central organ of the international community, he suggested, what he called 'the old measures of self-help' (effectively every nation for itself) would prevail.

It is true that, as Suganmi reminds us, 'Article 51 ... delimits the use of force in self-defence to those cases where an armed attack occurs against the member-states',[18] but contemporary concern about terrorism has made it possible to circumvent this limitation. Assuming that a terrorist attack on the US counts as an 'armed attack', and assuming that the terrorists concerned (such as al-Qaeda) could be linked to a particular country which was harbouring them or even preparing them for a specific mission and sending them, say, to attack the Twin Towers, then any US armed intervention that followed could be justified as a form of self-defence. It was on these grounds that the US argued at the end of 2001 that the Security Council did not have to authorise its use of force against Afghanistan.[19]

The so-called 'war on terror' has undermined the principle of non-intervention in one area, while the determination to intervene in the affairs of member-states for humanitarian reasons, based on the 'Responsibility to Protect', has undermined it in another. This might be thought no bad thing, the right approach for a 'post-Westphalian' age in which the absolute authority of the nation-state has rightly been undermined. However, those who herald the end of the 'Westphalian' age of absolute authority for the individual nation-state need to recognise that the authority to intervene in the internal affairs of a state must be given some clear backing in law.

Increasing instances of intervention, whether for pre-emptive or humanitarian purposes, make it all the more important that decisions, whether of individual nations, the Security Council or the General Assembly, should come within a legal framework. As Gray writes:

> Whereas commentators used to discuss the problem of the inactivity of the Security Council, now they concern themselves also with difficulties over the legitimacy of its action.[20]

However, Annan's high-level panel, proposing criteria that would legitimise the use of force by the Security Council, once again failed to establish that breaches of such criteria should be determined by the International Court of Justice. The lack of legal oversight where the Security Council is concerned confirms a disturbing sense that it feels able to act as its own arbiter, and as the (in many instances perhaps laudable) calls for intervention in the affairs of member-states increases, this is bound to become an increasing problem.

Robert Cooper[21] argues that what he calls the 'legalistic' model of international relations will no longer suffice – i.e. a system whereby states maintain sovereign and autonomous control of everything domestic so long as they conform to certain 'international norms'. He argues that this was the principle underlining the formation of the UN, calling the UN Charter something 'written in and for another age.' Other writers make the same point. Mark Leonard talks about the United Nations' doctrine of 'non-interference in internal affairs', referred to in Article 5 of its Charter, as a 'political do-not-disturb sign'.[22]

What these writers do not seem to recognise is the fact that the need to be 'legalistic', at least in the sense of having clearly defined legal norms and a body to apply them, was never so necessary as when intervention in the affairs of nation-states becomes the rule rather than the exception. There may be a case for saying that in a post-Westphalian age there should be more such intervention, but it is not clear that there is any *legal* framework for such action. The Security Council has given itself the power to make binding resolutions, but without the legal mechanisms to give such resolutions validity. It is impossible to envisage it working either fairly or effectively if it insists upon wrapping itself in what one writer calls a fog of law rather than developing a clear and binding legal framework for its activities.[23]

The financial framework of the UN

The UN has no equivalent of the European Union's 'own resources'. Under Article 17 its budget is determined by the General Assembly, which employs a scale of assessment in order to ask for more of richer countries, a well-established practice among IGOs. If countries fail to pay their dues, they are violating their treaty obligations, and if they fall more than two years behind in their payments they can lose their vote in the General Assembly (a sanction unlikely to worry members of the Security Council).

The system led to a series of financial crises generated by defaults on payments, which was supposedly resolved by an informal practice of determining the budget 'by consensus'. Effectively the requirement for such a consensus meant that the wealthier states determined a ceiling on UN funding. Since the assessments are revised every three years (as opposed to the European Union's seven), this produces regular crises over funding. The UN has no borrowing powers and can do nothing in the face of a powerful state's refusal to pay. In 2006 a New York think-tank, Global Policy Forum, estimated that members' arrears to the Regular Budget were in excess of a billion dollars, or about 10% of the UN's annual expenditure (if the spending of all its programmes, funds and specialised agencies, excluding the World Bank and IMF, are taken into account). Where the contributions to the EU budget are made legally binding upon member-states and are paid, commitments by members of the UN to, for instance, designating 0.7% of GDP to aid programmes have never been honoured by more than a handful of countries.

However the figure is arrived at, what is striking is not only the unreliability of UN funding but its paucity. Special programmes often limp along on very limited budgets. UNDP (the United Nations Development Programme, designed to help countries in their economic development) does not fare as badly as some others with its 4,500 staff and a budget (in 2007) of five billion dollars. On the other hand UNCTAD (United Nations Conference on Trade and Development) forty years old and designed to integrate developing countries into the world economy, has only four hundred and fifty staff and a budget (all figures given are for 2007) of 100 million dollars. Then there are two less well-known bodies created in later years, IFAD (International Fund for Agricultural Development), with four hundred staff and a hundred million dollars, which focuses on rural poverty, and UNIDO (United Nations Industrial Development Organ), about twice as large and aiming to promote the growth of small and medium-sized enterprises. Finally there is the World Food Programme, approaching its fiftieth birthday, with a three billion dollar budget and 10,000 staff, designed to meet emergency food needs and – like the other two funds mentioned – help with economic development. Some of these will be looked at in more detail in Part III.

With the exception of the World Bank, none of these UN programmes and agencies has a very large budget (though some do have a large number of staff). By way of comparison, the EU, representing a much smaller group of nations (admittedly including some of the world's richest) has an annual budget which is more than ten times bigger than that of the UN at around one hundred and fifty billion dollars.

Compare, for instance, the totals for structural funds and various regional development programmes administered by the EU, an annual figure of something like fifty billion dollars guaranteed for the whole period 2007–13.

Not only is there a lack of funding, but there is also a clear need for all these programmes to be properly coordinated. The lack of central control described in earlier sections applies to these agencies as much as it does to more well-known bodies like the IMF and the World Bank. UN funds are often wasted, since the UN lacks authority in developing countries and cannot oversee its spending in the way that the EU can oversee the use of its structural and cohesion funds. UN agencies become 'milch cows' for corrupt governments, not because they are themselves corrupt but because they have no way of preventing this from happening. Once again this will be given further consideration in Part III.

If poorer countries are to prove willing to make the sort of changes to their economies that would, for instance, help to reduce their carbon emissions, then they will need some financial support in order to do so – just as the poorer nations of the EU, as was seen in the last chapter, needed such support in adapting to the demands of the single market and the common currency. Help given to their vulnerable economic sectors – or sectors made vulnerable by their commitment to carbon reduction – will be necessary. This is one of the reasons why UN agreements on tackling the urgent problem of climate change have proved so difficult. Without a proper budget the UN lacks the carrot; without binding legislation the UN lacks the stick.

The lack of control over bodies at one remove from the UN, the 'agencies' and related bodies like the WTO, the IMF or the World Bank, together with the lack of 'own resources' which makes it extremely difficult for the UN to plan in the medium or even short term through bodies like UNIDO and UNCTAD, (and even here it has little control over their activities in particular developing nations), means that it has proved extremely difficult for the UN to be effective in the economic and social areas where so much needs to be done. For this reason Part III outlines a proposal for a Global Food Security Programme whereby member-states agree to share sovereignty in a particular area and create (as in the formation of the European Coal and Steel Community) a 'higher authority' with binding powers.

Of course the decisions of the Security Council may well have funding implications too. Money is usually found for military intervention (and kept in a separate budget) even though it is not always found for the UN's other activities. Even in the military area, however, there can be difficulties, with funds for peacekeeping being withheld even by countries that voted for such actions in the Security Council. On the other hand some military operations, enthusiastically supported by most members of the Security Council and accepted by the others, have no problem finding financial support from the enthusiasts themselves. The intervention in Iraq during the early 1990s would be an example.

It is worth pointing out in this context how much easier both the funding and the organisation of the UN's peacekeeping activities would be if it was able to maintain some military forces of its own. This was the original intention of those who framed the Charter. According to Article 43 each member-state undertook 'to make available to the Security Council, on its call and in accordance with special agreement or agreements, armed forces, assistance and facilities, including rights of passage.' These forces were supposed to be ready to be mobilised at a moment's notice. Article 45, for instance, talked about 'immediately available national air force contingents for combined international enforcement action'. The original vision was of command and control by the UN itself – essentially the UN would have its own forces under a Military Staff Committee, which was established under Article 47 of the Charter. But this proved impossible in the conditions of the nascent Cold War.

Therefore the system of collective security was 'decentralised', which essentially meant that authority was delegated (under Chapter VII) to a particular group of states to take military enforcement action. In effect this was a similar arrangement to that under Chapter VIII where regional organisations, like the EU and NATO, are used by the Security Council for enforcement actions. Command is decentralised to the states which form the multinational force – the 'coalition of the willing' prepared to take action. But the effect of this is to loosen the UN's grip. Rather than managing its own forces – or at least managing the forces of member-states through its own military staff committee – it lets a particular nation or (more often) group of nations assemble forces of their own and then direct them in the conflict, reporting to the Security Council on what actions they have been taking. The states themselves know that this is a less effective arrangement than one under direct control of the UN. Agreements have to be reached between states and military units from different countries put together, often over a lengthy period of time, before any effective military action can be taken. However, these individual states also know that this cumbersome system allows them a greater degree of individual control over what military enforcement measures are taken. It may even allow them to place their own military measures under the UN umbrella. It is the same old story. For the sake of freedom at national level, states are prepared to tolerate a cumbersome and ineffective organisation at international level.

Conclusion

It may well be true that, as White observes, the UN Charter was from the outset 'constructed as a constitutional document and not as an international treaty'.[24] But if he is correct to say that the UN is 'a system founded on law' and not on a 'conference model', it must be able to show how those who break the law are held to account. White claims that the UN Charter saw itself as a constitutional document rather than an international treaty, its 'We the Peoples of the United Nations' echoing the famous 'We the People' of the United States Constitution. Thomas Greer believed that Roosevelt took the view that 'the conception of the United Nations was not that of an *ultimate* organisation',[25] implying the need for change. If so, this must – as he recognises – propel the UN into the arena of making and applying law.

This raises the question of whether it is possible to reform the UN. There is no doubt that reforms have been and are being proposed. One well-known proposal from the 1960s envisaged a radically reformed General Assembly with legislative competence with regard to disarmament and the maintenance of peace. Indeed, attempts to argue that more power should be vested in the General Assembly go back to a proposal from the Philippines Delegation to the UN in 1945 to endow it with legislative authority to enact rules of international law which would be binding on the organisation (the proposal was defeated at a drafting session by 26 votes to 1). Instead of the Security Council there would be an Executive Council of seventeen members elected by the General Assembly. The International Court of Justice would have compulsory jurisdiction over a range of international disputes. There would be a full-time UN peace force numbering hundreds of thousands.[26] A decade later Rajni Kothari proposed that ECOSOC become the UN's 'principal executive organ' and that a World Parliamentary Assembly be established (and a world police force), while Mazrui focused on enhancing the role of UNESCO.[27]

Another thirty years on, it is noticeably how much less ambitious attempts to reform the UN are than they were then. Excitement is generated by the idea of adding a few members to the Security Council or limiting its remit or by the launch of a new body like the International Criminal Court. Fundamental reform is on hardly anyone's agenda.

Is there much chance of significant reform of the UN? The view of this book is that there is not. If it is correct in its assessment of the overweening powers of the Security Council, then it is difficult to see how fundamental change is possible. Moreover, the excessive power of the Security Council and the ineffectiveness of the other elements of the UN, such as the General Assembly, ECOSOC and the ICJ, are part and parcel of the same failure. C.K. Webster made a prescient remark when he declared that the UN Charter was an attempt at 'harmonising the Great Power Alliance theory and the League theory'.[28] What he realised was that each of the veto-wielding Five 'Great Powers', participating in a Security Council with binding powers but no binding obligation to uphold international law, was effectively immune to the harmful consequences of any legal challenge to its interests. Some, like Brierly, even saw in the way the UN developed a return to the nineteenth Century principle of a concert of powers. Such a harsh view is perhaps unsurprising in an eminent international lawyer – compare the comments of Prof. Christine Gray cited above from a contemporary perspective.[29]

Outside the collective security area it is clear that the UN could not apply what the last chapter considered to be the precondition and instruments of an effective sharing of sovereignty. Giddes rightly points to a key difference between the EU and the UN in that for the former 'formal sovereignty has been pooled, such that each member takes on board decisions handed down in the EU courts'.[30] In the UN, as this chapter has stressed, there is no equivalent control exercised by the International Court of Justice.

Linked to the lack of an equivalent to European law, with its power to override national laws in appropriate areas, is the absence of the instruments which the last chapter identified as crucial to the development and enlargement of the European Union. The UN lacks 'own resources' – effectively independent budgetary powers, the condition for providing support to vulnerable economic sectors. Instead, certain states prefer the control won by being able to drip-feed the UN with money, as one might control an alcoholic in the family by releasing funds only for specific purposes and on particular occasions. Secondly, the UN lacks the equivalent of systems for regional development which possess not only the resources to support less well-off parts of the Union but also the means of enforcement to ensure that assistance is not wasted (which isn't to deny that it sometimes is).

On the one hand, the loose connections between the UN and its 'agencies' produce a system in which the IMF and World Bank are not bound by the charter to follow relevant UN resolutions. The result is to have bodies like the World Bank and IMF free floating in space, rather than being brought within a UN framework. On the other hand those bodies which clearly do represent the UN's thinking are often poorly-funded, badly coordinated and cannot control the way funds are used in a number of countries where they are made available. It is hard to disagree with Zamora that 'the international economic system is ill-served by a UN system in which a multiplicity of agencies operate in uncoordinated fashion to deal separately with economic issues that are interrelated'.[31]

It would be foolish not to recognise the important role which the UN still plays. To reiterate the point once again, this book is not arguing for the replacement of the UN. It is calling for a supplementary body formed on supranationalist lines which, it argues, is able to do things which the UN can't – enact binding legislation and provide substantial practical assistance to member-states who need help in, for instance, curbing carbon emissions or climbing out of extreme poverty.

The search for global governance must recognise one clear advantage of a body like the UN over a body like the projected Global Union. The UN is a system designed to include everyone (only Western Sahara, Taiwan and the Vatican State are missing, since they are not recognised by everyone as states). In this the approach of the UN is similar to that of the Council of Europe, whose fifty-odd members include, for instance, both Russia and Georgia, taking in everyone with any 'geographical claim'. The principle is to have everyone round the table first and then see what can be agreed upon.

This makes sense. What, it might be asked, is the point of a 'global union' which (initially at any rate, and probably for some time thereafter) contains just a small percentage of the world's countries, when global problems like climate change require discussions with countries like Russia and China that might not wish to share sovereignty in the manner of a Global Union? Any proposal limited to a few countries could therefore be seen as essentially impractical because important emitters of greenhouse gases, for instance, are excluded.

On the other hand – the other side of what is an impossible dilemma – the Global Union does have one clear advantage. Because it entails a real sharing of sovereignty and penalties for non-compliance, it has a chance of being effective, at least among its own members. Its member-states are likely to abide by its rules, as by and large do the member-states of the European Union. The dilemma is made clear where crucial contemporary issues like climate change are concerned.

It can be argued that the UN is capable of achieving a comprehensive settlement. The United Nations Framework Convention on Climate Change (UNFCCC) was an international treaty signed by practically everyone in the world. However, they did not achieve the targets they set themselves, for reasons that have to do with all the limitations of what are essentially non-binding agreements and the UN's lack of resources both in the offering of carrots and the wielding of sticks. A Global Union would at least permit the achievement of agreements that were binding and enforceable – at first on nothing like one hundred eight-nine states, and probably on very few of the 'worst emitters', but with some prospect of being able to enlarge over time after success had been demonstrated. Fashionable talk of 'effective multilateralism' needs to pay much more attention to these deeper questions of structural constraints upon UN action.

The clear implication would seem to be that both institutions, the comprehensive 'talking shop' (at least outside the collective security area) and the more limited (in terms of membership) but expanding group of states willing to share sovereignty and therefore make themselves subject to binding agreements, have their value. One makes up in being effective among its members for what it lacks in terms of being comprehensive. The other makes up by being comprehensive for what it lacks in terms of being able to subject its members to binding agreements. Both institutions have a valuable role to play. However, the point of this chapter has been to demonstrate that the UN is unlikely to be able to succeed as the only effective international institution with a role to play in global governance. The structural issues which a number of academics, parliamentarians and *fonctionnaires* prefer to ignore will not go away.

6
Other Potential Global Authorities

Introduction

In the last chapter the focus was upon the UN. The intention was to examine whether it might – possibly as a result of substantial reform – provide the way forward towards effective global governance. The conclusion was that it is highly unlikely to do so.

Nevertheless, it might be argued that there are plenty of other actual and potential global organisations. Several have been mooted as possible life-savers for the world in 2009, a time when global economic crisis has led to frequent trawling around in search of better institutions for dealing with the current economic turmoil and the political fallout it is bound to bring.

Six institutions or sets of institutions will be dealt with in this chapter. The first section examines what are broadly speaking financial and economic bodies like the IMF (International Monetary Fund), World Bank, WTO (World Trade Organisation) and OECD (Organisation for Economic Cooperation and Development), some of which were mentioned in the last chapter because of their loose links with the UN. The second considers informal meetings between heads of state. The emergence of the G20 (Group of 20) as a more rounded and representative body than the G7 and G8, including as it does developing nations like Brazil and India, could arguably develop into a 'G 200' with global authority. The third section analyses a body with a primarily security concern but whose reach is increasingly global, namely NATO (the North Atlantic Treaty Organisation), comparing it with the less well-known OSCE (Organisation for Security and Cooperation in Europe). The fourth section examines bodies that might have emerged for particular historical reasons but which can still, their supporters argue, provide a very important springboard for the coming together of nations in the twenty-first century. The (British) Commonwealth of Nations would be an example. The fifth section examines the idea of forming a new organisation. This is precisely what this book attempts to do, but the section here will consider proposals for other new organisations, such as John McCain's 'League of Democracies' and Eduard Balladur's 'Union of the West'. The sixth and final section of this chapter considers the idea of informal global networking activities which can somehow bypass the work of troublesome nation-states in achieving world peace. This 'constructive anarchy' approach argues that nation-states do not need to agree a sharing of sovereignty, because the very process of globalisation forces them to give up a significant proportion of the powers they would like to keep. The problems highlighted in this book are therefore not so much solved as bypassed. No new institutions for global governance need to be created because global governance will emerge anyway, not from arrangements between states but from irresistible developments at 'sub-state' level fostered by the communications revolution and other modern developments.

Such a list may not be exhaustive, but it will hopefully be able to cover the main candidates for effective global governance. In the process the hope is that the chapter will provide a further opportunity to focus more sharply on precisely what the requirements are for such an organisation to act successfully. A later chapter will then provide further evidence of these requirements by examining the relations of the EU with countries that are not (in some cases not for the foreseeable future and in other cases never) actual or potential candidates for membership of the Union.

Financial and economic bodies

Though a few of these organisations, for example NAFTA (the North American Free Trade Association comprising the US, Canada and Mexico), are focused upon particular regions, this section will concentrate upon those which may reasonably claim a worldwide remit, namely the IMF (International Monetary Fund), the World Bank, the WTO (World Trade Organisation) and the OECD (Organisation for Economic Cooperation and Development).

The International Monetary Fund

As mentioned in Chapter 5, the IMF is ostensible linked to the UN as a 'specialised agency', but in reality it has nothing like the sort of close connection which EU agencies have with the Commission. It has its own charter, governing structure and finances, which have effectively enabled it to pursue a course independent of any parameters that might have been set by the Economic and Social Council of the United Nations.

The IMF originated with the Bretton Woods agreement at the end of the Second World War. It was specifically designed to maintain exchange rate stability and monetary cooperation between states, ensuring a balanced growth of trade and helping members in balance of payments difficulties. It does not finance specific investment projects but it does loan large sums of money, originally to more developed countries but for the last thirty years to developing countries too. The oil shocks of the seventies, the collapse of communism in the eighties and the currency collapse caused by rapid shifts of global capital in the nineties and in the new millennium (part of the impact of globalisation), have all led to countries being in sudden and urgent need of IMF support. Hence its role as what Andrew Baker calls 'the crucial institution in the international financial architecture'.[1] Indeed, as recession caused by the so-called 'credit crunch' began to deepen in early 2009, there were widespread calls to provide the IMF with extra funding in order to be able to meet what was certain to be an increase in demands upon it as lender of last resort.

The terms of that support – what the IMF calls 'conditionality' – have been controversial, for instance in requiring public expenditure cuts in order to reduce government debt (the IMF has hardly been Keynesian for the last thirty years, despite Keynes' involvement in its origins). Stiglitz talks of 'formulaic orthodox prescriptions' along the lines of public expenditure cuts, privatisation and trade liberalisation.[2] But whatever the terms of its provision (and there are recent signs that these are changing) no one denies that such funding has been needed and is likely to be needed even more in the immediate future. In that context current proposals to increase the funding available to the IMF are understandable.

Furthermore, it is arguable that the present world financial crisis has parallels with that of the 1930s. Once again the temptations of protectionism and competitive devaluations are there. The need to avoid the chaos of the 1930s while restoring growth and currency stability is paramount, and many see the IMF as the ideal body to coordinate such a recovery. Whether or not the 'Friedmanite' proposals of earlier decades were justified, it is likely that different policies will be followed in the context of the current urgent need to boost world trade.

It is remarkable to reflect that a leading article in *The Economist* accompanying its feature article quoted at the start of this book, 'What a way to run the world', contained a passage on the IMF which questioned whether there was any further need for an institution 'originally set up to monitor exchange rates' (in fact this task was always conceived to be part of a far wider remit to avoid a repeat of the catastrophic depression of the 1930s, precisely the fear that so many have today). The leading article suggested that the IMF 'could become a committee of oversight, but the main financial regulation will stay at the national level'. That was July 2008. Within six months the deepening financial crisis, had driven people into talking about the need for financial regulation at a trans-national level and the key role which the IMF could play in such an arrangement.

However, there are some difficulties in envisaging a wider role for the IMF. The body has one hundred and eighty-five members, making its membership almost universal. Its voting system, however, is not democratic, at least in a formal sense. Votes are weighted roughly according to a country's importance in the global economy. This, of course, is something fluid, requiring constant reappraisal, but any changes require an 85% majority of votes. Given the fact that the US has over 16% of the votes, this gives it a veto over any changes. This doesn't mean no change will happen – some action has already been taken in order to recognise the growing importance of China and other fast-developing countries in the world economy, and in order to increase the voting capacity of low-income countries – but it means the change will be limited. The impact of changes made so far has been slight in terms of the overall balance of power, and some countries which have been asked to increase their funding of the IMF in 2009, such as China, have raised the question of further reform to voting procedures. Whether or not this takes place, fundamental reform in the direction of one country one vote, as in bodies like the UN General Assembly, is not on the agenda.

Woods points to another way in which the IMF is 'undemocratic', namely its tendency to talk only to the finance ministers and central banks of the countries to which it is lending money, rather than drawing other potential participants, such as NGOs and representatives of civil society, into the discussion.[3] This has partly been because such bodies were unlikely to approve of the 'Friedmanite' texture of its conditions. But it also represents the nature of an institution which is dominated by the wealthiest minority of countries, who then decide the conditions for making a loan in consultation with a few members of the elite in the recipient country. Though the highest body in the IMF is the Board of Governors, many decisions are delegated to an Executive Board of 24, with one member each for the largest countries (such as the US, China, Russia, the UK, France and Germany), while the smaller (economically speaking) countries are represented in clusters (constituencies) by a single representative who has somehow to bring together their separate interests. Despite its delegated responsibilities, the Board does not move outside the informal parameters set by the largest 'stakeholders' in the institution. Baker suggests in his book that the Executive Board doesn't even discuss a loan of which the US disapproves. A similar 'informal arrangement' has ensured for the last fifty years that the head of the World Bank has been an American and that of the IMF a West European.

There is nothing wrong with the 'he who pays the piper calls the tune' approach if it is recognised that this is an arrangement to suit a commercial enterprise with major shareholders seeking to have their interests respected. It is not a recipe for global government. Though the membership of the IMF is broad it does not have a broad distribution of power (as many of its members are themselves keen to point out). Its loose ties with the UN are misleading – perhaps deliberately so, as Chapter 5 suggested, since they give it an aura of respectability. The Economic and Social Committee of the UN, the official organ of the UN with which it might be expected to consult, has had no influence on the very different economic outlook of the IMF itself. It is difficult to say that it is 'impossible' for it to change into a more democratic institution. But for it to lose its present dependence upon the major 'shareholders' who provide its budget, whilst accepting a degree of control from the UN which it has never before countenanced, must be reckoned an extremely unlikely scenario.

The World Bank

The World Bank is the second institution that goes back to the Bretton Woods agreement of 1944. It provides low-interest loans and interest-free credits to countries that are either (broadly speaking) poor and creditworthy, in which case IBRD (International Bank for Reconstruction and Development) helps them, or the poorest countries of all, in which case the IDA (International Development Association) comes to their aid. As with the IMF it initially focused upon helping 'developed' countries recover from the aftermath of war (its first loan was to France), but its more recent focus has been upon providing help to poorer nations.

The World Bank is closely tied in with the IMF – indeed, to benefit from an IBRD loan, it is necessary to join the IMF first, and many of the same criticisms apply. Like the IMF it has weighted voting roughly based on the size of each member-state's economy and therefore an effective US veto over any changes to the organisation (amendments to the Articles of Agreement require an 85% majority and the support of at least 3/5 of member-states; the US has over 16% of the voting strength). Indeed in the case of the World Bank its president is 'by tradition' a US national.

As with the IMF, it is difficult to see the World Bank assuming a more important role globally. It has the same problem of a weighted voting system, appropriate to a commercial organisation that wishes to give power to its largest shareholders but not to a public institution seeking a wider mandate. Moreover, the failure to consult widely with a range of agencies over loans which it has made, another charge similar to those levelled at the IMF, has led to criticism of the World Bank for failing to find ways of lending without falling victim to corruption. Too many of its loans have ended up in the private bank accounts of government officials. An unfortunate faith in the market's power of self-policing (which hardly seems appropriate in 2009) has led to a failure to involve itself in regulating the loan process.[4] Some go even further and suggest that the bank legitimates exploitation or supports loans that lead to environmental degradation.[5]

These criticisms illustrate a further problem with expanding the global role of either institution. The free market philosophy which undergirds both – deregulation, privatisation and limiting the state's involvement in the economy – looks out-of-date in the present economic crisis. The approach of both IMF and World Bank has meant reliance upon a limited range of private-sector contacts, shutting out other 'actors' who might have helped to prevent corruption and waste. Though both institutions remain 'lenders of last resort', the terms of their lending are liable to be put under increased scrutiny. They may receive more money but at the same time there will be demands for more control over what they do with it. Additional funding is therefore extremely unlikely to be accompanied by calls for either to play a more prominent part in 'global governance'.

The World Trade Organisation

The World Trade Organisation (WTO), officially born in 1995, inherited the role of General Agreement on Tariffs and Trade (GATT) in regulating the world's trading system. The original plan at Bretton Woods was the creation of an International Trade Organisation (ITO) which would be the third pillar of the post-war economic system alongside the IMF and the World Bank. Its charter would extend as far as rules of employment, thereby introducing a social element to the regulation of world trade. In the end that plan was killed off by US opposition, leaving GATT as the salvageable element of what was originally planned.

Given this background, the formation of the WTO might be seen as a return to a wider conception of trade relations which considers social as well as economic aspects. In fact, as the widespread protests at the 1999 meeting of the WTO in Seattle suggested, this wider conception has yet to be achieved. In an interesting paper produced by the University of California in 2001,[6] Andrew Guzman argues that expanding the remit of the WTO to include non-trade issues is essential, precisely because it has been relatively successful in regulating international trade. This success has made the effects of a well-run trading system in non-trade areas, such as those of labour law, human rights and the environment, all the more important. Guzman is rethinking some of the thoughts that failed to come to fruition with the ITO at Bretton Woods.

Guzman argues that unless it expands its remit the WTO will lose its status as the most effective and reliable of international institutions. His arguments concerning the strengths of the WTO are important and need to be stressed. It is one of the few organisations with both a broad if not quite universal membership (it currently has one hundred and fifty-three members, thereby representing about 80% of the world's nations) and a democratic voting system. Unlike the World Bank and the IMF, which are effectively steered by their largest shareholders in a system which proportions voting power to overall economic weight, the WTO gives equal weight to each member. Power, it can fairly be said, lies with the membership as a whole rather than with a minority of member-states or a board of directors.

Moreover, the WTO emphasises the importance of being a rules-based organisation, with the rules clearly defined and with a definite timetable for considerations of any alleged breaches. Guzman points out that it has a dispute settlement procedure which is the envy of other international institutions and which can be effective, not least because no state that loses a case can block the adoption of a ruling. The fact that more cases are being brought to the WTO than in the past could reasonably be considered a sign of the success rather than failure of its organisation. If a decision is not honoured, then the Dispute Settlement Body can agree to authorise trade sanctions against an offender, though as Guzman points out these are not sanctions which are large enough to force compliance. There are some 60,000 pages of jurisprudence governing the workings of the WTO dispute mechanism, and decisions are not always weighted in favour of the most powerful; Venezuela and Brazil, for instance, successfully brought a case against the US for discriminating against their gasoline imports. On the other hand Guzman quotes a revealing comment from the US *Journal of Commerce* in 1995, declaring that if the country lost both cases pending on access to the Japanese auto industry, the US would exercise its right to leave the organisation within six months.

Guzman makes some important points about why a country – even a powerful one like the US – might seek to work within the rules of the WTO. He refers to the 'reputational costs' of violating them, and points out that even the US would be reluctant to abandon an organisation with so many agreements and regulatory practices already in place. At the same time, his ideas about extending the remit of the WTO look less plausible, particularly when consideration is given to the problems encountered during the 'Doha Development Round' of trade negotiations, begun in 2001 and still ongoing. Deadlines for completing the Doha round have come and gone since January 2005. The Ministerial Conference, the top decision-making body in the WTO, has effectively been suspended because of the problem. Intended to meet at least biennially, it has failed to meet since 2005. Meanwhile, the centrifugal force of desiring a solution has caused individual nations to spin off into bilateral or regional deals, making a global accommodation even harder. In such a context, it seems difficult to believe that much progress could be made towards extending the WTO's remit.

Though it might fairly be said that the issues are complex and agreement in the future not unthinkable, it is difficult to avoid the view that the WTO is bogged down in the difficulties of trying to secure agreement between one hundred and fifty countries for whom the sharing of sovereignty (at least in this context) is unthinkable. As its own self-effacing website points out, the WTO is a 'negotiating forum'. Indeed the website cites a radio discussion in which various people were suggesting things for the WTO to do. One participant then said: 'Wait a minute. The WTO is a table. People sit round a table and negotiate. What do you expect the table to do?' The image neatly encapsulates the difference between a supranational system which creates a higher authority and an inter-governmental system which does not.

Ironically, in one sense the WTO is too modest. Although the table analogy might apply to its Ministerial Conference, we have already seen how its dispute-resolution panels, consisting of independent experts who interpret and enforce its rules against national governments, can be described in different terms. Here there is indeed the sort of arrangement whereby an organisation is able to bind member-states to act according to certain rules. The main problem is that a system which applies to a particular sub-division of the organisation – these panels – is not applied at the very top of the organisation. For that reason the implementation and enforcement of these rules (if necessary by sanctions) is not carried out in an effective manner.

Like most of the other main forums under consideration in this chapter, the WTO ultimately acts by 'consensus' – which means unanimity. Guzman sees its agreements as akin to a 'contract'. The idea recalls the 'social contract' mentioned in Chapter 1, the move described by Hobbes whereby individuals choose to give up some of their powers in order to receive the benefits of security. However, Hobbes' *Leviathan* entailed the creation of a national authority with binding powers, just as the suggestion in this book is for an international authority with binding powers. Otherwise the 'contract' becomes no more significant than one of de Gaulle's treaties, which like roses and maidens have their day and disappear. A contract which cannot be ignored or broken requires an authority with coercive mechanisms that the WTO 'table' obviously lacks.[7]

Organisation for Economic Cooperation and Development

Described as 'much cited but little studied', the OECD probably deserves to be considered alongside the other organisations treated in this section.[8] Formed in 1961, it developed out of the Organisation for European Economic Cooperation (OEEC) which was set up in 1947 to administer aid under the Marshall Plan to restore the economies of Western Europe after World War Two. Like the World Bank and the IMF, therefore, the OECD can trace its origins back to the determination to provide a secure economic and financial order after 1945.

It is certainly true that the OECD is talking about a wider range of issues than it used to. It has traditionally been known for its reliability in collecting statistical data on economic performance, data which can be used for economic forecasting. However, though primarily an economic organisation, it has developed broader social and political interests. It describes its purpose as being to bring together the governments of countries committed both to 'a market economy' and to 'democracy'. Though some of its aims, such as liberalising financial services, might seem more controversial in 2009 than they did before the credit crisis, it is noteworthy that the organisation interests itself in promoting 'effective and accessible health systems', access to education and combating social exclusion and environmental waste. It also wants to promote the participation of citizens in decision-making.

However, a wider range of discussions is hardly enough to transform it into a body capable of acting to implement change. In terms of staffing and resources the OECD is hardly large. It has its headquarters in Paris, a secretariat of 2,500 and a budget (in 2008) of about three hundred and fifty million euros. Indeed it has been estimated that the cost of its secretariat is lower than the cost of sending officials to its meetings and maintaining permanent delegations to it. One former Deputy Secretary General, Pierre Vinde, described it as a 'permanent inter-governmental multi-sectoral conference'. Whether this is quite the case or not, such comments reflect the fact that the OECD is more a forum for officials to network than an administration tasked to get things done. As with the WTO, its 'table' status reflects the lack of supranational powers. It is another organisation working by 'consensus' (unanimity) through a governing council which includes representatives of each member country.

The principle of unanimity throws some doubt on the capacity of the OECD to survive expansion, since it tends to produce effective working only among states that are already capable of reaching a relatively easy consensus. Supporters see the workings of the OECD, with its 'peer review' system, formal abstentions (roughly equivalent to opt-outs in the EU) and *actes innomés* ('gentlemen's agreements' that are unsigned but officially recognised by its governing council) as an example of sophisticated processes enabling member-states to find consensus.[9] Others might feel that such systems are only effective when a group of nations is brought together with sufficient common understanding to be able to act as a 'gentleman's club' in the first place.

Partly because of its origins in the rebuilding of Europe after the Second World War, the OECD lacks the breadth of membership that can be claimed by the WTO, the IMF and the World Bank. Thirty member-states are currently members, including the United States, Japan and most European countries – indeed a majority of its members are members of the European Union and all of them would be described as from the 'developed world'. Developing countries are notably absent from the mix, although China, Brazil and India have a form of associate membership (they enjoy what it calls 'cooperation programmes'), and there are plans to enlarge OECD membership to include these and other developing nations.

Unlike other international organisations that permit virtually automatic membership, the OECD has an accession process. Countries must be committed to an open market, democratic pluralism and respect for human rights, and must demonstrate that commitment in terms of possessing the will and ability to adopt its 'legal instruments'. However, candidate countries may express reservations about certain instruments, and the matter is then hammered out in committee until 'consensus' is reached. Since both Russia and Israel are currently candidate countries, this is likely to prove – in the words of the OECD's own official website – 'a time-consuming process'.

In a speech in Berlin in February 2009 before leaders of all the institutions considered in this section, German Chancellor Angela Merkel spoke of the need to foster 'greater cooperation and networking by national governments, international organisations and other stakeholders, *and to further develop these capacities institutionally*' (my emphasis). This last point is, of course, crucial, since cooperation and networking have been going on for a very long time, certainly since before the credit crisis, and have continued apace since with mixed results.

Merkel spoke specifically of a 'charter', saying that it might be built up from various OECD instruments promoting financial cooperation, together with important social provisions as contained in the ILO (International Labour Organisation)'s 'Decent Work Agenda'. The Charter, she suggested, might be launched by a G20 meeting of heads of government.

In response to Merkel's speech, the Director-General of the OECD, Angel Gurria, wanted to know whether 'we should seek to develop binding rules or voluntary initiatives'. This is the absolutely crucial question – and it is difficult to see how 'binding rules' could be effectively applied by any of the financial institutions mentioned in this section.

It is interesting to compare Merkel's comments with another speech she made, this time to the World Economic Council on 30th January, 2009. Here the Chancellor looked to the UN for a possible way of coordinating an international response to the world economic crisis. However, she did not suggest the Economic and Social Council (ECOSOC), which has been a principal organ of the UN for the last sixty-three years. Indeed she specifically commented that it wasted years of its time writing up reports. Instead she wanted a new body which would operate like the Security Council – in other words a body with binding powers. Here was the answer to Angel Gurria. Merkel was prepared to suggest an altogether new body as an alternative to 'another table'. Though there would clearly be other problems with an Economic Council formed on Security Council lines, the German Chancellor's use of the Security Council as a point of comparison was very interesting. The financial crisis has thrown up a whole collection of proposals for reforming institutions like the IMF to make them the focus of effective international action; but the most plausible suggestions are those which look to the creation of new institutions altogether.

G7, G8, G20 ... G200?

The G7 was a forum of finance ministers set up in response to the economic turmoil of the early 1970s. This was when the post-war boom came to an end and the world economy was thrown off-balance by the end of the international financial system founded at Bretton Woods in 1944. The exchange rate instability this produced was compounded shortly afterwards by a huge jump in oil prices. In 1975 French President Giscard d'Estaing invited heads of state from the major industrialised countries (the US, France, West Germany, the UK, Italy and Japan) to a summit in France at Rambouillet, where regular meetings were proposed to try to bring stability to the world economy. At a subsequent summit in Puerto Rico the six became seven through the addition of Canada.

Andrew Baker concludes his study of the G7 by wondering whether the G7 will:

> ...be sufficiently enlightened to curtail the foreign ministers and central banks' current control of global financial governance and extend participation in key debates and dialogues to a wider range of government agencies and social interests.[10]

It is a prescient remark for a book written in 2006, shortly before the world was plunged into financial crisis. However, it is difficult to give a positive response to his question concerning whether the G7 would show 'enlightenment' or 'extend participation' in the way he suggests.

For one thing, the G7 has had considerable difficulty 'extending participation' simply in terms of widening its membership. Russian participation (which turned the G7 into the G8, beginning from the summit in Birmingham in 1998) has remained a bone of contention. In 2005, a year before Russia assumed the rotating presidency of the G8, US Senator and later Republican presidential candidate John McCain was calling for Russia to be suspended from the group for what he regarded as its lack of commitment to economic and political freedoms. As a further complication Russia is still excluded from meetings of finance ministers, who continue to come together as the 'G7' rather than G8.

Such difficulties over deciding its own membership illustrate a more general difficulty which the group has. Over the years the G7 has widened its remit in order to discuss and make pronouncements on issues outside the narrowly economic, such as security and the environment, relations with developing countries and 'making globalisation work'. With a wider remit it has become more concerned about broader political issues and therefore, perhaps, about who may join it. At the same time, however, it remains an organisation without a constitution or a headquarters.

The arrival of the G20 format in the light of a further set of economic crises in the 1990s might seem to have solved the membership problem. In fact the G7 had already held meetings with different groups of emerging countries, (variously known as the G22 and G33), before settling on a regular pattern with the G20 at a meeting of finance ministers and central bank governors in 1999.

Though the G20 can claim to represent 90% of global GNP and 80% of world trade, it still represents only 10% of the world's nation-states. Its membership includes the European Union as a single member (with the President of the European Central Bank) alongside individual EU countries such as the UK, France, Germany and Italy, a pattern of 'double representation' which in different forms applies to the WTO and OECD as well. Part III will come back to this in the context of assessing the role of the European Union as a potential single member of a Global Union. Like the G7 and G8, the G20 lacks even the permanent staff ('secretariat') enjoyed by organisations like the OECD and the World Bank. It remains effectively an informal gathering of world leaders like its less representative predecessors. It is doubtless useful, but useful in the way international summits are useful. Indeed the G20 explicitly referred to its meetings in Washington in November 2008 and in London in April 2009 as 'summits'.

As for Baker's reflections about 'curtailing the finance ministers and central banks' current control of global financial governance', it is true that the world's twenty leading economies came together in Washington at the end of 2008 in order to discuss the global financial crisis. A communiqué from the meeting expressed confidence that stability and prosperity would eventually be restored to the world economy through 'partnership, cooperation and multilateralism'. The IMF, it was hoped, would take the lead in drawing lessons from the current crisis given its 'universal membership' (a democratic feature whose effect is somewhat lessened, as we have seen, by its weighted voting procedure).

Worthy as these sentiments are, they have an obvious limitation. Whether it's the G7 or the G20, they come from a body that has no sovereign powers and cannot make rules or laws which its members have to observe. Instead members are free to cooperate or not with whatever decisions are made. To turn itself into a more effective body, the G20 would at the very least have to acquire a constitution providing it with sovereign powers binding upon member-states, and be backed up by a secretariat. It is certainly aware of the need to introduce more regulation into financial institutions and regularly talks about 'improved governance', but awareness of a problem and determination to deal with it count for little without mechanisms of enforcement. The G20 does not appear – despite an emphasis upon enhanced international cooperation – to be able to propose significant structural change for its own organisation beyond enlargement.

It would seem reasonable to conclude from this that the G20 will remain primarily a discussion forum, albeit a more representative one than the G7 or 8. If it does expand further into a G50 or even a G200, then it will still represent a round-table discussion, perhaps comparable to General Assembly meetings of the United Nations. It will not be able to issue decisions binding upon members.

As the debate over Russian membership of the G7 showed, there were those who thought that new member-states should fulfil certain 'criteria' (whether these were fairly applied to Russia is another question). The G20 refers to its first meeting in 1999 as bringing together what it calls 'systemically important' industrialised and developing economies. It is not easy to see what 'systemically important' means, beyond the idea that these should be the world's actually or potentially largest economies. There is nothing in such an idea to suggest any sort of political criterion or requirement that a member display democratic credentials. Moreover, the sort of concerns with poverty relief and development that the G20 has laid emphasis upon would surely call for an invitation to the 'systemically *in*significant', those countries (the majority) who for one reason or another are unable to develop their economies into the front rank. The G20 is based upon the perception that there are more 'big players' than there used to be; a G200 would have to recognise that the 'small players' needed representation too. There is no sign yet that the G20 is prepared to think in such terms.

The Commonwealth and the International Francophone Organisation

It is a mark of the seriousness with which people are looking for new institutional arrangements that in a speech to the Royal Commonwealth Society in London in February 2008 the Shadow UK Foreign

Secretary, William Hague, called for the Commonwealth to be 'expanded' (it currently has fifty-three members). Pointing out that as an organisation with 600 million Hindus, 500 million Moslems and 400 million Christians it crossed divides of 'religion, ethnicity and wealth', he declared that it should take on new members.

Hague is right to point out that the Commonwealth, unlike organisations like the G20, has a wide membership range both in terms of wealth (Canada, New Zealand and Australia are members alongside a swathe of poorer African and Asian nations) and in terms of culture. However, created in 1949 as a body to bring together the colonies, former colonies and dominions of Britain, it would be difficult for such an organisation (whose head is the Queen) to be perceived by other countries, without such historical links to Britain, as a genuinely international organisation. Even Hague's speech, which talked about the Commonwealth as a 'foreign policy tool' and about the advantages to British business of trade with a commonwealth that often had the same institutional and legal arrangements as Britain (because of the colonial past) was as much about the advantages of an expanded Commonwealth to Britain's interests as to those of the wider global community.

The Commonwealth might be compared to the International Francophone Organisation (IFO), another grouping of about fifty nations which first met in 1986, and whose members at its most recent summit in Quebec in 2008 numbered 68. Like the Commonwealth it lays great stress upon bringing together nations which come from both hemispheres, are both rich and poor and (though united by the use of French) which display considerable cultural diversity.

Though focusing upon the maintenance and spread of the French language, the IFO clearly sees this as inseparable from broader social and political issues. The Quebec summit produced statements on climate change, a global partnership on food and agriculture and an international conference on renewing the financial system. French Presidents tend to be as prominent at IFO meetings as British Prime Ministers are at meetings of the Commonwealth, and to make pronouncements on the same broad range of social and political issues.

If there is a specifically British interest in the Commonwealth, there is also a specifically French interest in the IFO, now provided with a new headquarters in Paris, the *Maison de la Francophonie*. For precisely this reason it is doubtful whether either organisation could throw off its perceived links to a 'mother country' which determined the past of so many of its members. Nor can one imagine a situation in which Mr. Hague's 'expanding' Commonwealth poached members of the IFO or vice versa (the relation of Canada as a member of the Commonwealth to Quebec as a member of the IFO might create one or two difficulties between the UK and France). These are organisations wedded to particular pasts, which makes it very difficult to see them as springboards for some form of global governance.

Moreover, as in the case of so many other organisations mentioned in this section of the book, the absence of sovereign powers is crucial. The Commonwealth, for instance, has regular meetings (biennial meetings of heads of state), the heirs of what used to be 'imperial' conferences going back to 1887. It has no written constitution but it has made declarations concerning its aims, at Singapore in 1971 and at Harare two decades later. The aims are ambitious and wide-ranging, including world peace, the eradication of poverty and opposition to colonialism. However, as the Singapore Declaration makes clear in its first article, 'The Commonwealth of Nations is a voluntary association of independent sovereign states'. The sharing of sovereignty, which this book argues is the essential prerequisite of effective global governance, plays no part in its organisation. As the Singapore Declaration goes on to say, it is concerned with 'consulting and cooperating' rather than in the establishment of a legal framework which can be binding upon member-states.

In a similar manner, the IFO has biennial summits of heads of state like the Commonwealth, a Secretary General, an annual meeting of foreign ministers and a permanent council of representatives accredited by the member-states which prepares and follows up on each summit. Yet none of this adds up to more than another forum for consultation and cooperation between sovereign states. There is also a strong sense of linkage to French national interests which produces the same difficulties for the IFO as links to British interests produce for the Commonwealth, a concern reflected in the reluctance of Algeria to participate in the IFO.

None of this is to belittle either organisation. The Commonwealth and the IFO have impressive lists of members, but they have achieved that size partly because they do no not seek to impose any binding rules upon their members. As with the UN, they have set out to achieve comprehensiveness, but it has come at the expense of effectiveness.

NATO and the OSCE

The North Atlantic Treaty Organisation (NATO) is an alliance of 26 countries from Europe and North America. Formally speaking, its purpose is determined by the North Atlantic Treaty signed in Washington in April

1949 (and known as the Washington Treaty). This talks of the need for a security pact in order to 'promote stability and wellbeing in the North Atlantic area', a geographical limitation which was largely determined by the concerns about a possible spread of communism into Western Europe from the East. There was a particular fear in the early 1950s that Germany might suffer a fate similar to that of Korea. Both countries had been partitioned, and in Korea's case this had been followed by an invasion from the communist north which had to be repulsed. The fear was of a similar move westwards from communist East Germany, a concern exacerbated by the conflict over West Berlin, effectively a capitalist island in the communist east which had already been subject to a blockade and a year-long airlift of supplies from the west (in 1948–9). In the late 1950s the formation of the Warsaw Pact, bringing together the armed forces of the Soviet Union and most of its Eastern European allies, embedded a bipolar balance of power on the continent of Europe which lasted until the fall of the Berlin Wall and the collapse of communism in all the countries east of the iron curtain during 1989–91.

That specific concern leading to the formation of NATO has now disappeared. The Warsaw Pact has been dismantled, and in the words of the Belgian Foreign Minister, Karel de Gucht, addressing a NATO meeting in 2008: 'The Iron curtain is no more. The risk of a great continental war has disappeared'.[11]

In such circumstances it might have been argued that NATO had outlived its usefulness by the 1990s. Indeed Article 12 of the Washington Treaty talked of reviewing the Treaty after ten years or at any time thereafter, in the light of the 'factors then affecting security in the North Atlantic area'. It might have been expected that by 1991 the North Atlantic no longer needed a body specifically concerned with the security needs of that area.

However, rather then *dis*band NATO chose to *ex*pand. Under Article 10 of the Washington Treaty members of NATO may take a decision, by unanimous agreement, to invite 'any other European state' to contribute to the security of the North Atlantic area and accede to the Treaty. Consequently, following the fall of communism a number of East European states applied to join, many of them subsequently becoming members. The Czech Republic, Hungary and Poland became the first former members of the Warsaw Pact to join NATO in 1999. Five years later seven more countries from Eastern Europe joined, including the three Baltic states of Latvia, Lithuania and Estonia, which prior to 1990 had been part of the Soviet Union. Several Balkan countries and two other former parts of the Soviet Union, Ukraine and Georgia, are also at various stages of applying for membership.

Interestingly, a 1995 study on enlargement appeared to extend the criteria for membership beyond the narrow considerations of strategic security which had determined earlier expansion (for instance the accession of Turkey and Greece in 1952). The study, produced shortly after the European Union's 'Copenhagen criteria' setting out its own conditions for eastward enlargement, put similar emphasis upon a functioning democratic system based on a market economy and including the fair treatment of minorities (alongside the commitment to contribute to military activities essential to any security organisation). It is difficult to conceive of Turkey being able to fulfil such wider conditions in 1952, but at that time the concern for security against the threat of communism was a paramount consideration, and Turkey's strategic position next to the Soviet Union undeniable. Presumably the continued membership of Turkey in NATO means that it is regarded as fulfilling those conditions now.

Arguably the 1995 study was a broadening of NATO's aims in response to the disappearance of its original *raison d'etre* in the form of the containment of communism.[12] This raises the question of whether NATO might eventually expand into something approaching a global organisation which, whilst its primary aim would be security, might have the sort of wider political and economic remit that NATO developed in the 1990s in the context of enlargement. Such an expansion would require a treaty amendment, unanimously agreed, ending the limitation of membership to European states, but such an amendment is not, perhaps, unthinkable. Talk of 'Global NATO' has been doing the rounds since an influential article in Foreign Affairs in 2006,[13] but it lacks precise definition. To some it is a question of global missions but not global membership; for others it could one day include countries like New Zealand, Australia, South Korea and Japan; for others again it is the heir to a wider Atlanticist vision that pre-dated the Cold War and is associated with names like Clarence Streit and Walter Lippmann.

It is true that NATO's focus has been upon the 'Euro-Atlantic' area. However, it is also clear that in a globalised world defending the security of a particular area may require activities *outside* that area, and therefore will encourage even a security organisation with a geographically limited remit to develop a global reach. This is what has happened with NATO, particularly through the invocation of Article 5 of the Washington Treaty after an unusually effective terrorist attack on the Twin Towers in New York in 2001. This article was used in order to treat a terrorist attack as an 'armed attack' on a particular member of NATO, which Article 5 declares will be met by a concerted response on the part of all NATO members, including participation in military action. Such a response effectively took NATO outside the Euro-Atlantic area even though its remit was limited to defending that area, on the grounds that the source of that armed terrorist attack on a NATO member could be traced to Afghanistan.

Thus in August 2003 NATO began its first mission outside the Euro-Atlantic area, assuming command and control of the International Security Assistance Force (ISAF), initially in and around the capital of Afghanistan but later throughout the country and, potentially, region. In doing so it is calling upon an ever-increasing commitment from its members. Though such actions are still specifically related to the security of the Euro-Atlantic area, it could be argued that the sort of global reach required to defend the security of that particular area is not so different from the sort of global reach required to defend the security of the world as a whole. Hence the temptation to detach itself from its specifically North Atlantic roots.

However, three factors militate against the possibility of NATO becoming an effective global organisation. One is that its enlargement, even within the Euro-Atlantic area, has not been free of controversy. NATO continues to be perceived as a threat by Russia, with whom it has a 'partnership' agreement but without the prospect of Russian membership. There is no doubt, as its response to the prospect of NATO enlargement into Ukraine and Georgia has shown, that Russia sees itself as endangered by NATO, a potentially encircling force encroaching upon its borders (and the fact that those borders are difficult to draw makes the situation even more problematic). In the speech of Karel de Gucht quoted above, he says that 'NATO and the EU will have to determine where to draw the line between the legitimate place of Russia in Europe and its ambition to obtain a veto on everything the EU and NATO do.' It is an interesting remark, because NATO specifically defines itself as an inter-governmental organisation, in which 'the 26 member countries retain their full sovereignty'. This means that *every* country inside NATO has a veto on what the organisation does. The real problem is therefore likely to be that Russia doesn't agree with many of the policies which NATO is pursuing. Without going into the finer points of this disagreement, it points to the difficulty any organisation is likely to have trying to change itself from a regional into a global organisation, namely that it carries with it the baggage of specific historical engagement in a particular area. NATO was born and developed as a way of containing Soviet power; it cannot easily turn itself into something that will be seen differently by those who, even in a post-communist world, still feel themselves to be the object of a similar policy of containment. The idea of a 'Greater NATO', like the idea of a 'Greater Europe' or a 'Greater EU', is fraught with difficulty.

The second factor militating against NATO as a global organisation also flows from the fact that it is inter-governmental, according full sovereignty to its member-states and therefore eliminating any form of sovereignty-sharing. As with other organisations that adopt an inter-governmental approach, this means that it relies upon member-states' voluntary contributions rather than possessing 'own resources', and even for the exercise of its security functions accepts that the forces supplied by member-states will be under national command and control until supplied for a particular operation. There is no 'NATO army'. Moreover, expanding its remit to include areas such as promoting democracy, a market economy and better treatment of minorities, as outlined in the 1995 enlargement study, has not entailed a significant expansion of resources in these areas. The EU accepted that the Copenhagen criteria had to be backed up with the provision of funding support in these areas, running to an annual figure of tens of billions of euros. There is no conception of this within NATO. It may have widened its remit, but the attractions of membership are likely to remain exclusively in the area of national security.

The third factor arises out of the second. For there is no doubt that despite being an inter-governmental organisation NATO manages to organise and implement a number of effective security operations, not least the one which brought an end to the Balkan conflict at the end of the 1990s. The reason for this is that it requires a high level of voluntary agreement between its members. This is, once again, what made Karel de Gucht's observation about Russia is so interesting. In an arrangement that is fully inter-governmental a member regularly exercising its veto is likely to bring the whole organisation to a halt, in the way that disagreements between the veto-wielding powers in the Security Council can make that organisation ineffective.

NATO's effectiveness relies on its being a community of the like-minded. But that is precisely what makes it very difficult to conceive of it expanding to become a global organisation. Its reliance upon consensus means that there is no voting in NATO. Countries discuss an issue until they can reach a common position, which may include 'agreeing to disagree' but never includes outright dissent. This is effectively the philosophy of the club. It works where there is the maximum affinity between members, whatever the decisions that have to be made. It does not work where adversaries have to work out a *modus vivendi*.

It is interesting, in this context, to consider the less well-known Organisation for Security and Cooperation in Europe (OSCE). Like NATO, the OSCE emerged in a Cold War context, although at a later stage, the period of *détente* in the early 1970s, when there was a real prospect of a thaw in relations between East and West. Originally the Conference on Security and Cooperation in Europe (CSCE), the organisation pioneered the Helsinki process which secured a number of security and human rights reforms.

The 56-nation membership of what is the largest regional security organisation in the world includes not only the US, Canada and Western and Central European nations, but also crucially the Russian Federation, together with a number of states from Central Asia and the Caucasus, such as Armenia, Georgia and Turkmenistan.

Like NATO, the OSCE operates by consensus. Like NATO it is a regional organisation recognised by the United Nations and which may be authorised (by the Security Council) to take action on its behalf in conflict prevention and border management. Though it does not have the military capacity of NATO, it is involved in activities crucial to security, such as disposing of vast quantities of surplus and environmentally dangerous weapons and weapons-related substances after the Cold War. Like NATO it has a parliamentary assembly of three hundred and twenty members,[14] with a wide spread of representation including those that NATO doesn't reach (the US has seventeen members, the Russian Federation fifteen, while the largest four European powers, Germany, Italy, France, the UK, have thirteen between them).

Naturally the OSCE has the same shortcomings when viewed as a potential global organisation as many others considered in this and the two previous chapters. It is another body seeking to work by unanimity rather than the sharing of sovereignty, while its staffing and central budget are small, limiting the work it can do in order to offer incentives to new members to cooperate or for existing members to stay. Yet it seems strange that so much of the talk is of a putative 'global NATO' rather than a 'global OSCE'. As a body whose roots lie in détente between East and West, the Russian Federation has remained a member – and indeed it is often members of the OSCE who join the UN in troublespots where Russia has been involved, such as Transdniestria and Abkhazia. The OSCE is broadly speaking an acceptable organisation to Russia, which might suggest that if any body was to be capable of breaking out of its regional roots, the OSCE was placed to do so. With a parliamentary assembly that is officially part of the organisation and a range of economic, environmental and social activities, it arguably has a broader range of interests and greater institutional depth than NATO. Yet it remains relatively obscure as an 'actor' on the international scene. It is difficult to explain this, though those who complain that NATO is little more than a projection of US power at least have one explanation to offer.

New organisations

Unsurprisingly, alongside calls for the strengthening or expansion of existing institutions (such as the globalisation of NATO), there have been a number of proposals for new organisations. John McCain, the defeated US Republican presidential candidate in 2008, proposed a 'League of Democracies', an idea which developed out of discussions about a 'community of democracies' in the 1980s and 1990s. In 2000 a 'Conference of Democracies' was set up and at its first meeting in Warsaw a Declaration was signed in which participants declared that they would 'respect and uphold...core democratic principles and practices'. On the whole it has not received much favourable support, not least because it faces the difficulty of defining a 'democracy' and the Convening Group has faced criticism over those it invites to its conferences. Moreover, even if the problem of membership criteria were to be ironed out, the democracies might still find it difficult to agree a common strategy – the example of the 'democracy caucus' at the UN suggests that they would find it extremely hard – or to move beyond occasional meetings (South Korea 2002, Chile 2005, Mali 2007) to the development of a real organisation.

More recently, former French Prime Minister Eduard Balladur proposed a 'Union of the West' (*Union occidentale*),[15] an interesting reversion to a notion ('the West') that often seems to haunt Europe during times of perceived decline. Balladur's concern about 800 million Europeans and North Americans accounting for only 50% of the world's GDP and falling has a Spengleresque quality of sensing a decline in the 'Abendland' as irreversible as the setting sun.

Before considering Balladur's idea in more detail, it is worth considering other permutations based on geography. James R. Huntley, for instance, proposes bringing together those involved in the Atlantic-Pacific system.[16] Huntley's book is an interesting reminder that for the US its Pacific rim is as important as its Atlantic rim. Japan and Australia are seen as key allies alongside European countries. European talk of an *acquis atlantique*, and even talk of the 'West' as such, tends to forget this.

Indeed the term 'the West' is not as clearly definable as Europeans tend to think. America looks both east towards Europe and west towards Asia. It thinks of developing Asia-Pacific Economic Cooperation (APEC) as a way of strengthening both its ties and its interests in (what it would consider) the West, just as it looks to the development of NATO and (perhaps) a 'Union of the West' with a US-EU Council in (again, as it would see it) the East. It would do so in pursuit of what has come to be called 'open regionalism', building up economic and trade ties without compromising its sovereignty, an approach closer to that of The Association of South-East Asian Nations (ASEAN) than the EU. To Europeans the other plank of US policy would be with what they call the 'Far East', but to the US they are simply partners across one sea rather than the other. Arguably Europeans would learn something of the limitations of their idea of the 'Union of the West' if they were to put away their Europe-centred flat maps and invest in a globe.

Balladur's proposal is seen as an interesting departure for a Gaullist in its 'Atlanticism', but in one respect it is consistent with a traditional Gaullist approach to Europe, that is to say in its hostility towards, or at least downplaying of, the sovereignty-sharing aspects of European Union. Balladur's 'Union of the West' envisages a US-EU Council roughly speaking on the model of the EU's European Council, the quarterly meeting of Heads of State which under the now finally ratified Treaty of Lisbon has become one of the seven official institutions of the Union. However, this would not entail that a 'Union of the West' meant an extension of the principles of the European Union westwards, since that would involve an extension of the whole network of balancing institutions, both those which are predominantly inter-governmental (though the European Council does not decide everything on the basis of unanimity) and those which are based upon the sharing of sovereignty.

The UK is often attacked for seeking to water down the level of 'integration' in the EU through its enthusiasm for expansion of the EU eastwards, such as through the accession of Turkey. But such an approach has also been associated with Gaullists, most famously when de Gaulle himself, having vetoed UK membership twice in the 1960s, tried at the end of his presidency to secure British entry in the context of a reworking of the European Economic Community (as it then was) as an intergovernmental organisation. In this respect Balladur's 'Union of the West' may be seen as coming from firmly within the Gaullist stable.

Balladur makes a perfectly valid point when he stresses what in English is often called the 'variable geometry' of the EU. However, it is one thing to acknowledge the complex pattern of arrangements cutting across membership of the EU; it is another thing to regard the difference between full membership (even with 'opt-outs' from particular aspects of membership) and some sort of 'association' or 'partnership' as insignificant. Balladur's *acquis atlantique* is simply not comparable with the sovereignty-sharing *acquis communautaire* which binds together the nation-states of the European Union.

Can the problem be bypassed?

The final approach examined in this chapter is one that seeks to undermine the trawl through actual or potential global organisations entirely, by claiming that such a search is rendered unnecessary by the world we now live in. Where there are global tools like the internet and the intricate array of networks and pressure groups spawned by it, where there are global corporations and financial flows, where there are dozens of 'actors', to use the jargon, – NGOs, lobbyists, think tanks and a thousand other networks, all of them exercising different kinds of power – then the sort of approach which tries to bring together the two hundred or so nations of the world in an organisation within which they might finally learn to act together is no longer appropriate. It is like trying to shuffle the pack in a different way when the game has moved on from cards to dominoes. The pack-shuffling approach continues to assume that power lies chiefly, if not exclusively, in the hands of the nation-state. But, the argument goes, that is no longer the case in the globalised twenty-first century.

It is certainly true that any approach to global governance must not treat the two hundred nations of the world as if they were planetary power systems orbiting in a vacuum and the only task was to ensure that they avoided a collision. Before the end of the twentieth century and the fashion for talking of globalisation, there was already recognition that various forms of mutual accommodation and norms of conduct mitigated the apparent anarchy of relations between states. Works like Charles Beitz's *Political theory and international relations*[17] criticised the view that world society was a Hobbesian state of nature among warring states precisely because he felt that such a view failed to capture the complex patterns of interaction already characteristic of international relations. Once globalisation had taken hold the point became even clearer a generation later, when there was even more willingness to subsume the nation-state within a mass of trans-national and private networks.[18] At the same time definitions of 'governance', as opposed to 'government', often sought to contrast the traditional state authorities who exercise 'government' with (the argument went) more effective but less established authorities at the sub-state level.

In an article published by *Foreign Affairs* in 1997, Anne-Marie Slaughter proposed a new world order based on the idea that 'the state is not disappearing, it is disaggregating into its separate, functionally distinct parts'.[19] The 'parts' she was referring to included courts, regulatory agencies and executives, all of them 'networking with their counterparts abroad, creating a dense web of relations that constitutes a new, transgovernmental order'. The Article followed a number of others in *Foreign Affairs* which accepted that the management of relations between states was ineffective but opposed the creation of centralised rule-making bodies to supply the deficit. Instead she directed attention towards 'new players' away from state level, who would produce what Slaughter called 'cooperative problem-solving by a changing and often uncertain cast'.

The idea was interesting in that it provided a refinement of the 'balance of power' idea, but through a balance that was found at the sub-state level. As with Chris Brown's 'chandelier' model of the balance of power, also proposed in 1997,[20] a new sophistication was introduced into the balance by seeing it as multi-levelled and capable of adjustment in several different places. Slaughter's levels went further than Brown's by including sub-state actors with multiple allegiances and global reach.

Slaughter worked up her ideas into a powerful and influential book, *A New World Order*.[21] On the one hand she traces what she calls the powerful 'horizontal networks' at sub-state level, and works them in with top-level networks like the G7 or G8 (these become 'executive networks'). On the other hand, she also recognises the importance of what she calls 'vertical networks', which include those which delegate individual governing authority to a 'higher' supranational organisation. In fact Slaughter's book contains some of the clearest descriptions available of the difference between international organisations which are 'genuinely supranational' and those which are 'primarily convening structures for horizontal networks of national officials'.[22]

The trouble with Slaughter's book is the implicit assumption that an increase in these so-called 'trans-governmental' activities must automatically lead to global harmony. The idea seems to be that the beams may be rotten but the house will not collapse because of the dense undergrowth that has grown up around and inside it, a forest of networking webs. However rotten the superstructure, there's an increasingly supportive mechanism at the base. What is missing from this analysis is the recognition that these webs do not necessary support the house; instead they may be working like termites to undermine it.

'The densest area of trans-governmental activity is among national regulators', says Slaughter in her article in *Foreign Affairs*, and the chapter of her book on regulators is sub-headed 'The New Diplomats'. The article talks of bureaucrats 'charged with the administration of anti-trust policy, securities regulation ... banking and insurance supervision.' We are told that 'national regulators track their quarry through cooperation'. A new phrase, 'positive comity', is introduced in order to describe this creative and harmonious sub-state networking. We are told how in 1988 the central bankers of the world's major financial powers achieved significant reform of the world banking system through the Basle Committee on Banking Supervision, an organisation composed of central bank governors, rather than through organisations like the G7, IMF or World Bank. We are supposed to believe that this is a trouble-free way of building solid foundations for the world's financial system. Similar enthusiasm is shown for the International Organisation for Securities Commissioners, ('no formal charter or founding treaty') and the International Association of Insurance Supervisors, while in the book (written in 2004, while there was still a degree of irrational exuberance about the world economy around), she extols the work of The Financial Crimes Enforcement Network (FINCEN).

If all these organisations were indeed able to manage the world's financial systems at this regulatory sub-state level, it would be all to the good. But no one reflecting on the world's financial system in 2009 could see Slaughter's arguments as anything but hopelessly naïve. What she misses is the fact that the opportunities provided by the communications revolution are as much for a networking that will *undermine* the 'world order' she talks about as for a networking that will *support* it. It was the communications revolution which made it possible for huge quantities of debt to pass through a system of such complexity that even the 'experts' lost track of what debt was where, until a huge asset bubble was created and finally exploded, leaving borrowing and lending facilities in chaos and millions thrown out of work. The sub-state 'actors' that Slaughter had such faith in were both manipulators and manipulated in this disastrous story. 'Expanding trans-governmental outreach' is no longer a source of confidence in mending the 'world order'.

All this is doubly ironic because Slaughter has such a strong and positive sense of the arrangements applied within the European Union.

'Vertical government networks,' she points out, 'pierce the shell of state sovereignty by making individual government institutions – courts, regulatory agencies, or even legislators – responsible for the implementation of rules created by a supranational institution'. In the view of this book, that is precisely the advantage of such a network, and it agrees with Slaughter's view that 'the coercive power of vertical networks is much greater than that of horizontal networks; it is thus not surprising that they are much harder to find'.[23] Indeed, she goes on to say that 'the model for this world order in many ways is the European Union', lauding the 'genius' of the European Union as a 'model for other regions of the world'. However, because she also thinks that the rest of the world differs from the European Union in critical ways ('EU members share a common region, history, culture as well as political and economic ideologies'), she does not see this 'model' as exportable,[24] and therefore both extols it and dissolves it in a general stew of other networking possibilities. Nothing could make clearer the need to present the sharing of sovereignty not as a 'European model' but as a model which happens to have taken root in Europe, even though its proper application is worldwide.

At the end of her book Slaughter returns to laud the EU as a 'vibrant laboratory for how to establish the necessary degree of collective cooperation among a diverse group of states while retaining the dominant locus of power at the national level.' It remains a collection of distinct nations, she points out, 'even as it works to create the governing power and institutions at the supranational level necessary to solve common problems and advance common interests for all its members'.[25] 'We might thus expect', she continues, 'the European Union to support the creation of global government networks. In fact, however, it is the United States that has led the way in supporting these networks at the global level'. It is a strange remark, and it illustrates the way in which she takes a 'more-the-merrier' approach to these networks that fails to weigh their relative merits. Among those she mentions are Asia-Pacific Economic Cooperation (APEC), which has 'refined the network form of regional governance', the Global Competition Network and even 'coalitions of the willing', such as the informal military alliance used to intervene in Iraq in 2003 when Security Council support was not forthcoming. Different 'networks' are lumped together by Slaughter without enough analysis of their real value or purpose. She recognises better than most what is distinctive about the structure underpinning the European Union, but then drops it into the general pick'n'mix of networks as a choice item.

Conclusion

The approach outlined in the previous section to some extent rode on the back of a burgeoning interest in 'globalisation studies' which is now more than a decade old. The chapter on 'Globalisation and Governance' in Scholte's introduction to the subject, for instance,[26] talks about 'supraterritorial constituencies', 'multilayered public governance', 'substate transborder governance' and 'nonofficial participation in official policymaking'. At the same time, it is difficult to avoid the feeling that the mushy world of 'global governance' represents the pursuit of a chimera. 'Global issue networks' or 'global policy networks' become the new magic wands with which to salvage some hope from the apparent impossibility of improving the system of world government.[27] Yet Scholte himself was prescient enough to observe the limitations of these arrangements a decade ago:

> The post-sovereign state has increasingly shared tasks of governance with relatively autonomous local, provincial, regional and transworld agencies. In the resulting multilayered public sector, governance has tended to lack a clear centre of command and control of the sort that the sovereign state once provided.[28]

In the light of the global economic crisis at the end of the first decade of the twenty-first century, this lack of 'a clear centre of command and control' is only too apparent. Despite his recognition of the work of 'norm entrepreneurs, activists crossing borders, members of the Global Compact and trans-national social networks', Thomas Weiss concludes his critical survey of the UN by saying:

> ... we have to do more than throw up our hands and hope for the best from norm entrepreneurs, activists crossing borders, members of the Global Compact and transnational social networks.[29]

This chapter has examined various ways in which we can try to 'do more', as Weiss puts it. No organisation has proved adequate to the task. Some, like the IMF and World Bank, are undemocratic when seen as potential organs of global governance. Some are tied irrevocably to particular historical roots, like the Commonwealth or the International Francophone Organisation. Many rely upon a degree of harmony or mutual self-interest among their members that will always keep their numbers limited – it is difficult to see NATO or the OECD expanding for this reason. Many are little more than summits in which world leaders can enjoy the limelight but achieve very little in terms of binding agreements. They provide a forum for the Masters and Mistresses of the Bland to express their hopes for a better world before they return home and continue to act exclusively in their own countries' interests. Such meetings are the heirs to those which Saint-Simon derided nearly two centuries ago:

> Assemble congress after congress, multiply treaties, conventions, compromises, everything you do will lead only to war; you will not abolish it, the most you can do is to shift the scene of it.[30]

None of the potential global authorities entails a supranational system whereby rules are developed and enforced against particular member-states (Slaughter's 'vertical enforcement networks'), except in particular areas such as the WTO's dispute resolution mechanism. In fact if one had to choose one existing organisation as an organ of global governance it would be the WTO, comprehensive, democratic and determined to enforce rules of trade and (in intention) social and environmental conditions of trade that are binding upon members. However, the WTO is currently unable to move, bogged down in the Doha round, and crucially lacks a supranational arrangement at the top of its structure.

The case for a new organisation therefore remains a compelling one. It is always difficult to justify the case for a new member of an already crowded 'club', though new 'entrants' are constantly being proposed, as the section on McCain and Balladur's proposals demonstrates. However, a new organisation has to justify itself by being genuinely different from the other alternatives on offer The argument of this book is that it should be based upon the sovereignty-sharing mechanism outlined in Part I. None of the global organisations considered so far, actual or potential, has that characteristic.

7
Other Regional Unions

Introduction

The previous two chapters examined the UN and other actual or potential organs of global governance. However, it is important to recognise that there are other significant regional organisations besides the European Union, some of which have recently grown in importance. It is therefore appropriate to consider how far they, as much as their European counterpart, might be the basis for a Global Union. How, if at all, can the European Union be differentiated from unions or partnerships between nations that have grown up in other parts of the world, such as the African Union, ASEAN (Association of Southeast Asian Nations) and MERCOSUR (the South American Common Market).

It is clearly not possible to examine all the different regional – and occasionally inter-regional – arrangements that currently exist and whose number is tending to expand. In Africa alone, for instance, there is COMESA (Common Market for Eastern and Southern Africa, dating from 1994), CEUCA (Customs and Economic Union of Central Africa, dating from 1966), EAC (East African Community, dating from 2001), ECCAS (Economic Community of Central African States, dating from 1983), ECGLC (Economic Community of the Great Lakes Countries, dating from 1976), ECOWAS (Economic Community of West African States, dating from 1975), MRU (Mano River Union, dating from 1973), SACU (South African Customs Union, dating from 1969), SADC (South African Development Community, dating from 1992) and WAEMU (West African Economic and Monetary Union, dating from 1994). Most of these groupings, which involve between two or three and up to a dozen states, concentrate on economic and financial cooperation, seeking to build up trading partnerships within particular regions. Some, however, specifically talk of political aims such as the promotion of a stable security environment, particularly in areas where there have been persistent outbreaks of violence.

Nevertheless it seems reasonable to concentrate upon the most influential and well-known community of states in any particular region. Hence this chapter will focus, where Africa is concerned, only upon the African Union, which dates from 2001 as successor to the Organisation of African Unity (OAU), founded in 1963. The African Union (AU) is the only body which spans the whole continent, having fifty-three of the fifty-four African States as members. In a similar manner, the focus in the case of Asia and South America will be upon what are considered to be the most important organisations in each region, rather than upon providing an exhaustive account of them all.

The African Union

On the face of it the African Union can lay claim to being a very different creature from its predecessor, the Organisation for African Unity. Its institutions show a certain similarity to those of the EU. Indeed Soderbaum goes as far as to suggest that 'whereas the OAU could be compared to a continental regional model of the United Nations, the AU is loosely modelled on the EU'.[1] Apart from the Assembly of Heads of State and Executive Council, there is a pan-African Parliament based in Midrand, South Africa, and an African Union Commission based in Addis Ababa, Ethiopia, with ten commissioners and a number of support staff. The Assembly of the African Union is akin to the European Council. It is composed of heads of state, meets annually and requires a two-thirds majority for its decisions to be binding. It is considering transferring some of its powers to the Parliament, a trend that could be broadly compared to the EU, where the Parliament has been acquiring more powers at the expense both of the Commission and the European Council. Meanwhile the Executive Council could be described as the African Union's 'equivalent' to the Council of Ministers. It is composed of ministers from the various African states, has a Permanent Representatives Committee (the equivalent of the EU's COREPER (Committee of Permanent Representatives), which consists of nominated permanent representatives of the member-states, and prepares the work of the Executive Council.

The inaugural meeting of the pan-African Parliament was held in March 2004. It was decided that the parliament would be a consultative and advisory body but would eventually receive full legislative powers. At present the two hundred and fifty-five members of the African

Parliament are not directly elected, but are chosen by the legislatures of the fifty-three states. This also bears a certain parallel to the EU, where the first direct elections to the European Parliament were in 1979, before which MEPs were delegates from the various national parliaments. The AU similarly aims at direct elections to the pan-African Parliament.

There is also a plan for an African Court of Justice, though one which is likely to concentrate on human rights abuses rather than develop a system of Community law binding upon individual countries. Further proposals include both a central bank and an investment bank, though they have so far fallen short of developing proposals for a common currency.

The African Union has been developing its structures at least in part as a response to the problem of conflicts between African states, another parallel between its development and that of the European Union. While the European Union has sought to develop a Common Foreign and Security Policy, so the African Union, following a proposal at Lusaka in 2001, created a Peace and Security Council responsible for monitoring and intervening in conflicts, which has an African force at its disposal.

It is frequently pointed out that the force has had little success so far in Darfur. At the same time, it should be borne in mind that the EU's own efforts to put together a Common Foreign and Security Policy stemmed from its failure to prevent the Balkans descending into bloody conflict in the 1990s – a conflict which it was unable to stop on its own. Whatever criticisms may be made of the various actors in that dispute, it is hard to deny that peace was restored neither by the UN nor by the European Union but by NATO.

It might seem from this that the African Union is well on the way towards developing an organisation south of the Mediterranean which can mirror that to the north. An EU Commission report of 2004 spoke of helping African countries 'integrate with their neighbours as a step towards global integration, and to help them build institutional capacities and apply principles of good governance'. The report is not very precise, making it difficult to know how far it anticipates a sovereignty-sharing system south of the Mediterranean. Soderbaum makes the point that there is always a danger of the EU seeing itself as the 'mother of all regional organisations' whose example the rest of the world is slowly learning to follow.[2] However, the evidence is that this is not the case. Whatever the superficial parallels between the EU and the AU, the latter is not moving towards the sharing of sovereignty.

Part of the explanation for this lies in the historical background. Europe's emergence after World War Two was a result of its finally managing to develop a mechanism which could lessen the chances of internal conflict, that is to say reduce the risk that there would be further wars between European states. Earlier chapters examined the Franco-German 'engine' of the EU, and its origins in the Coal and Steel Community of 1951, and suggested that the sharing of sovereignty, the key move in its formation, was a European answer to the problem of allowing Germany to recover economically without allowing it to become a danger again militarily. A long history of wars between European states was the background to the Schuman Plan. Europeans did not have a strong sense of an external threat (though they were to develop one as the Cold War intensified after 1948), but they had a very strong sense of the ruinous consequences of their own internal squabbles.

In the case of Africa, despite the civil wars between states that obviously afflicted the continent in the last century (and still do), there has been less of a sense that there is an urgent need to control the activities of 'rogue states', in the way that Europe has had to control its 'rogue states'. Europe's problem was that one power (Germany in the twentieth century) might come to dominate (at the least) the whole continent. Africa had no 'German problem' after World War Two: instead, it had a problem dictated from outside its borders through its long history of colonial occupation. For this reason the rhetoric about a united Africa, and even a United States of Africa, doesn't translate into a determination to implement strong practical measures to share sovereignty between nations, or to strengthen (once formed) the necessary associated institutions.

The history of the African Union reveals a combination of, on the one hand, a longing after African unity and a pan-African approach to solving problems on the continent, and on the other, the jealous guarding of (hard-won) rights to sovereignty as independent nations. African Union summits therefore proceed in a curious manner. Their calls for ever-increasing union would rarely be heard in Europe and would shock the most 'Europhile' of sensitivities (imagine anyone in France or Britain echoing President Gaddafi's declaration in 2007, ahead of a forthcoming African Union summit in Accra, Ghana, that 'our micro-states have no future'). Yet at the same time there is a reluctance to share sovereignty in particular areas, a reluctance which in Europe has been largely overcome, even in countries like the UK. Unsurprisingly, having so recently won their independence as nations from European conquerors, African countries are unlikely to be too receptive to those ex-colonial powers now trying to interest them in sharing sovereignty.

Indeed some writers suggest that participation in organisations like the African Union, rather than reflecting a willingness to share sovereignty, may actually represent a determination to affirm its inviolability. Talking in general terms, Acharya and Johnston claim that 'in most cases, regional institutions outside Europe were designed to protect sovereignty'[3] rather than to share it. States came together in order to reaffirm their solidarity against threats from outside their region, whether it was perceived US economic pressure on South America or the continuing weight of the colonial past on Africa. Jeffrey Herbst goes even further. 'However, signing international human rights accords, designing new regional and continent agreements, and participation in the vast United Nations conferences are reaffirmations of African countries' sovereignty and thus helpful in augmenting the domestic power bases of leaders.'[4] The more organisations and bodies that can be dreamed up, the better. Participation rights are collected like honorary degrees.

The irony is that the way institutions appear to be developing in Africa often awakens an excited response from outside the continent, claiming that a real sovereignty-sharing organisation is about to emerge. The feeling is that unlike the more 'informal' Asian networks, African organisations are seeking to give a real structure to their regional arrangements. However, Herbst offers a different explanation. The wider organisations, and the enthusiasm to weave participation in them into the lives of individual countries, are part of a concerted effort to embed the absolute sovereignty of individual leaders in their own countries. An African leader who enthusiastically supports the African Union is not preparing the ground for the sharing of sovereignty, but acting in such a way as to make clear, both to domestic and foreign audiences, that the absolute sovereignty of his or her country is being and should be respected. Mayall arguably has a more accurate view of the approach of African leaders and leaders of other former European colonies when he remarks that:

> The EU model has been accepted – at least rhetorically – in many but not all parts of the former colonial world, albeit as a means of attacking the problem of under-development, not of confronting the problem of sovereignty.[5]

There are also clear practical and administrative reasons for doubting whether the sharing of sovereignty might develop within the AU in the near future. In this respect the problems that undermined the Organisation of African Unity threaten to be equally damaging to its successor. For even granted that the states might be willing to share sovereignty, a key condition for the successful sharing of sovereignty is that the administrations of member countries be up to the task of fully participating in, for instance, the African Union Commission. However, many of the states in Africa lack an administration which can make a reasonable financial contribution to the organisation's budget or participate fully in the technical subject matters of the various committees that would draft proposed legislation. These countries' leaders would be reluctant to agree to such proposals if they had not participated fully in their formulation.

These practical problems are compounded by the fact that countries without administrative competence (in common parlance, 'failed states') are already part of the AU, rather than being drawn into the organisation once they have succeeded in demonstrating their viability. Unlike the EU, which expanded gradually over decades and required of its applicants a process of careful preparation through acceptance of all points of the *acquis communautaire* (though there are certainly arguments about whether these requirements have been enforced sufficiently strictly), the AU has simply started with everyone (bar Morocco) and is trying to build administrative structures around dozens of members, many – if not most – of whom are simply unable to manage the requirements of a supranational system. In this respect, whatever its talk of developing as a supranational authority, its approach has been more that of the UN than the EU – i.e. get everyone round the table without preconditions first and then see what, if anything, they might be able to agree upon.

The EU steadily increased its number of member-states in response to their preparedness to develop the political, social and economic competences that would satisfy the demands of the *acquis*. It only grew, in other words, after right-wing dictatorships and communist regimes had collapsed and their successor states had demonstrated both their willingness and their ability to adapt to a new system of governance. If they were unwilling or unable to do so, they would not be allowed to join, whatever their geographical status as European. Precisely the same approach is being taken towards EU enlargement into the Balkans, where states have first to demonstrate that they can and will abide by the terms of the *acquis*. This will inevitably entail laying to rest the conflicts of the past.

The African Union has not been willing to impose such demands upon its own member-states and therefore, despite the appearance of EU-type institutions, it is extremely unlikely that it will be able to operate with comparable effectiveness for the foreseeable future. Grafting supranational institutions onto an organisation that has begun by involving everybody with the minimum of commitment in terms of sharing sovereignty is unlikely to be successful, as recent attempts by the United Nations to sharpen up its own organisation have shown.

Hence for both practical and ideological reasons, it is not so surprising that the achievements of the African Union (and of the OAU before it) have been modest. The sort of practical successes it can point to are limited to measures such as the harmonisation of technical standards, the construction of roads across national frontiers or the agreement to common tariffs on certain imports. Very little has been achieved in terms of promoting economic convergence and overcoming the huge differences in wealth within Africa itself (let alone between Africa and the developed world).[6] Whatever the achievements of the AU in setting up various institutions that appear similar to those which operate in the European Union, it is difficult to see how they could move towards a real sharing of sovereignty.

ASEAN (The Association of South-East Asian Nations)

ASEAN is a body of ten Asian countries originally formed (as a group of five) in 1967 in order to promote economic growth, social progress and regional stability. It was a product of concerns engendered by the Vietnam War and the spread of communism, with its plans for economic integration primarily designed with the political end of withstanding communist expansion in mind. The whole area was affected by the three-way 'Great Power rivalry' of the US, China and the Soviet Union, between which the 'minnows' had to find a way of swimming together. However, as the threat from communism started to decline, so more attention was focused upon the demands of economic integration. The ASEAN Free Trade Area (AFTA) aims to abolish customs duties among member-states and, by progressively reducing tariffs upon imports, to establish eventually (by about 2020) a common market.

However, it is not difficult to see differences from the approach adopted by the EU. AFTA is reminiscent of EFTA (the European Free Trade Area) which was launched and promoted in Europe specifically as an *alternative to* (what was then) the European Economic Community. ASEAN, unlike the EU, has no supranational authority, precisely the sovereignty-sharing organisation which countries such as the UK, who supported EFTA as an alternative to the EEC at the end of the 1950s, sought to avoid.

Eliassen and Arnesen classify the ASEAN approach as one of 'informal' as opposed to 'formal' (by which they mean institution-based) integration. They describe an active form of cooperation based on production and business networks that often operate along ethnic and cultural, rather than national, lines. This is unsurprising in an area representing a huge cultural and linguistic mix (in terms of language families and different religious traditions, for instance, the area is far more diverse than is the EU). They conclude that 'the inclusive style of Asian network-style integration' stands in contrast to 'the continental European emphasis on formal institutions'.[7]

This fluid, networking approach, both within and outside the economic area, extends to a willingness to contract or expand the network of states involved according to the demands of particular issues. The largest body is the 'ASEAN Regional Forum' (ARF), which considers security issues in the Asia-Pacific region. This is a group comprising twenty-six member-states including the EU, Canada, Russia, Australia and the United States. In the economic area another very wide forum has emerged known as APEC (Asia-Pacific Economic Cooperation Forum). Established in 1988, this body includes the countries around the Pacific Ocean, thereby including Canada and the US, Australia, New Zealand, China, Japan, Chile and Mexico as well as the ASEAN countries. Then there is 'ASEAN + 3' (APT), an organisation which includes China, Japan and South Korea as well as the ASEAN countries. Telò refers to 'a promising "concentric circles" system' which has developed through the emergence of various bodies whose size and range is determined according to the demands of particular issues.[8] Higgott concurs, saying that 'the range of interactions is unprecedented'.[9]

On the other hand, it is important not to forget the political factors that led to the various permutations of states in South and East Asia, and which to some extent obviate the need to discover some particularly 'Asian' way of working. The formation of APEC was partly a Japanese initiative to give itself a multilateral dimension from which to resist US criticism of its economic policies, which in the context of its massive inroads into the US market in the 1980s were viewed as threatening. ASEAN + 3 (sometimes called APT) was connected to an attempt to overcome the economic crisis of 1997 without succumbing to all the IMF conditions for financial assistance (for instance by facilitating currency swaps). APEC, on the other hand, was partly a US move to legitimise its own involvement in East Asian affairs (by way of contrast, the US effectively prevented the East Asian Economic Group from getting off the ground). Such political factors may or may not have been decisive, but they are significant.[10]

Higgott is surely right to insist that these flexible forms of interaction do not obviate the need to develop new *institutional* mechanisms. Indeed it is very often participation in these 'concentric circles' that has awakened ASEAN to the need for further institutional development. For instance, some ASEAN countries feared that they would be swamped by APEC, and in particular by the US, which they saw as preferring to pick them off one by one for bilateral trade deals (a similar concern affects Latin American countries, as the next section observes) rather than seeking to reach multilateral agreements with the ASEAN group of nations as a whole. Indeed, bilateral deals not only took place with the US but also between particular Asian nations, such as Singapore and Japan. Bilateral activities will inevitably be in competition with attempts to upgrade AFTA to an ASEAN Economic Community by 2020.

Moreover, the alphabet soup of different organisations does not necessarily reflect a promising network of interactions. Not all interactions are useful. Yeo Lay Hwee remarks concerning ASEM (the Asia-Europe Meeting), for instance, that:

> Although ASEM has generated many meetings, activities and initiatives and even established a concrete institution, the Asia-Europe Foundation (ASEF) to encourage more interactions and exchanges between the peoples of Europe and Asia, the reality is that ASEM remains essentially an informal inter-governmental forum without any mechanisms and institutions capable of actual problem solving. ASEM is still not a tool capable of enhancing multilateralism and global governance capacity directly. It is primarily an instrument used for networking, information gathering and confidence building.[11]

The argument of this book is that such 'mechanisms and institutions capable of actual problem-solving' are vital, and indeed that without the appropriate mechanisms and institutions the endless circulation of people fulfilling their 'dialogue commitments' around the world is of limited value.

Indeed some of the rather vague language – almost jargon – used to describe the 'ASEAN way' is not entirely convincing. Foong Khong and Nesadurai talk of an emphasis upon non-interference in the internal affairs of others and a 'consultative diplomatic culture' which 'suggests institutional features that are low in intrusiveness, high in agent autonomy, and that prize process over product'.[12] But to 'prize process over product' in effect means, rather as African leaders have been accused of doing, to relish the conferences and the bodies in the presence of which leaders can affirm their own sovereign authority in their particular countries ('high in agent autonomy' as it is put here), rather than anything concrete that can come out of them. As with Africa and the Arab League, it is a system in which affirming the importance of regional integration establishes your credentials as a leader respected at home and abroad, and thus *cements* your sovereignty. Achieving the integration that you talk about, on the other hand, would have the effective of *diminishing* your sovereignty. Prizing 'process over product' is really a way of prizing one product (sovereignty kept inviolable) over another (sovereignty shared). The conference and diplomatic circuits fill up with those who participate in order to show that they retain precisely the authority which, were the discussions ever to reach any real resolution, they would have to give up.

Arguably, then, any contrast between 'formal', institutionalised European ways of integration and more 'informal' Asian ways can be taken too far. Many of the problems of regional organisation are the same for Asia, Africa and Europe, whatever their cultural differences. Luong Dinh's argument that sovereignty-sharing remains taboo for many East Asian governments can be viewed in terms of power politics and economic realities as much as in terms of underlying cultural differences. However, this does not affect her argument that 'regionalism in East Asia is primarily focused on facilitating inter-governmental and functional cooperation in low politics and less sensitive areas'.[13] It therefore remains highly unlikely that external pressures may eventually push an 'inter-governmental' AFTA open to comparison with EFTA towards an AEC which bears some similarities with the EEC, forerunner of the European Union.

It is true that ASEAN represents a part of the world which is much more ethnically and culturally diverse (for all the latter's emphasis upon diversity) than the EU, and undoubtedly the sort of connections that play upon cultural links, such as Confucian or Islamic business networks, are very important. But it would be an exaggeration to see this as removing the nation-state from the picture. The extent to which nation-states are willing to share sovereignty in the various groupings they enter into remains a question of the utmost importance.

The ASEAN group represents a part of the world has had to confront powerful trans-national dangers, arguably more than any other. It has not only faced the economic meltdown of the later 1990s but also the surge of China as an economic power and terrorist attacks from many sources, of which the most infamous was the Bali bombings (all of which are liable to exacerbate intra-regional conflict and the problem of refugees). It has also encountered severe health problems centred on environmental dangers such as cities blanketed in smog, often caused by illegal forest fires started in other countries, not to mention potentially very dangerous infectious diseases like bird 'flu. Such threats make cooperation vital, whether in financial and economic areas or in response to security and environmental threats, but they have not pushed the countries of the region towards supranational solutions.

This is not to deny that there have been efforts to achieve closer integration. Right at the beginning of ASEAN's life (it was founded in 1967) it declared South-East Asia a 'Zone of Peace, Freedom and Neutrality' (1971). It has remained conscious of large and powerful neighbours around it (China, Japan and the US). As recently as November 2005 a declaration was made on the establishment of an 'ASEAN Charter', which was finally adopted in November 2007. It included the establishment of a 'legal personality' for the organisation, (not to mention a flag, an emblem, a hymn and an ASEAN National Day – 8th August), and recognised the importance of human rights. But it refuses to countenance any infringement of sovereignty. Burma/Myanmar's admission, despite objections to its appalling human rights record, underscored this. ASEAN members declared a preference for 'enhanced interaction' over 'flexible engagement'; when unpacked, the jargon means that doing more and more things together will never challenge the principle of sovereignty.

The ASEAN Charter faces precisely the problem which the United Nations faces, that of being at once committed to international law, including what the Charter calls 'international humanitarian law', and to non-interference in the internal affairs of member-states, a principle it explicitly affirms. Humanitarian intervention to end abusive action by member-states within their own territories is thereby ruled out, a problem that the UN has been trying to come to terms with through its emphasis upon the 'Responsibility to Protect' commitment which was discussed in Chapter 5.

If there are any signs at all of a different form of organisation, they come less from the impact of human rights abuse in Burma/Myanmar or the regional impact of Indonesian forest fires, than from the constraints of economics. The ASEAN Charter refers (in Article 2) to the need for adherence to ASEAN's 'rule-based regimes' in order to eliminate barriers to regional economic integration. In a similar manner ASEAN Vision 2020 (a strategy for the economic development of the area over the next decade) refers to strengthening the ASEAN 'dispute resolution mechanism' to ensure the legally-binding resolution of economic disputes. Such language suggests acceptance of the idea that 'informal networking' cannot always be sufficient. This may lead in time to the sort of rule-based adherence to an open market that is imposed by EU law.

Interestingly, the Charter also talks of narrowing the development gap within ASEAN and of alleviating poverty. This is an important principle for a population of over half a billion people with a combined GDP of close to a trillion euro, but with much larger disparities between levels of wealth among member-states (rich Singapore has about eighteen times the wealth per head of poverty-stricken Laos) than obtains in the case of the EU (where the ratio is about 3:1). Once again it is difficult to see how effective action can be taken without own resources and a commitment to direct them towards development projects and infrastructural works in poorer regions. Though ASEAN does have such projects, it has yet to develop a clear funding mechanism for supporting them. Progress towards mechanisms which might effectively deal with human rights issues is less likely, though some might argue that in the disappointment of some members with what they saw as the weakness of the Charter there is potential for change.[14]

Overall, despite the development of the ASEAN Charter it is clear that ASEAN has so far chosen to avoid the supranational route taken by the EU. While some argue that it has chosen a clearly different path based upon 'what works best for Asia', it is not always clear that it *does* work best for Asia. It may be that the imperatives behind developing a rules-based organisation with some sharing of sovereignty will eventually find its way into ASEAN as it seeks to ensure regional cooperation and development over the next decade. However, such developments are highly unlikely in the short term.

MERCOSUR and UNASUR

The South American continent has a different history to that of much of Asia and all of Africa, in the sense that it has – at least formally – been independent for nearly two centuries. Inspired by the principles of the French Revolution and Napoleon's invasion of Spain in 1808, an initial effort to throw off Spanish colonial rule was followed by a more successful liberation movement after the Spanish Revolution of 1820. By 1822 Spanish South America was free and Brazil was 'quietly separating' from Portugal.[15]

One of the great 'liberators' of Spanish South America, Simon Bolivar, planned a federation on the model of the United States in the northern half of the Americas. However, his dream of a United States of South America was not to be. He formed Grand Colombia (which in modern-day terms would include Colombia, Venezuela, Ecuador, Panama and some parts of other countries), but despite seeing this as a springboard for a united South America he couldn't even hold this part of the continent together. In 1830 he gave up and a year later the independent countries of Colombia, Ecuador and Venezuela came into being, their origin as 'Grand Colombia' still reflected in the similarity of their national flags. Ironically Bolivar ended up as one of the few people to have a country named after him (Bolivia). By 1875 Latin America was 'seventeen republics and one empire, which did not survive the 1880s (Brazil)'.[16]

However, despite comprising a score of separate nation-states by the end of the nineteenth century, South America was not made the subject of further colonisation.

In 1823 the US proclaimed the Monroe doctrine, which resisted any political intervention by European powers in the Western hemisphere. Whether or not the US was in a position at that time to enforce the doctrine, the Americas remained the only part of the globe where there was no serious rivalry between European powers in the nineteenth century, and therefore no 'carve-up' of territory on the African model.

Indeed for much of the nineteenth century the United States was looked at favourably in Latin America as a counterweight to the imperial forces of Spain, France and Britain. This was to change after the Spanish-American war of 1898 and the Mexican Revolution. Hobsbawm sees the early twentieth century as the time of a rise in 'anti-Yankee anti-imperialism', something which 'the obvious taste of Washington in the first third of the century for gunboat diplomacy and landing marines did nothing to discourage',[17] though it never led to formal colonisation.

Where in the post-war generation after 1945 it was from European powers that nations in Africa and Asia were winning their independence, in Latin America the revolutionary movements looked to escape from what they saw as indirect control through military governments supported by the US. The famous deposition of the Batista regime by Fidel Castro in 1959 remains the most well-known example. However, this remained the only clear success of that generation. Other radical movements were put down by the US (for instance the reforming government in Guatemala in 1954) or 'petered out in a romantic death', as Hobsbawm puts it, citing the case of Che Guevara or the priest and rebel Father Camillo Torres in Colombia. When the socialist Salvador Allende won election to the presidency of Chile in 1970, he was overthrown by a military coup three years later (there is an argument about whether it was organised or merely supported by the US). A similar controversy remains about the extent of US involvement in destabilising the Sandinista government in Nicaragua in the 1980s (it was over an incident during this campaign, when the US mined Nicaraguan waters, that the US 'rejected' a decision of the International Court of Justice, as discussed in Chapter 5). Recent US concerns about radical governments in the Southern parts of the Americas, for instance the Chavez government in Venezuela, therefore have a long pedigree.

Whatever the justice of claims about US 'imperialism' in the region, it remains the case that military regimes remained in power in most Latin American states, including the two largest, Brazil and Argentine, until the end of the 1980s. When change came, it not only brought an end to brutal internal repression but also helped relations between states. In 1988 Brazil and Argentine signed a Treaty of Integration, Cooperation and Development and abandoned aggressive nuclear programmes. Their reconciliation, like that between France and Germany which led to the foundation of the European Coal and Steel Community after World War 2, facilitated the creation of a regional union, MERCOSUR, in 1991 (the four founder members included the 'Big 2' and two buffer states between, Uruguay and Paraguay, the South American equivalent of Benelux). MERCOSUR, like the ECSC (and later the EEC) was motivated both by political concerns to preserve fledgling democracies and by the economic desire to develop an effective common market in the new post-communist global era.

The political element should not be under-estimated. A strong and concerted MERCOSUR response to General Orviedo's attempted coup in Paraguay in 1996 helped to preserve democracy there and led to the introduction of an explicit 'democracy clause' which makes such a form of government a condition of membership (hence recent concerns about Venezuela's joining).

However, despite the tensions between some Latin American states, there was not the same need to 'de-legitimate nationalism', as Vasconcelos puts it,[18] which Europe felt after its many wars. The main source of oppression had either been abusive military dictatorships within particular countries terrorising their own domestic population or else the 'imperialism', overt or covert, which many believed, was being exercised by their huge neighbour to the north. Hence MERCOSUR did not feel impelled to 'tame the nationalist beast' by moving in the direction of sharing sovereignty. Though it admired the EU and sought in many ways to imitate it (moving early on towards a common external tariff), it remained inter-governmental.

Whether MERCOSUR can really prove effective without a degree of shared sovereignty is, however, a moot point. Like the ASEAN nations, MERCOSUR faces the power of bilateral trade deals with the US which threaten to make impossible any effective common trade policy, in particular a customs union with a common external tariff. In 2002 moves to include Chile as a full member of the organisation were suspended after the country signed such a deal. Even when external powers do deal with MERCOSUR as a bloc, for instance in the EU-MERCOSUR 'framework agreement' of 1995, little benefit has resulted. This is partly because of differences between the two over agriculture and services, but it also flows from disagreements within MERCOSUR itself, which is often unable to approach inter-regional discussions with a common position.

Without any equivalent of the European Court of Justice, able to arbitrate in disputes and issue binding decisions, disagreements between members of MERCOSUR have been difficult to resolve. One between Uruguay and Argentine over the building of pulp mills along their common border ended up going to the International Court of Justice for arbitration. Another, over the effect of Brazilian car exports on Argentine, led to a temporary tariff war between the two countries. Given the inability of MERCOSUR's institutions to provide a platform for resolving differences between member-states, it is difficult to disagree with Brazilian President Cardoso's statement to the Fifth Euro-Latin American Forum in 1998, 'we are going to have to improve the institutionalisation of MERCOSUR'. However, this can only be effective if the institutions are effective. A MERCOSUR parliament, established in 2006 and beginning regular meetings in the Uruguayan capital Montevideo in 2007, has as yet no powers beyond persuasion.

Other regional groups in South America have similar problems. The Andean community, currently Bolivia, Colombia, Ecuador and Peru, has been affected as much as MERCOSUR by bilateral trade deals with the US (both Peru and Colombia have signed them, prompting Venezuela to leave the group). Meanwhile Mexico has been drawn into NAFTA (North American Free Trade Agreement) with the United States and Canada.

In such circumstances it is interesting to note that, despite severe problems at regional level, the idea of building a South American

Community of Nations to bring together the whole continent, first mooted at the end of the 1990s, has moved some way towards realisation. The Community was formally launched at a summit in Peru in December 2004 and a 'constitutive treaty' was finally signed in 2008 in Brasilia, when the name 'Union of South American Nations' (UNASUR) was adopted. A headquarters and permanent secretariat were established at Quito in Ecuador, its parliament in Bolivia and a bank (limited to financing development projects rather than realising a common currency) in Venezuela. There was agreement to create a single market with a common external tariff in all goods by 2019. A number of ambitious infrastructure projects were supported, including an 'interoceanic highway' across the continent and a South American Energy Ring bringing together arrangements for supplies of natural gas to several countries (though this has run into difficulties).

However, it is difficult to imagine that UNASUR will not have the problems that the African Union or the UN has, namely that of appealing only to the lowest common denominator by bringing everyone together to begin with and then attempting to get them to agree on common actions. Starting with a smaller group of nations, like the MERCOSUR Four or the Andean Four, and then agreeing to share sovereignty in particular areas before enlarging over time, would have been closer to the model followed by the EU in building up a sovereignty-sharing organisation.

Though some believe that there are particular problems in South America arising from the size of Brazil, which tends to overshadow its neighbours, the country has often taken the lead in supporting both MERCOSUR in the 1990s and UNASUR in the present decade. However, the view of the current Brazilian President Lula da Silva that bitter divisions between members of UNASUR, like Venezuela's Chavez and Colombia's Alvaro Ulribe, are a sign of 'lively debate' is too sanguine. Without supranational mechanisms 'liveliness' easily becomes unresolved conflict, because there is not yet a system in place in which it pays each country to support the common interest, even if its individual interests are temporarily frustrated in doing so. Equally complacent is the remark of Allan Wagner, Secretary-General of the Andean community, that the continent will have 'complete union' like that of the EU by 2019 (the projected date of the full implementation of a single market and common external tariff). For one thing, the EU is not a 'complete union' in the sense that not all of its members' policies are under the aegis of Community law – it is a compromise between areas that are deemed appropriate for sovereignty-sharing and those where it is thought that decision-making powers should lie exclusively with individual member-states. Secondly, the EU has mechanisms, which have been explored in previous chapters, such as the Commission, the Court of Justice, and a separate budget in the form of 'own resources', which allow it both to bind member-states to commonly agreed positions and to provide some material encouragement for them to do so. UNASUR lacks these mechanisms. The declaration of the distinguished Brazilian political scientist Moniz Bandeira that 'we will get our own Maastricht Treaty and very soon' remains unconvincing when there is no equivalent of the *acquis communautaire*.

Da Silva declared that UNASUR showed how South America was becoming a 'global player'. This can only be the case if it has the mechanisms in place that provide individual countries with the incentive to adopt common positions, even if such positions appear to provide difficulties for their own immediate national interests. This incentive is something that the mechanisms of sovereignty-sharing provide. Whilst there is much that might seem to bind the nations of South America together (a common religion, bearing in mind that 95% of the continent is Catholic, and a common language, if Spanish and Portuguese are regarded as mutually intelligible), the fear is that their present institutional arrangements will no more allow them to avoid the bitter conflicts arising from particular rivalries and disagreements than will the informal networking arrangements of multi-cultural ASEAN. They will continue to be picked off by bilateral deals with the US, which arguably does not want them to form a powerful regional union. The EU is perhaps more prepared to encourage such a development and has supported a number of 'region-to-region' meetings, but they have not so far borne a great deal of fruit.

Conclusion

The only other geographically significant body that might have been considered in addition to the three discussed in this chapter is the Arab League, though geography is clearly not the decisive determinant of League membership – Turkey and Iran were never considered. Here too, despite a very strong sense of 'Arab' identity between member-states, the suggestion of a sharing of sovereignty, contained in the Protocols that emerged from a meeting in Alexandria at the end of 1944, was eliminated in the Charter of the Arab League when the organisation was formed a year later. As Michael Barnett and Etel Solingen put it, 'the post-Alexandria negotiations transformed an organisation whose ties were supposed to bind into one that clung to sovereignty as an organising principle'.[19] As with the African Union, so with the Arab League, leaders' statements can often be highly misleading. Demands for a high level of regional integration can bring considerable kudos to individual leaders in both areas. The way to embed your sovereign rights in your own country is to make a grand speech about the need to bring together all the countries in the region. A declaration that all barriers should be removed is the surest way of firming up the 'keep off' signs in your own area.

It is clear that, to a greater or lesser extent, the EU has been a model for other regional unions. However, the conclusion of this chapter is that nothing like the sharing of sovereignty, which is the cornerstone of the EU, has been achieved in the other regional unions it has considered. Organisations like ASEAN, the OAU (predecessor of the African Union) and MERCOSUR have been around for well over a generation, but have still not yet begun to develop along such lines.

The experience of the European Union would suggest that it is necessary to have political, social and economic mechanisms in place, based on an acceptance of the principles of a sharing of sovereignty, before states are admitted to a regional (or, as will be proposed later, a global) union. The six have slowly expanded to twenty-seven states on the basis of member-states being able and willing to countenance the economic conditions of a stable and functioning social market economy, the administrative ability to implement the *acquis* and the political requirements of democratic rule and respect for minority rights. Notwithstanding the view that the EU has, all the same, expanded too fast, for instance in admitting Romania and Bulgaria in 2007 despite widespread corruption in both countries, it is clear that the gradualist approach has been able to bind member-states to a particular social and economic pattern. Only when military rule had been shaken off in Southern Europe and communist dictatorship in Central and Eastern Europe, could the countries in those areas join. Only when the Balkan states are committed to peaceful coexistence will they be party to a new enlargement of the EU.

This does not seem to be the pattern in other regions. Lumping all the states in a particular area together from the outset, as in the African Union, whatever their relative levels of political stability or economic development, and then seeing 'what they can do together', effectively rules out the construction of supranational mechanisms. In Latin America there seems to have been a decision to exchange MERCOSUR and the Andean Pact for a continent-wide organisation, without first establishing the sovereignty-sharing arrangements which could then be used as a springboard for effective enlargement. Both Africa and South America have a strong sense of their identity as continents. However, partly because they have been party more to invasion or interference from outside than to rogue states attempting to dominate the continent from within, they have not felt Europe's need to develop a means of curbing the power of individual nation-states. Only ASEAN has remained limited in size (though often participating in larger groups like ASEAN plus Three), but despite various pressures upon the region it has remained an organisation for which the sharing of sovereignty, in Toshiro Tanaka's words citing Luong Dinh, is 'taboo'. Though some would say that this reflects an 'Asian way' that should not be denigrated by Europeans who are viewing it from outside, it is equally clear that for a lot of Asian commentators too it is *not* working.

Organisations like the AU and MERCOSUR may imitate the institutions of the European Union, for instance with talk of continent-wide parliaments, but they do not have the instruments which would make those parliaments effective. Essentially, they reproduce the failings of the UN. There too, as Chapter 5 suggested, an institution has arisen with everybody as a member but without the powers, outside the Security Council arena, to enable it to act effectively, binding its member-states to decisions. There too, there is a sense that new bodies are thrown at problems, often at the cost of bureaucratic overload, but they are institutions without real authority, and apart from their own endemic weaknesses they are often inadequately coordinated from the centre.

It would seem reasonable to conclude that no other regional bloc has advanced as far as the EU. However much it may serve as a model for at least some of the members of other regional unions, (and it clearly has, as the quotations cited in this chapter from leaders of countries in these other regions, like Brazilian President Lula da Silva and Philippines President Gloria Arroryo, clearly show) these other unions have not yet moved towards a real system of shared sovereignty. In this respect the EU is still (so far as large regional unions are concerned) *sui generis* – one of a kind.

Part III
A Global Union

8
Current EU Thinking

Introduction

Part I of this book presented the development of the European Union as a sovereignty-sharing organisation. Part II sought to justify the claim that the sharing of sovereignty had developed effectively only within one regional organisation, the EU, and that no other actual or potential organs of global governance had developed in such a way. It remains in Part III to suggest *how* the European Union might become the catalyst for the development of a Global Union, that is to say a global sovereignty-sharing organisation.

Given the arguments in Parts I and II, it might be expected that there would be some enthusiasm within the European Union itself for such a role. In reality there is little evidence of such enthusiasm. Chapter 8 will outline some of the present approaches adopted by the EU, Chapter 9 will present in more detail the idea of a Global Union proposed by this book and then the last chapter will consider the prospects of some change of thinking within the European Community.

'Effective multilateralism'

When it comes to its relations with the wider world, the European Union's emphasis is understandably upon dialogue and cooperation with other existing organisations. Whenever there is discussion of the possible contribution of the EU to global governance, we encounter the word 'multilateralism'. There is hardly any book, article or for that matter report from the European Commission itself that does not use it several times over.

Take the difficult question of the EU's relationship with the UN. The Commission statement of 10th September 2003, 'The European Union and the United Nations: the choice of multilateralism', set out the official EU approach, which was that 'The EU's commitment to multilateralism is a defining principle of its external policy'.[1] In December 2003 the EU linked its declaration that 'effective multilateralism' was the way forward to the announcement that strengthening the UN was one of its priorities. This made it clear it that the UN was the route through which the EU was seeking to achieve a 'global player' role commensurate with its economic and social strengths. In doing so, it was prepared to shelve consideration of the ways in which the EU and the UN were very different organisations.

A similar approach is visible in many of the articles, papers and books emanating from various think tanks and university departments, often co-written with members of the European Commission. Take, for example, a recent book edited jointly by two lecturers at the Dutch-speaking part of the divided University of Louvain/Leuven,[2] Jan Wouters and Tom Ruys, and a legal adviser at the European Commission, Frank Hoffmeister, entitled *The EU and the UN: An Ever Stronger Partnership*.[3] The book's chapters examine the range of cooperation between the EU and the UN which are intended to illustrate this 'stronger partnership'. They cover areas such as employment, social affairs, dealing with refugees, public health and financial issues, and look at the EU's involvement in organisations such as UNESCO, the World Bank, the WHO (World Health Organisation) and the IMF (International Monetary Fund).

The buzzword throughout the book is 'multilateralism'. Chapter 10 is headed 'The EU's Human Rights Policy in the UN: an example of effective multilateralism?' Chapter 14, concerning UN-EU cooperation on crisis management, is entitled 'Putting effective multilateralism into practice'. Chapter 16, which considers EU-UN cooperation on security, is similarly entitled: 'In search of "effective multilateralism" and a balanced division of tasks'. We are encouraged to believe that despite any fundamental differences the EU and UN, because of 'multilateralism', are singing from the same hymn-sheet.

The points made in the book are perfectly valid as far as they go. They detail various forms of cooperation between the EU and the UN, and they indicate that the range and intensity of cooperation, despite various difficulties, are growing. A similar approach is pursued by Wouters in *The UN and the EU: Partners in Multilateralism*, a work published at around the same time.[4] It makes a number of perfectly valid points concerning the contribution of the EU to the UN budget (38% of its regular funding, 50% of the budget for UN funds and programmes), the increasing presence of EU delegates on UN bodies, often as 'observers' but sometimes as full participants, and the growing capacity of the EU to play a role both in UN development programmes and UN peace-building programmes. Wouters does not exaggerate this – he is admirably cautious about the modest size of the EU's present peacekeeping capacity (in a telling note, he points out that the EU provides 40% of the money but only provides 6% of the 'blue hats' – personnel keeping the peace). He makes a perfectly good case for an important EU contribution to UN peacekeeping and other activities.

But nowhere in all these detailed descriptions of the EU's involvement in this particular UN agency or that particular agency is there any questioning of the EU's decision to seek out the UN as the means by which it may eventually achieve a role as a 'global player' commensurate with its wealth. To some extent this is perhaps a danger run by 'academic' textbooks which threaten to be co-productions with EU officials. The preface to *The EU and the UN: ever-stronger partnership*, indeed, is written by the EU External Relations Commissioner of the time, Benito Ferrero-Waldner. She takes the opportunity to call the EU and UN 'natural partners'. But *are* they really 'natural partners'? Or are they unnatural partners forced together by a combination of inertia and political convenience?

Another book entitled *The European Union at the United Nations: The Functioning and Coherence of EU External Representation in a State-Centric Environment*,[5] was published in 2008. The author was a European Commission Delegate to the UN in New York, and once again there is very little (among several hundred pages detailing various patterns of representation in order to determine 'EU voting coherence' in the UN) which addresses the question implicit in the title: is a 'state-centric' environment really the place where the EU is liable to find what Ferrero-Waldner blithely calls 'a natural partner'?

Many of the contributors to these books find themselves coming up against institutional constraints upon 'effective multilateralism' without considering whether there is a wider message implicit in the difficulties they are recording. One place, however, where such wider considerations *can* be found is the first chapter of *The European Union and the United Nations: ever-stronger partnership*, in which Frank Hoffmeister and Pieter-Jan Kuijper consider 'The status of the EU at the UN: Institutional Ambiguities and Political Realities'. The problems they describe are familiar enough to all those who have studied the very different organisational features of the two institutions. Indeed, when Hoffmeister and Kuijper start to consider how 'UN rules may be more conducive to EC membership' (according to Article 4 of the Charter, for instance, the UN is open to all 'peace-loving states', and the EU is not a state), they suggest that this can only happen if a new international organisation is founded.[6] This is a fairly drastic proposal, given that the EU and the UN are supposed to be 'natural partners'. One minute they are blissfully married; the next minute the husband wants a new wife! They propose that this new international organisation is to be founded 'under UN auspices'. They imagine the General Assembly convening a conference which would negotiate a 'new multilateral convention'. In other words, despite showing very effectively how difficult it is for two such very different bodies as the EU and the UN to produce 'effective multilateralism', they suggest that the UN convenes a conference to sort the matter out!

Despite the manifest failures of the UN itself, the heirs of Robert Schuman are unable to come away from New York as the original Schuman came away from the launch of the Council of Europe in London in 1949, determined that something different had to be done. When Jean Monnet examined the early post-war attempts to facilitate cooperation in Europe through an international organisation of sovereign states, he saw that they were not going to succeed on their own. Of the Organisation for European Economic Cooperation (OEEC) he wrote that 'I could not help seeing the intrinsic weakness of a system that went no further than mere cooperation between governments'. Of the Council of Europe he remarked 'It confirmed my belief that this approach would lead nowhere.'[7] Yet a worldwide army of some 400 Jean Monnet 'professors of integration', not to mention a host of Jean Monnet 'Centres of Excellence' with European Union co-financing, regular Jean Monnet conferences and even Jean Monnet 'multilateral research groups',[8] appears incapable of making the same leap of imagination away from existing inter-governmental organisations, the leap that was so importantly made by the figure in whose name they hold their various chairs.

If 'multilateralism' is not the term being used, then as the previous chapter made clear 'strategic partnership' is the likely alternative. The idea of bringing other 'collective actors' into a stable relationship with the EU developed in the 1990s with a 'strategic partnership' offered to both African states and (in 1999) those of Latin America. High-level meetings would 'constitute the overarching 'roof' for all the other sub-regional cooperation models the EU uses',[9] such as MERCOSUR or (since 2002) the African Union. An *Interim Report on an EU Strategic Partnership with the Mediterranean and the Middle East* was produced in 2004, giving rise to the attempt to deepen Euro-Mediterranean links, while another 'strategic partnership' has been developed with the African, Caribbean and Pacific (ACP) countries.

The bi-regional summits associated with these 'partnerships' often run into difficulties. On the traditional conference model, they offer opportunities for grandstanding and added prestige back home, but achieve little of substance. They stand for little more than a constant growth of 'dialogue commitments'. However, they have continued into the twenty-first century and remain an integral part of the EU's thinking.

The argument of this book is that whatever the value of 'effective multilateralism' and 'strategic 'partnerships', the EU needs to develop a much more radical approach based upon a belief in its own distinctive form of governance. Once it does that it can recognise that while, of course, it will want to work 'in partnership' with the UN, the OECD, the WTO and other bodies with a largely inter-governmental makeup, its particular strength is different to theirs.

'Effective inter-regionalism'

When it is not struggling to be effectively multilateral, the EU is trying to be effectively inter-regional, promoting cooperation between the EU as one regional union and other similar unions ('inter-regionalism'). Earlier chapters of this book have tried to suggest that this is not a satisfactory way forward either, though many have seen it as hugely significant. In 1987 the German foreign minister Hans-Dietrich Genscher, teaming up with European Commissioner Claude Cheysson, dubbed it a 'landmark on the road to a new world order',[10] and it was still at the heart of Mark Leonard's upbeat hopes for Europe as the basis for a new world order twenty years later.[11]

The reason for the unsatisfactory results of the first form of 'multilateralism' is that the EU is one kind of organisation and these other institutions – the UN, OECD, IMF, World Bank, WTO – are another. But it is also the case, as Chapter 7 tried to show, that regional groupings like MERCOSUR, the African Union and ASEAN, are different in kind from the EU. The same problem of mixing incompatibles arises in the context of 'inter-regionalism'. The sort of language used to promote the group-to-group approach fails to give proper weight to this. Björn Hettne, for instance, suggests that the EU strategy 'encourages multidimensional intra-regional links as well as institutionalised inter-regional relations'.[12] But behind the jargon lies the inescapable point that other regions have not integrated in the key sense of sharing sovereignty. Indeed for some of them membership of a regional union is largely concerned with boosting their image in their own nation-states, a thoroughly 'Westphalian' approach.

Inter-regionalism is not necessarily the means of ensuring a stable global order. It depends on what the 'inter' in inter-regionalism adds up to. After all, 'Great Regions' might well start to act like nineteenth century Great Powers, competing blocs like those in Orwell's 1984. This brand of multipolar arrangement, much hyped by those who fear what they believe to be a 'unipolar' world of US domination (as opposed to the bipolar world of East-West confrontation which it supplanted), is not necessarily any more stable than the others. This is a point made by members of the so-called 'neo-realist' school of thought. If realism views the state as the main actor in international affairs, neo-realists see European integration as altering the nature of the players without changing the game; international politics remains a process involving tense and dangerous rivalries between various units. Thus Waltz claimed that the emerging world was one of four or five great powers (a very nineteenth century scenario) 'whether the European one is called Germany or the United States of Europe'.[13] As Filippo Andreatta puts it:

> The fusion of different states into one does not alter the anarchic relationship between the new unit and all the other ones which have not participated in the union.[14]

There is therefore reason to be suspicious of those like Hettne who want to draw on the idea of inter-regionalism as the basis of a new world order.[15] Hettne contrasts a regionalism where there are 'complementary' regional arrangements with one in which each region becomes an autonomous and separate element in a multipolar system. He prefers the former arrangement, rightly considering that the latter contains the seeds of an Orwellian conflict between power blocs. But what is the nature of this 'complementarity'? How does it enable regionalism to be the key to what he calls a 'post-Westphalian governance pattern'? He talks of the locus of power moving 'irreversibly' to what he calls the 'trans-national' level, but it is difficult to see where the confidence in irreversibility comes from. Why shouldn't power stay in the mutually antagonistic regions, as the neo-realists fear it will?

The conclusion is that there are limits to the value of 'effective multilateralism', 'strategic partnership' and 'inter-regionalism'. Neither a deeper involvement with existing organisations nor a closer relationship between the EU and other regional unions can achieve as much as an attempt by the EU to reproduce its own unique system of shared sovereignty at a global level.

Success and failure: Europe and its 'near abroad'

In 2003 EU Development Commissioner and former British Minister for Overseas Development, Chris Patten, observed:

> Over the last decade, the Union's most successful foreign policy instrument has undeniably been the promise of EU membership. This is unsustainable. For the coming decade, we need to find new ways to export the security, stability and prosperity we have created within the enlarged EU.[16]

Patten does not make clear the grounds for such 'unsustainability' – whether it be the geographical limits of Europe or the 'enlargement fatigue' that has made many EU citizens and their leaders unenthusiastic about further enlargement. Since 1993, when the Copenhagen criteria were elucidated to prepare for the admission of the post-communist Central and Eastern European states, there has been explicit mention of the EU's capacity to absorb new members. In any case there is bound to be a limit to enlargement, and therefore at some point the question of the EU's relationship to countries outside its own borders has to be faced.

If there is one overwhelming piece of evidence that an 'institutionalist' approach has merit, it is the relative failure of the EU in its relations with the 'near abroad'. As Telò remarks, '...in the countries where no promise of full membership is possible, "democratic conditionality" hardly works, including within the multilateral framework of the "Barcelona process"'.[17] Similarly, Joffe is scathing about the EU's recent attempts to create a 'ring of friends' around its borders. Becoming 'friends' or 'neighbours' of the EU, he points out, 'only provides proximity to the EU, not access'.[18]

This 'ring of friends' policy is heir both to the 'Barcelona process', which brought together the northern and southern edges of the Mediterranean in 1995, and to various policies towards Eastern and South-Eastern Europe (effectively the Balkans and those countries of Eastern Europe which are not already members of the EU). The two areas were brought together into one European Neighbourhood Policy in 2004. The results were not successful, and recent initiatives during the French Presidency of 2008 to establish a Mediterranean Union have rekindled the idea that a new Barcelona Process might arise.[19] The proposal entails a specific Mediterranean substructure which would be created within a reorganised ENP – a policy which is in effect re-creating the former distinction between the two areas.

In the case of Eastern Europe, eventual membership of the EU remains a real if distant hope. Article 49 of the Treaty on European Union (TEU) explicitly states that 'every European state can apply to become a full member of the Union'. In the case of the countries on the southern rim of the Mediterranean, on the other hand, the option of membership is not available, even as a distant hope. The facts of geography cannot be redrawn (though there can be some boundary cases where there is a dispute over whether a country is in Europe or not, as in the case of Turkey). Morocco's application to join the European Community in the 1980s, for instance, was rejected on the grounds that it was not in Europe.[20] The expectation on the part of these Southern states has to be limited to something less than eventual membership – in other words some sort of 'association' or 'partnership'.

Does this matter? Is there necessarily a huge divide between a close partnership with the EU on the one hand and membership on the other? Does the idea of a 'concentric circles' approach not suggest that the 'outer circle' has its own distinct advantages even if it isn't able to penetrate the 'inner circle'? Does non-membership of the EU make a huge difference in the case of Norway and Switzerland, for instance? Both are economically successful; both are closely involved in a number of EU processes – for example, both are part of the Schengen Agreement on visa-free travel between states of the EU. Is it not possible for a close or 'strategic' partnership to amount to something very close to membership? A closer look at Europe's relations with its 'near abroad' throws interesting light on this.

The EU and the Southern Mediterranean

For the countries south of the Mediterranean, the prospect of full membership is unrealistic even in the long term. Apart from Turkey, this is an area which is clearly outside Europe and therefore has no chance of becoming a member of the European Union. It has, however, been the subject of a number of attempts by the EU to involve it in a close partnership which, whilst it does not amount to membership, nevertheless offers tangible benefits.

The approach has sometimes been labelled 'soft regionalism' or 'open regionalism',[21] but as with other fashionable phrases this has to be treated carefully. Vasconcelos defines 'open regionalism' in two ways reflecting different American and EU approaches. From the American viewpoint, he says, it means the creation of large free trade areas. Defined in this manner countries south of the Mediterranean could, as part of an 'open regionalist' relationship with the EU, expect to have the sort of relationship with it that Mexico has with the US. However, 'open regionalism' from an EU perspective means something more than it does for the US, he claims. It 'goes beyond free trade alone to embrace conditionality and political cooperation, as well as development aid'.[22]

What is one to make of the European 'addition' here? Can (and some might say 'should') the EU 'export democratic norms' south of the Mediterranean, as the title of an article by Luis Martinez suggests?[23] When various trade deals are tied to the evidence of commitments on human rights and democracy ('conditionality') does this produce the sort of progress on these crucial issues that has undoubtedly been seen in Southern and Central/Eastern Europe over the last three decades since the collapse of military and communist dictatorships respectively?

The first thing to emphasise is that many of the lands south of the Mediterranean have an economic dependence upon Europe stemming from the age of imperialism, when they were colonised by various European countries, such as Italy in Libya, Spain in Northern Morocco and Western Sahara, France in Algeria and Britain in Egypt. The South Mediterranean area now relies on Europe as a market for agricultural and energy products (oil and gas), and cannot develop without access to European markets. At the same time Europe is keen to find a market for its industrial products south of the Mediterranean, and to see the removal of trade barriers to these. Under the 'Barcelona Process' mentioned above, which dates from a conference in Barcelona in 1995, it has been trying to forward its economic aims through a series of bilateral agreements with individual countries.

Unsurprisingly, the 'Barcelona process' has been seen as exposing the industrial sectors of the South Mediterranean countries to unfettered competition with European industry. Indeed, the emphasis upon phasing out trade barriers and generally liberalising trade is very much in line with IMF prescriptions. Moreover, the emphasis upon free trade is not linked to the free movement of labour. Large-scale legal and illegal migration to Europe[24] from the south has been a concern of the EU for some time. This in turn is linked to relative wage levels and to the fact that employment opportunities south of the Mediterranean have not kept pace with demographic growth. Consequently there are many attempts to reach Europe from North Africa illegally, with scores of deaths when boats capsize in bad weather. To this extent, Europe's 'open regionalism' doesn't seem so very different from that which operates between the US and Mexico under the NAFTA accord, where there is a similarly protective attitude on the part of the former towards the free movement of labour.

The intention behind the Barcelona Process was to make the bilateral agreements a staging-post on the way to a single Southern Mediterranean market, but there has been little progress on this. There was talk of a 'zone of prosperity' being created. The intention – and the justification – behind the often painful process of trade liberalisation was that it would attract foreign investment. Yet such investment south of the Mediterranean has been minimal. By way of comparison, the former communist states who joined the EU in May 2004 have managed to attract a great deal of foreign direct investment (FDI), thereby maintaining employment levels through the decline of the formerly state-managed heavy industrial staples of the communist era and in many cases achieving high levels of growth.[25]

The Copenhagen criteria, when applied to candidate countries from Central and Eastern Europe, contained much that involved developing the sort of administrative structures that ensure a working as opposed to a 'failed' or 'failing' state. Everyone knew that the Czechs and Poles were keen on a market economy; but did they have bureaucracies capable of meeting its demands? Much of the training that went into the pre-accession years involved developing the administrative skills necessary for adhering to the *acquis communautaire*. The result was that the ex-communist countries, which were always more than willing to move towards a market economy, could also cope with its demands, since for all the talk of governments 'leaving it to the market' to create wealth (and even fewer take this line now that recession is upon us), the reality is that governments need to lay down and maintain the conditions for a market economy to work successfully. By the time these states joined the EU there was *already* a great deal of foreign direct investment going into them. They had (for the most part) a skilled workforce, sound political institutions, a secure working environment and a fast-developing infrastructure. Business moved in not only because tax rates and labour costs were low, but because it was possible to organise payments and credit transfers, for instance, without either confusion or corruption. The EU was supporting them throughout this transition.

The states of the Southern Mediterranean, on the other hand, lacked the sort of support which enabled the countries of Central and Eastern Europe to attract investment, and this has had unfortunate consequences (at least outside the oil-and-gas sector). Investors look at other potential areas of investment with similar advantages in terms of labour costs, such as China and South-East Asia, and see them as more attractive in terms of overall infrastructure and administrative organisation, not to mention political stability. For this reason the foreign investment moves further east. The problem is not that the South Mediterranean countries do not want to become 'market players', but that they do not receive the sort of backing that would enable them to 'play' successfully. It might therefore be asked whether they are really offered any more by the EU than by the US in its 'US – Middle East Partnership Initiative'. Both the EU and the US are arguably pursuing 'open regionalism' in much the same way.

The EU and Eastern/South-Eastern Europe

Where the countries of Eastern and South-Eastern Europe are concerned, the picture is more complicated, since these are all areas that are geographically part of Europe and it is difficult to see how the EU can indefinitely postpone expanding outwards into these areas. As has already been pointed out, full membership of the EU is a realistic prospect for each one of them, though in many cases it remains some way down the line. Though these countries can be grouped in a number of ways, this section will divide them into three. The first group, the Balkans, represents a region whose members are likely to be part of EU enlargement relatively soon. The second group, which could be called 'Europe's far east', comprises countries where membership is in prospect but after a possibly considerable length of time (decades rather than years). The third group is a single country, Turkey, which is in the unique position of being both officially accepted as a candidate country and yet rejected as a potential member by some very influential figures inside the EU. In one sense it is ahead of the others, being further up the queue; in another sense it is behind them, since it is the most likely to be rejected when its case finally comes to be decided.

It is true that some of the countries in these three groups (such as Albania and Turkey) are also in the Euro-Mediterranean group, since parts of South-East Europe are part of the Mediterranean coastline. However, the grouping made in this section remains a useful one. In each case the prospect of full membership exercises an influence on the countries concerned in a manner that does not apply to the prospect of 'partnership' in the case of the Euro-Mediterranean group.

a) The Balkans

The EU and the Balkans is the subject of an interesting study by Dallago.[26] Given the destabilisation of the 1990s and the descent of the region into violent conflict, there is every reason to view this area as a test case of the EU's claim to be able to control undesirable outbursts of violent nationalist feeling through a supranationalist mechanism – as it arguably did on the one occasion where such feeling exploded worryingly among its own member states, namely when Haider's far-right Freedom Party became a coalition partner in Austria's government in 2000. EU sanctions encouraged Haider's resignation as head of the party, which remained a junior partner in the coalition but with much-reduced authority. Earlier, warnings to Meciar's government in Slovakia during the 1990s that it must meet democratic norms before joining the EU contributed to his loss of power there.

Karen Smith argues that the desire for 'leverage' contributed to Romania and Bulgaria's fast-track entry to the European Union. She points out that the Copenhagen Council of December 2002, by declaring that the countries would become members on a specific date, 2007, acted in an unusual way, 'because previous European Councils had been so hesitant to set a definite date for the accession of specific candidates'. However, she goes on:

> The risks of alienating Bulgaria and Romania were considered too great not to give a firmer indication of when those two countries might finally accede, although the pressure on them to comply with the conditions could be more difficult to maintain.[27]

Whether or not those who say that the entry of Romania and Bulgaria was premature are correct, it is clear that the experience of conflict in the Balkans in the 1990s had produced a sense that membership of the European Union was the one sure way of ensuring that more outbreaks of violence were avoided. Bound within a supranationalist union, states would be much less likely (though it could never be pronounced impossible) to resort to war.

Hence while the EU was understandably criticised for a failure to respond to events outside its borders in the 1990s, such criticism is consistent with a view that the EU has effective structures with which to prevent such events where member-states themselves are concerned. Indeed it is consistent with a position arguing that the prospect of membership has already had a positive impact in preventing further outbreaks of ethnic and nationalist violence. Telò is right to say that 'the Yugoslavian tragedies of the 1990s shattered the rhetorical idealistic approach of a general benevolence and final victory for democratic values'.[28] However, the soul-searching that resulted focused upon building up an effective Common Foreign and Security Policy and an ability to mobilise effective peacekeeping forces where needed for intervention in areas outside the EU. It did not involve a questioning of the positive effect EU membership could and already had had upon dampening and resolving precisely the sort of tensions that gave rise to the Yugoslav conflict.

Since the Zagreb Summit in 2000, the EU's policy towards the Western Balkans (Serbia, Kosovo, Croatia, Bosnia-Herzegovina, Albania, Montenegro and Macedonia) has been determined by the 'Stabilisation and Association Process'. In each case specific mention has been made of 'reforms with a view to accession', a process which would involve 'aligning their legislation more closely with that of the Community'. A summit at Thessaloniki in 2003 took the process a stage further. Bilateral 'Stabilisation and Association Agreements' would be reached with each country, based on their progress towards accession. It has always to be borne in mind that candidate countries are involved in the EU's economic market long before they formally accede. There is a process of gradual acclimatisation, assisted by various EU instruments.

At the Thessaloniki summit EU External Relations Commissioner Chris Patten declared that 'the map of the EU will not be complete until the countries of the Western Balkans are included in it.' He made sure that various pre-accession programmes were grafted onto the Stabilisation and Association Agreements. These included a European Integration Partnership Programme, support for institution-building through 'twinning' programmes, effectively the secondment of civil service advisers to help with the administrative preparations for membership, and participation in educational exchanges such as Socrates and Leonardo. The former CARDS (Community Assistance for Reconstruction, Development and Stabilisation) programme for Community assistance to the region, which applied to the budgetary period of 2000–06, would be incorporated into the new IPA (Instrument for Pre-Accession) for the new budgetary period 2007–13.

The countries were now receiving help specifically targeted towards accession. As the EU's own website makes clear, 'considerable investment is required if the candidate countries are to bring their institutions and standards in line with the Copenhagen criteria' (the criteria for accession developed in 1993 with a view to the first tranche of Eastward enlargement into the post-communist countries). However, in 2006 some hesitations about the membership aspirations of the Western Balkan countries were voiced at a Salzburg summit in March, when EU leaders explicitly spoke of the Union's 'absorption capacity' as a criterion governing enlargement. The new External Relations commissioner, Olli Rehn, at once voiced his misgivings in the 23rd June edition of the *European Observer*:

> If we go wobbly about the 'Western Balkans' European perspective, our beneficial influence will be severely eroded, just when the region enters a difficult period for talks on Kosovo's status.

Rehn knew how keeping open the prospect of full membership was essential to the political healing process in a region so recently torn apart by civil war.

Those countries from the region that the EU defines as 'candidate countries', as opposed to 'potential candidate countries' (the former being further along the track towards membership, specifically Croatia and Macedonia from the Western Balkan area) receive additional funding in order to adopt and implement (once they have become members) the community's cohesion policy and manage its structural funds. As was made clear in Chapter 4, this is a very important part of the EU's budget (it has now overtaken the Common Agricultural Policy in size and stands at around fifty billion euros per annum), involving programmes of regional assistance which provide significant infrastructural support and help to overcome large disparities in wealth between richer and poorer nations in the Community. Candidate countries know that they will be able to tap into these funds – though they also know that such funds have to be bid for on the basis of creditable projects which will be closely monitored, with funding withdrawn in the case of non-compliance with community rules.

Furthermore, co-funding from the European Investment Bank and various other international financial institutions is opened up for candidate countries. This is not just a question of funding being made available directly, but also of providing the sort of confidence in their future which makes international lenders willing to invest in countries that they know will soon be full members of the EU.

It is reasonable to conclude that a country that is clearly on the path to membership of the EU has a range of financial incentives to adopt and respect the *acquis communautaire*, both in terms of developing the administrative capacity to operate a functioning market economy and in terms of social and political reforms needed in order to enshrine respect for human rights and the needs of minorities. Whilst no one could claim that the Western Balkans have been transformed from a battlefield into a model of multicultural pluralism, the real incentives to membership have made the EU much more successful in maintaining peace in the Balkans after the war than it was in ending the conflict in the 1990s. Its progress in the Balkans contrasts sharply with its lack of progress in the case of the South Mediterranean countries that have no hope of eventual membership.

b) Europe's 'Far East'

The countries in this part of Europe effectively have their membership on a back burner. Though there is little argument about their geographical qualifications for joining the EU, other considerations make it unlikely that any of them will do so in the near future.

In the first place, there is the question of size. The new members who joined in 2004 and 2007 were relatively poor and it was generally perceived that their incorporation into the community had come at a cost in the short term; future enlargements, it was said, would be possible 'only when they could be afforded'. In the case of the Western Balkans the countries, though poor, were relatively small in population terms; but a country like Ukraine, with a population of forty-six million, would represent a substantial increase in numbers, far in excess of all the Western Balkan states combined. Though ratification of the Treaty of Lisbon may have streamlined the EU enough to make it capable of coping with a large number of additional members (such as the West Balkan states), it will not make it any more capable of absorbing the economic costs of additional members who are both poor and populous (whatever the arguments for the economic benefits of doing so long term).

In the second place, there is a political consideration – Russia. As the Russian foreign minister Sergei Lavrov pointed out in an interview,[29] Russia has 'special interests going deep into centuries' in the countries which form its own protective 'ring of friends' around its borders, countries which like the Balkan states (now inside the EU) were once part of the Soviet Union. Lavrov sees Russia as having its own 'privileged partnership' with these countries, and emphasises that his country has its own close economic and social ties with Ukraine. Concern about being seen by Russia as interfering in its own neighbourhood has led certain EU members to support a brake on membership for countries like Belarus and Ukraine. In the case of Belarus, the lack of progress towards anything approaching the economic, social and political conditions enshrined in the Copenhagen criteria means that few problems are created by Russian interests in the area. In the case of Ukraine, however, it is much harder to accept.

Ukraine clearly took some steps towards democracy through the so-called 'Orange Revolution'. President Viktor Yuschenko's declaration that 'we have chosen Europe; it is not just a question of geography, but a matter of shared spiritual and moral values' was applauded in many European countries, particularly those which had seen similar 'velvet revolutions' themselves. The EU played a role in the affair. It sent a large number of election monitors and a special envoy, Nicholas Bigman, while its High Representative Javier Solana mediated in negotiations between government and opposition parties.

However, its role as a pro-active defender of Ukrainian democracy did not extend to an offer of (even distant) membership of the EU. Instead the country was strongly advised by the European Commission in 2005 not to apply for membership, (advice it took). An EU-Ukraine 'Action Plan' was created, aiming at economic integration – not radically different from the 'Free Trade Area' promised under the previous PCA (Partnership and Cooperation Agreement). The Action Plan was reluctantly signed in February 2005, though with a List of Additional Measures that talked of a new Enhanced Agreement once the political criteria set out in the Action Plan were fulfilled, but with no firm commitments. Ukrainian reluctance was partly explained by the fact that the very idea of an Action Plan conceived within a 'European Neighbourhood Policy' was seen as an insult; Ukraine does not think of itself as being 'in the neighbourhood' of Europe but as being in Europe itself – reference is often made to the Vienna Geographic Society's determination a century ago that the geographical centre of the continent was in the Transcarpathian region of Western Ukraine (an area which belonged to Czechoslovakia between the world wars, enabling the newspaper magnate Robert Maxwell, who came from the region, to call himself a 'bouncing Czech' – presumably a bouncing Ukrainian would be thought to have less bounce).

The trouble is that the sort of institutional harmonisation on offer in the Action Plan is an approach suitable mainly to developed countries such as Norway and Switzerland which don't want EU membership but do want access to its market. The point which needs always to be borne in mind, when comparisons are made between a country such as Ukraine and countries like Norway and Switzerland, is that the latter are able to bear the high cost of bringing their regulations in line with the *acquis*. Moreover, they already have a sophisticated administrative infrastructure. They can easily put a body in place to manage competition policy or appoint a set of lawyers and judges trained in the regulation of the market economy. Ukraine – like the Southern

Mediterranean countries trying to work on the 'zone of prosperity' – would have to develop such procedures almost from scratch. The costs have to be met (despite various forms of assistance from EU funding) largely up-front, and it is very hard to create the political will to do so if the prospect of access to structural funds and the Common Agricultural Policy (which only comes with membership) is nowhere on the horizon. As the European Commission itself recognised, 'an important part of the incentives of the ENP – for instance in terms of market access and integration and other economic benefits will only bear fruit later. This creates a real difficulty for partner countries in building the necessary domestic support for reforms.'[30] What the Commission did not point out was that the quality of this 'later fruit' would depend upon the prospect of membership.

After 2005 Ukraine moved into four years of instability, with two rounds of national and four of local elections. Meanwhile continuing failure in the reform of government, the judiciary and the media meant that the country failed to implement many of the agreed Action Plan priorities, though there were some significant agreements with the EU on satellite navigation systems, energy and aviation. The danger was of a mutually reinforcing slowdown on both sides, as Ukraine became more resentful over the limited scope of what was offered and the EU equally resentful over Ukraine's failure to make proper use of the little it had been offered.

Ukraine is often painted as a country of two halves, with a Europhile West and a South and East more oriented towards Russia. However, this is an oversimplification. In the economic sphere, even the oligarchs who benefited from the privatisations of the 1990s look favourably upon membership of the EU and the opportunities on the world market which that would offer – even if one takes the cynical position that they simply want a global environment in which to spend their ill-gotten gains. They have supported Ukrainian membership of the WTO and resisted close involvement with the Russian-dominated SES (Single Economic Space), despite the fact that Russia remains a vital trading partner. In the foreign policy sphere, though the parties stress their differences for internal consumption, it is noteworthy that even the hardline communists in Ukraine support membership of the EU (as opposed to NATO). Whether it was the so-called 'Orange elites' who were in power, or the government of Yanukovich, the same position was taken. Yanukovich's government may have sought to distance itself from the 'Euro-romanticism' of his predecessor as President, Yuschenko, but it did not revoke the 'Action Plan' for

Ukraine under the European Neighbourhood Policy. As Wolczuk points out, 'relations with the EU are considerably less divisive in Ukraine than are relations with Russia, the US and NATO'.[31] Indeed it should not be forgotten that EU membership was originally tabled by the Kuchma leadership before the 'Orange Revolution'.

Hence there has always been a broad political agreement on closer ties with the EU. This is something which, it is fair to say, the broad majority in Ukraine desires, not just its 'pro-western half'. However, progress with regulatory alignment, for the reasons mentioned earlier, has been slow. The introduction of a new European Neighbourhood Policy (ENP) 'Instrument' in 2007 at least meant that Ukraine received more support for civil society and other organisations; ironically, the country was receiving 'cooperation tools' which had previously been used for countries that were to be part of EU enlargement, such as Twinning and Technical Assistance and Information Exchange (TAIEX). Negotiations finally began in earnest on the 'New Enhanced Agreement' (NEA) which had a stronger measure of conditionality – i.e. a means of ensuring that measures were legally binding on both sides. Shapovalova describes the NEA as 'in spirit' an integration agreement.[32] Certainly its provisions represent a narrowing of the gap between the EU's Neighbourhood Policy and its Enlargement Policy. Then in 2008 Ukraine moved forward again, applying to join the WTO with EU encouragement and being accepted into the organisation in May of that year.

In July 2008 the name of the NEA was changed yet again, becoming an 'Agreement on Association.' This game of 'musical acronyms' is characteristic of the EU. It is difficult to avoid the view that the organisation is dancing around different titles in order to avoid giving Ukraine a direct commitment on future membership. Though a summit of EU heads under President Sarkozy in September 2008 did accept that Ukraine was a European country and shared 'European values' (thereby effectively promoting it from the 'European Neighbourhood' to Europe proper), it declared the door to future membership 'neither open nor closed'.

What is interesting about Ukraine is the fact that even a distant and uncertain prospect of EU membership is able to exercise a considerable influence upon its policies. Its real political divisions do not extend to a debate on the desirability of membership. It accepts that full membership will take more than a decade to achieve, but at the same time it will not accept anything less. Without a road-map to accession, however long the road, it will be impossible to exercise continuing pressure on Ukraine to reform its institutions and 'compel divisive political elites to restrain their personal ambitions for a common policy agenda'.[33]

c) *Turkey*

Turkey has to be placed in a category of its own because of its unique situation. In one sense it is further along the road to membership; it was accepted as eligible for membership as far back as 1963. However, its membership has been repeatedly delayed and remains controversial. Though a long-term member of NATO, it has seen many former members of the Warsaw Pact enter the EU before it.

The reasons are threefold. In the first place there is the sort of cultural difference that concerns those for whom the EU is built, however tenuously, upon the ideals of 'Christendom' and that it should therefore not accept a member whose overwhelming religious affiliation (despite its commitment to being a secular state) is Islamic (a criterion which would create difficulties for some of the West Balkan countries too). In the second place there is the important concern about the capacity of the EU to manage the entry of a large new member, one that by 2020, if demographic trends continue, would in fact be the most populous of all. Thirdly, where the official Copenhagen criteria themselves are concerned, many view Turkey as falling short, particularly in relation to the observance of human and minority rights and political stability.

Nevertheless, recent history would suggest that the prospect of membership has encouraged reform in Turkey. The large number of judicial and constitutional reforms passed by the Erdogan government after he became Prime Minister in 2003 did bring about significant change, and led to the formal opening of membership negotiations with Turkey in October 2005. Even accepting the fact that Turkey has not gone far enough, it is arguable that these reforms, passed in the anticipation of future membership of the EU, would have been impossible outside that context.[34] One might compare events in the previous decade when Turkey suspended its relations with the EU following its being placed in a separate category of applicant states. As Smith comments:

> The EU's leverage over Turkey diminished, and consequently the EU altered its policy. The Helsinki European Council in December 1999 classified Turkey as an official candidate, although it made it clear that membership negotiations would only be opened once the political conditions had been met.[35]

Arguably the same sort of tactics might have led to the reunification of Cyprus. The Turkish Cypriots, traditionally more hostile to reunification but desperate for EU entry, actually endorsed a UN plan to reunite the island; it was the Greek Cypriots who rejected it, having been told that their entry to the EU would proceed anyway. Had the prospect of membership been as dependent on reuniting the island for Greek Cypriots as it was for Turks, the UN plan might have been endorsed by both sides. Once again the Cyprus issue illustrates how the attraction of belonging to an effective supranational organisation can lead to compromises that other forms of persuasion, and certainly the sort of pressure exercised by inter-governmental bodies like the UN, cannot achieve.

Ironically the wider political context may come to the rescue of Turkey. Where Russian pressure effectively blocks even 'potential candidate' status for Ukraine, American pressure on behalf of Turkish membership has been overt and forthright. Interestingly, such pleas from President Obama on Turkey's behalf inevitably meet the response from opponents of Turkish membership like French President Sarkozy and German Chancellor Merkel that 'privileged partnership' is on offer as an alternative. Nothing could better illustrate the difference in kind between full membership and such 'partnerships' than the fact that these two leaders are willing to stand up to any form of persuasion in order to deny Turkey the former, while enthusiastically offering it the latter.

Conclusion

What comes out very strongly from a study of the EU's relations with its 'Near Abroad' is the fact that whatever its failings in the 1990s in preventing war in the Balkans, the prospect of membership for these states has enabled the EU to do a great deal to assist economic renewal and progress towards democracy since the end of conflict. Not only that, but where there is a prospect of eventual membership, however distant, (Turkey, Ukraine), significant pressure towards economic and political reform can still be maintained by the European Union. Where there is no such prospect, however, as in the case of the South Mediterranean, progress has been much more limited, despite the language of partnerships, however privileged, and summits, however frequent.

It would seem that between 'privileged partners' (reminiscent of the 'most favoured nation' status much used by the US in discussing trade relations with other countries) and 'members' there remains a great gulf fixed, which talk of 'multi-speed Europe' and 'concentric circles' cannot overcome. Full membership of the EU remains the aim for all those European states in the Balkans and Eastern Europe that lack it. In order to achieve it they are prepared to accept the sort of economic and political changes required by the *acquis communautaire*. These come at a considerable economic cost, but they receive assistance for their implementation and know the benefits that full membership will bring in terms of access to structural and cohesion funding, not to mention the advantages of the Common Agricultural Policy and eventual sharing in a common currency. Moreover, the prospect of such membership has immediate advantages in terms of their financial stability and commercial attractiveness. Eastern Europe is able to attract FDI (Foreign Direct Investment) in a way that the countries south of the Mediterranean are not.

As members of the EU, these countries will have to give up sovereignty in certain areas, thus being bound by EU law under threat of sanctions. However, for the sake of participation in a stable and prosperous environment they are willing to do so. They will be able to retain their identity as nation-states within a larger supranational organisation. In such a context they are willing to make a number of political changes which were unthinkable a decade ago. Without the prospect of EU membership, for instance, it is extremely unlikely that Croatia's Prime Minister Ivo Sanader could have steered the Croatian Democratic Union (CDZ), formerly the ruling party of hardline nationalist Franjo Tudjman, onto a moderate conservative path.[36]

The EU's success in dealing with candidate and potential candidate countries is only the extension of its earlier success in helping to end communist dictatorship in Central Europe and military dictatorship in Southern Europe. It contrasts with a relative lack of success where its 'privileged partners' south of the Mediterranean are concerned. The natural conclusion is that when there is a prospect of belonging to a prosperous and secure organisation like the EU, states are willing to accept internal reforms and a limited ceding of sovereignty.

According to Gideon Rachman 'the awful prospect is now dawning that the EU, if it were to discard enlargement, would be throwing away its only foreign policy tool'.[37] He is right to the extent that the EU has been markedly successful on the world stage only with those countries which have a chance of joining it. However, there is an alternative approach. Instead of trumpeting its questionably effective multilateralism, its strategic partnerships and its inter-regional dialogues, the EU could recognise what its own history has told it, namely that the system of shared sovereignty is its unique advantage as an organisation. It is this system that has brought so much to Europe in terms of stability and prosperity, as Part One tried to bring out, drawing in even reluctant joiners like the UK and keeping in reluctant members like Gaullist France. It should therefore seek to universalise it, so that even countries that are *not part of Europe* can have the opportunity to adopt such a system. This does not mean extending Europe beyond its natural frontiers; it means extending the sharing of sovereignty beyond the European Union. The next chapter will consider that possibility in detail, before the last chapter discusses whether it is realistic to think of the EU playing the role envisaged for it inside a Global Union.

9
A Global Sharing of Sovereignty

Moving beyond other organisations

The last chapter argued that whatever the value of 'effective multilateralism' and 'strategic 'partnerships', the EU needs to develop a much more radical approach based upon a belief in its own distinctive form of governance. Yet so far it has failed to do so.

The European Union is deeply conscious of the fact that it possesses huge legal, institutional, technical and financial resources – more than any other regional organisation on the planet. It has a huge budget of over one hundred billion euros a year, far more than the UN possesses and guaranteed for a seven-year period. Its combined wealth is greater than that of any country outside it. Even its military weight is considerable, if the armed forces of its separate members are put together and considered as one – the defence budget of the EU-27 combined is equivalent to half that of the USA and three times that of Russia.

At the same time, however, it recognises that defence and foreign policy lie in the area of inter-governmental cooperation, whereas many parts of that legal, institutional, technical and financial prowess fall into the sovereignty-sharing area. The EU may be able to achieve a 'single' market, but the most it can hope for is a 'common' foreign and security policy, seeking to coordinate the views of twenty-seven different governments in a highly sensitive area on a case-by-case basis. This is the root of the quips about the EU as economic giant but a political and certainly a military pygmy; in many (but not all) economic areas cooperation has made the EU strong, whereas in the military area cooperation has remained weak. More to the point, however, the EU has simply failed to find a role.

As a consequence its policy of 'effective multilateralism' is one of dependence on others. Take, for example, its first faltering steps in the area of 'hard power'. A number of small-scale military operations have been undertaken by EU forces under the ESDP (European Security and Defence Policy), initially in Bosnia and Macedonia and then outside Europe altogether in the Democratic Republic of Congo. The largest EU deployment to date involved about four thousand troops from over twenty EU countries, acting under a UN Security Council mandate to maintain humanitarian relief and protect civilians and UN personnel between 2008 and 2009 in Chad and the Central African Republic. Early in 2009 this 'bridging operation' came to an end and control was handed back to UN military forces.

Other small-scale activities have taken place – a monitoring mission in Georgia, a 'border assistance mission' at the Rafah Crossing Point in Palestine, a mission in support of 'Security Sector Reform' in Guinea-Bissau. Alongside these deployments attempts have been made to build up EU military forces. An ambitious plan adopted in 2004 by the European Council, entitled Headline Goal 2010, aimed to develop forces capable of rapid deployment to deal with 'crisis management operations' by 2010. Though these ambitions are unlikely to be realised, there is no doubt that the military capability of the EU has increased. There has also been progress with arms cooperation and joint procurement projects, some of it facilitated by the creation of the European Aeronautic, Space and Defence Company (EADS) in 2000.

Hence there has been a slow build-up of military capability, and there is an expectation of more. If over twenty members of the EU can work together in Chad under an Irish operational commander, then further cooperation may develop in future, drawing in its wake the demand for sufficient available troops and equipment to carry out its tasks. However, it is also generally accepted that such cooperation is best achieved under the auspices of the UN, (an Irish commander of a NATO force, for instance, would be unthinkable). Unsurprisingly, therefore, EU pronouncements in this area provide unreserved support for the UN. The European Council declaration of 2003 launching a European Security Strategy based on 'effective multilateralism' talked of 'a strong UN at its heart', while the European Security Strategy Implementation Report ('Providing Security in a Changing World') at the end of 2008 spoke of the UN as being 'at the apex of the international system' – though elsewhere it spoke of the need to 'continue reforming' the UN, without specifying what reforms it had in mind.[1]

However, seeing the UN as an ideal umbrella under which to further EU military cooperation comes at a cost. The downside is that the EU will be forced to act only where the UN finds it possible to reach agreement, and that provides a severe constraint. It is as if the only way to secure agreement for starting the car is to have the garage doors closed. As Chapter 5 discussed in detail, Security Council mandates require unanimity from the veto-wielding powers and may not reflect the view of the wider international community, most of which is not represented on the Security Council. Intervention will be impossible in any state that refuses to consent to a UN presence. The EU may feel that imagining itself and the UN to be natural partners provides the safest method of testing the waters for military cooperation among its member-states, but it is hardly likely to provide it with an effective foreign policy. It is more likely to guarantee it a series of 'bridging', monitoring and mopping-up operations on those few occasions where the UN is able to deploy its forces.

Concern over whether the EU could do anything effective in external relations has limited the scope of its activity so far. Hanging on to the coat-tails of the UN in order to pick up scraps of peacekeeping might not be too unkind a way of describing its efforts at a Community-wide policy of military engagement. Though its increasing involvement with the UN has led one writer to talk of 'compelling evidence that European voting cohesion has grown rather dramatically (*sic*) in the UN General Assembly over the course of the 1990s',[2] another talks about a 'dysfunctional multilateralism' in EU-UN relations and suggests that member-states revert to 'opportunistic, self-interested and self-promoting' behaviour there. In the intergovernmental environment of the UN General Assembly they behave like dogs off the leash. Jorgensen's view is that:

> We can question whether the EU – with its own remarkable integrative processes of multilateralism – is contributing to a more effective UN multilateralism.[3]

Opinion is therefore divided about the 'partnership' between the EU and the UN. The suspicion remains that in a desperate search for a world role mediated by others, the EU is forever trying to fit a quart into a pint pot. It is arguable that if, instead of trying to adapt itself to the demands and structures of other organisations, the EU were to be bold enough to seek to apply its own sovereignty-sharing structures on a global scale, it would be a far more effective 'global player'. The rest of this chapter offers one example of how it might do just that.

The McClintock system

For one of his regular contributions to *The Guardian*,[4] Timothy Garton Ash, Professor of European Studies in the University of Oxford, chose the title 'I've found a perfect new member for the EU. If only it were in Europe'. He explained why Canada would be a perfect member of the EU:

> It effortlessly meets the EU's so-called Copenhagen criteria for membership, including democratic government, the rule of law, a well-regulated market economy and respect for minority rights (Canada's a world-leader on that). Canada is rich, so would be a much-needed net contributor to the European budget at a time when the EU has been taking in lots of poorer states. One of Europe's besetting weaknesses is disagreement between the British and the French, but on this the two historic rivals would instantly agree. English-speaking Canada would strengthen the Anglophone group in the EU, Quebec the Francophone.

However, Canada is not in Europe – no one can stretch the frontiers of the continent that far, even though Iceland is reckoned a potential member of the EU and neighbouring Greenland once was a member (through its association with Denmark). Canada, like Morocco or Tunisia, must be ruled out even as a potential member of the EU by the facts of geography.

Nevertheless, Garton Ash has a point to make in what he calls his 'mildly amusing thought experiment':

> To look at Canada and its values is to understand how foolish it is to try to define Europe by reference to an allegedly unique set of 'European values'. Values matter, but these European values are shared by most Canadians more than they are by many Europeans.

Once it is recognised that there is no unique set of 'European values', then it becomes possible to think in terms of a global union, one that is not attempting to export Europe but to export a system which took hold in Europe for reasons that have to do with the particular circumstances in which that particular continent found itself after World War

Two. If some countries outside Europe, of which Canada is an example, wish to take part in such a system, there has to be a means of enabling them to do so.

One proposal for such an arrangement comes from John McClintock, an official of the European Union who has built a great deal upon his experiences (in Sierra Leone and pre-accession Poland) outside the Union before coming to Brussels to work inside it. He has been able to observe a system of sovereignty-sharing not only from within but also from the perspective both of a deeply troubled 'failed state' outside any such system and of a pre-accession country preparing for membership.

In *The Uniting of Nations: An Essay in Global Governance*,[5] McClintock outlines his proposed 'Global Union'. It is a product of the sort of treaty that led to the formation of the European Coal and Steel Community in 1951. In other words, it begins as a 'coalition of the willing' – a small (in all probability) group of states who are willing to share sovereignty in certain areas. It therefore starts small in two senses – both in terms of the number of states involved and in terms of the areas within which sovereignty is shared.

Just as the EU began with six countries and grew to (currently) more than four times that number of nation-states, so the GU would start small and aim to grow. In the second place, just as the EU began with an agreement to share sovereignty in terms of the management of the coal and steel sectors, and then grew into a common market, a common currency and common social and environmental policies (to say the least), so also the Global Union would begin with a sharing of sovereignty in a particular area (McClintock proposes food security in the latest edition of his book) and then extend the areas within which it shared sovereignty. This is not to say that such an extension would proceed automatically through 'spillover', as some of the 'neo-functionalist integrationists' are said to believe. It is simply to argue that the best way in which to demonstrate the general applicability of the sharing of sovereignty is first to demonstrate its efficacy in a particular area. Nevertheless the 'spillover' theorists are correct to say that whatever area is chosen will not be completely detachable from others and may in that sense encourage extension.

McClintock foresees that the Global Union will eventually consist of regional unions rather than individual countries. As yet, however, as Chapter 7 attempted to show, there is only one regional union in which there is genuine sharing of sovereignty – the EU. McClintock therefore suggests that in its initial phase the members of the Global Union would be the EU (which would be a single member) and other countries, each of which would be a member in its own right. There would then be no domination by the EU; the EU would be just one member of this Global Union, as would each of the countries from elsewhere which chose to join. Indeed, the Global Union could even begin with the EU and Canada alone as its two founding members.

For the sake of argument, let it be supposed that the Global Union has a wider appeal than that. Let us say that the second member of the Global Union besides the EU is Chile. Then a third member joins, say South Africa. Canada comes in as a fourth. But the fifth to join, let us hypothesise, is Peru. At this point we have two members from one region, Latin America, and, according to McClintock, the two countries from this region would between themselves combine to form a Latin American Union, within which they shared sovereignty. Individual countries from the same region would form themselves into regional unions when more than one country from the same region wished to join the Global Union. They would then participate in the Global Union as members of the Latin American Union, just as France and Germany would participate in it as members of the European Union.

It is unlikely that the countries involved would refuse to form regional unions, since they will only be sharing with each other what they are prepared to share anyway with countries from other regions in the Global Union. But the advantage of McClintock's proposal is that it allows the regional unions to emerge *at the same time as the Global Union*. It does not require the world to wait until the regional unions are operational before embarking upon the development of a Global Union. Since the regional unions and the Global Union emerge together, there is no danger of conflict between national blocs being replaced by conflicts between regional blocs. This is a useful precautionary move against the sort of 'multipolar' world that might prove as unstable as the 'unipolar' world of a single 'top dog', or the sort of instability which former Labour Defence Secretary and Chancellor of the Exchequer Denis Healey envisaged when he wrote that 'a continental sacro-egoismo could be even more dangerous to peace than a national sacro-egoismo'.[6] By following McClintock's proposal the nightmare of endless competing (or warring) blocs is avoided, because the world organisation develops hand in hand with the regional organisations.

The Global Union would entail the formation of appropriate global institutions to parallel those in the European Union, in order to reflect and manage the balance between supranational and inter-governmental that will be necessary in any organisation intended to regulate rather than supplant the nation-state – a *binding* rather than a *destroying* of nations. The sort of balance maintained at European level between Commission, Council, Court of Justice and Parliament would be reflected at global level. It is not, of course, necessary to argue for an exact replication of those institutions, but it *is* necessary to argue for the sort of checks and balances that prevent the European Union sliding either into a single superstate or a mere treaty alliance.

McClintock's proposal is not a 'complete kit' for the construction of a new world order, and it is immediately bound to raise questions. One is that of whether the EU would be prepared to join a Global Union as a 'single member'. This is not, perhaps, too much of a problem. In theory there is no reason why the EU should not do so (and the Treaty of Lisbon gives it 'legal personality'). The EU is already a member of a number of international organisations, like the WTO (World Trade Organisation). It is true that its member-states are also members of the WTO, and difficulties are common. Nevertheless, it should be possible to devise a system in which the EU is a member of the Global Union in its own right and the member-states, though not themselves members of the Global Union, have to be consulted on any decisions that are made.

In practice this is the way in which many disputes are resolved at the WTO (with the difference that the member-states of the EU are also individual members of the WTO). The question of whether a particular form of trade is a 'Community competency' or not is often far from cut-and-dried (quite apart from the question of whether that competency should be extended or narrowed). For instance, unanimity among member-states is needed for any agreements involving trade in audiovisual and cultural services where there is a 'risk' of prejudicing the Union's cultural and linguistic diversity. It is also required in the field of social, educational and health services where there is a 'risk' of disturbing the national organisation of such services. But clearly there is bound to be room for considerable disagreement over what constitutes 'risk'. Without constant interaction between the EU and its member-states it is difficult to see how any trade policy could be managed successfully at the WTO.

Any sovereignty-sharing arrangements at global level will have to proceed in a similar manner. The EU would participate as a single member, but would also have to maintain close contact with member-states. If there were irreconcilable differences over whether a particular policy fell under the remit of Community competence, then it could not proceed. This is not an unfamiliar way of working for the EU, besides which it has to be made absolutely clear that the sharing of sovereignty at global level will not be in any areas in which sovereignty is not shared at European level.

Another question concerns the ease with which the world can be divided up into distinct multi-member regions. What sort of 'regional union' would Canada aspire to, for instance? Its associates in a putative regional union would appear to be Greenland (the one country to have left the EU) the US, which as the most powerful country in the world is unlikely to share sovereignty in any area easily, or Mexico (the only plausible partner, unless a relaxation of geographical rules were to draw in a euro-sceptic UK, perhaps seeking a regional union with a more limited supranationalism). The global map does not divide easily into tidy regions.

Moreover, in those parts of the world which already have regional unions that are trying to develop (even though, as Chapter 7 has argued, progress so far has been limited), it might be politically difficult to create others. On the other hand, as Chapter 7 also made clear, Africa, South-East Asia and Latin America already contain a large number of regional groupings and sub-groupings. Some disappear, others come to life for the first time and membership lists grow larger or smaller. It is not difficult to envisage another organisation in each region, although it is hard to predict how it will develop.

It is important to reiterate why McClintock wants to argue for the simultaneous formation of sovereignty-sharing Global and Regional Unions. He sees a way of avoiding the sort of dangers of 'inter-regionalism' which make 'neo-realists' like Waltz imagine a repeat of the Great Power rivalries of an earlier age, whilst at the same time giving substance to 'partnership' between states by requiring that they share sovereignty in certain areas. He therefore feels that his proposal offers, to use the sort of phrases beloved of the EU, a safer form of inter-regionalism and a more effective form of multilateralism.

The points mentioned above show that there are clearly difficult questions raised by the McClintock proposal, and they would undoubtedly need more detailed consideration if the idea of a Global Union were to advance any further. However, his book is significant because it represents an important introduction to the argument for extending the sharing of sovereignty to a global level. Here at last is a suggestion that the European Union might actually respond to its own distinctive organisation in some other manner than by trying to link it or even weld it onto other so-called 'natural partners'.

Precisely because his suggestion for making this the focus of the European Union's approach to global governance is so unusual, McClintock is bound to leave a number of issues in need of further development. Yet the value of his approach becomes clear as soon as one considers the area in which sovereignty is to be shared.

Food security

McClintock's idea of a specific trigger for the formation of a Global Union concerns the setting up of a Global Food Security Community. The purpose of such a body would be to manage hikes in the price of food, which were severe in 2007 and 2008. Prices then fell, but started to rise again in 2009.[7] The one undeniable thing about them is their volatility.

He suggests that countries interested in resolving price hikes form a new supranational community open to all countries of the world as and when they want to join. The member countries would share sovereignty, but to begin with only in the domain of food security. The institutional structure would mirror that of the European Coal and Steel Community – the forerunner of today's European Union. It would have, as the ECSC had, a small secretariat, a modest legislature and a judiciary. Its objectives, to repeat, would be limited to the prevention of hikes in the price of food. If the community was successful in this, it could proceed to more ambitious tasks. But initially its aims should be modest. This is one of the lessons that Europeans learned from their experience of sharing sovereignty – the first expression of the European Union was the European Coal and Steel Community, which had only one objective: the organisation of the market in these two commodities.

The background to the problem of food security has been well documented and the severity of the problem is undeniable. The UN forecasts that one billion people will suffer from chronic hunger in 2009, up from eight hundred million at the end of the last decade. Severe food shortages not only have a terrible effect on the lives of millions of people in poor countries but also affect the rest of the world through political instability and waves of migration. At the same time it is well known that the earth can produce enough food even to feed six billion people adequately. It is therefore a highly appropriate issue around which to attempt to take effective action at global level.

The reasons for such price hikes are many and various and do not need to be discussed in detail here. They may originate from a drop in supply or a rise in demand or (as in 2007 and 2008 when the price of rice went up by 400%) from both. They may also result from speculation, where speculators buy the right to receive a delivery of food at some point in the future in the hope that the price will rise and they will be able to sell their entitlement on at a profit. They are often difficult to predict and may be the by-product of factors far removed from the naturally occurring rhythm of good and bad harvests. A drop in supply, for instance might be caused by the agricultural disruption produced by changes to the climate, while a rise in demand might be caused by the economic progress of countries like India and China. What is clear is that there are many reasons for expecting price levels, affected as they are by so many different factors, to be extremely volatile.

Food Security is not an issue which world organisations do not take seriously. In June 2008, at a conference in Madrid on 'Food Security of All,' the Secretary-General of the United Nations, Mr. Ban Ki-Moon, stated that 'the world will face ever more severe food crises unless and until there is public action to stabilise food supplies.' In July 2009 the G8 Summit in Italy focused on increasing food supplies to the hungry, and pledged about twenty billion dollars to be directed towards agricultural development, 'helping the poor to help themselves'.

However, the question arises as to *how* the world can most usefully take the 'public action' spoken of by Ban Ki-Moon, or use the money pledged by the July 2009 G8 meeting. One of the most important bodies where this issue is concerned is the United Nations' World Food Programme. This organisation has been in existence since 1963, with a mandate to deliver food to those who can neither grow it nor buy it.

As McClintock emphasises, one problem with the World Food Programme is that it buys its food on the world market, and therefore when food prices rise it is forced, like any other consumer, to buy less, as it did in 2006, cutting rations for Sudan's three million refugees in the Darfur region to half the daily minimum requirement for subsistence. For the same reason the organisation was forced, in March 2008, to issue an emergency appeal for funds. In 2009 it suspended food distribution to 600,000 people in Northern Uganda as a result of lack of funding and reduced its operations in Ethiopia and North Korea.[8]

Moreover, such a policy means that the World Food Programme contributes to the problem as well as to the solution. When food prices increase it needs to buy more food (there are more people who cannot afford it and who therefore rely on the World Food Programme). But by purchasing more food on an already tight market, it is simply increasing demand and engendering a further increase in the price of food.

A better system would be to buy food when the price was low, stock it as emergency reserves, and release it onto the market when prices began to increase. The price hikes created by such volatility would then be dealt with by releasing reserve stocks of food onto the market in order to lower the price.

In order to make this possible, the world would have to develop a system of strategic reserves (kept for release in an emergency). Most current stocks are operating stocks (kept by farmers and trading companies and not yet sold or by food processing companies and not yet used).

At the same time the traders in the country to which the stocks (of grain, for instance) were released would have to be prevented from selling the grain on to another country where the price was higher, rather than using it to support their own people. A government export tax would prevent this, but the traders might be able to influence the government to prevent it imposing one. To avoid the possibility of such pressure being exerted, the country would need to accept a legal obligation to introduce customs measures as a condition of its receiving stocks – *and this can only happen if the organisation releasing the food is a supranational one,* having a measure of political authority and a legal right to oblige its member countries to take particular actions. This is another reason why progress is unlikely to be made through the World Food Programme, since the countries that run it would have to take a unanimous decision to agree to confer an element of their national sovereignty onto the organisation. As has already been emphasised in countless places in the course of this book, the UN outside the Security Council operates in the manner of inter-governmental organisations, with all the attendant limitations of such an arrangement.

By pooling their sovereignty in this particular area states could overcome the problem of particular nations hoarding their national stocks rather than helping their neighbours (something McClintock witnessed for himself when working at a famine camp in Ethiopia during the 1980s). The stocks would be the property of the Community, stored by the Community in one or other member countries. The Community would decide, for each of its members, a 'release price', the price on the local market at which grain begins to be unaffordable. When the local market price reached this level, the Community would release some of its stock, for sale, on the local market.

It should be noted that this is not a question of 'giving food away'. The grain (if it is grain that is involved) would be sold at or around the release price. The revenue generated by the sale of the grain would be the property of the Community and would be returned to the Community budget. The Community would then use this revenue to cover its running costs and to replenish its stocks. A system of stocks managed and released by a supranational community of nations would be based upon the prospect of self-sufficiency, without the reliance upon hand-outs that is attached to the UN system of voluntary donations.

Voluntary donations, of course, are entirely unpredictable. 2009 has been a very bad year for the World Food Programme, simply because the financial crisis has understandably made countries less generous. After an appeal in 2008 which secured about two billion dollars in extra funds, donor countries have been much less generous in 2009 as they begin to be hit by the downturn. Thus the World Food Programme is not only bedevilled by volatility in food prices but also by volatility in its own available resources. Once again this is a point that was very strongly emphasised in the chapter on the United Nations, pointing out that it had none of the security of funding offered by a system of 'own resources' and very low funding levels overall when compared to those made available to a sovereignty-sharing organisation like the EU. There is a chronic problem of both under-funding and unreliable funding where the World Food Programme is concerned, forcing it to adopt a policy of endless crisis management and no strategic planning.

The claim being made is that the global problem of food security can best be dealt with by the sort of sovereignty-sharing mechanism outlined in Part I of this book in relation to the European Union. The three key ingredients in a successful supranational mechanism were European Community law, allowing for binding legislation in those areas where sovereignty was being shared, the possession of 'own resources' and the provision of support to vulnerable economic sectors.

The same would apply in a Global Union. There would be a form of Community law at global level, which would be binding upon member-states. There would be a Community budget, facilitating long-term investment. There would be targeted support in vulnerable areas where individual regions or industries required assistance. This would follow the principles that Part I described, namely the use of cohesion and structural funds not to undermine the workings of a market economy but in order to help it to function more effectively.

Some of the measures in Food Security will suggest the sort of support through guaranteed pricing that the European Economic Community originally applied to itself through the Common Agricultural Policy. Those measures turned controversial after the EEC became a victim of its own success, turning post-war scarcity into the later generation of embarrassing surpluses – though mistakes were also made, such as setting the original guaranteed prices at too high a level. But in the case of the CAP (Common Agricultural Policy) these were minimum prices designed to guarantee income for farmers, rather than maximum prices designed to help consumers. Nevertheless, the principle of adopting a means of keeping prices steady in the uncertain world of agriculture, where everyone agrees that extreme volatility in price levels is unavoidable, is the same in both cases.

Indeed, a Global Food Security Community could consider both avoiding too high a price (in order to protect consumers) and too low a price (in order to protect farmers). If farmers are to be encouraged to make an investment, they need to have a measure of security. Otherwise, however many billions are poured into agriculture by organisations like the G8, farmers will not feel confident enough to invest in a 'business' where returns are so much at the mercy of factors outside their control, however 'entrepreneurial' they may be. Farmers have to plan for years ahead and harvests, climate 'change' and shifts in demand play havoc with the prices they can expect and make such planning extremely difficult.

The Global Food Security Community could ease up the flow of reserve stocks onto the market when prices fall too low, in order to help farmers, and staunch the flow when prices were too high in order to help consumers. Once again, the point would be to bring stability to a business which is becoming, not least through climate change, ever more precarious.

European farming could have been undermined after World War Two by such uncertainty, and Europe instead might have imported the food it needed. Guaranteed prices (and import quotas to keep out cheap alternatives from elsewhere) were the reason why there was not a mass exodus from rural to urban areas in post-war Europe, and why European agricultural productivity eventually out-grew Europe's needs. Naturally, the idea of import quotas is a controversial one and is not being argued for in the context of the developing world's needs at present. What is being argued for is a secure environment for capitalist enterprise in the developing world, so that its consumers will be able to afford essential food and its farmers will feel confident enough to invest. Dollops of largesse from the developed world will not provide that secure environment on their own.

McClintock's proposal for Food Security allows for regular and substantial funding in selective areas, but it *also* involves close control and monitoring. It provides the resources for building up food stocks, but at the same time it controls and manages their distribution. It believes that UN agencies entrusted with the job would not only be under-funded but they would as often as not be milch cows for corrupt governments, the aid they disburse being taken into the control of individuals who are at one and the same time the main agricultural traders and members of (or highly influential with) the government. The proposal for a Global Union insists upon a supranational solution, taking the control of this sector of the market out of the hands of individual governments. In this sense a supranational mechanism is by far the best means of circumventing the problem of corruption which is at the root of much of the current hostility in the developed world towards helping developing nations.

The condition of this arrangement working is, of course, that a group of states agree to transfer sovereignty in agricultural markets. Is it conceivable that they would? It is surely conceivable that *some* would, and only a small number is required in order to make a beginning. The last chapter showed that the prospect of joining the European Union, however distant, was a substantial incentive for many European countries, which were willing to make internal reforms in order to secure membership. Countries are willing to be bound by a sovereignty-sharing arrangement, requiring that they submit to binding legislation in particular areas, if they feel that they are not simply being penalised for doing so. This is precisely what many of the poorer nations who are presently being entreated to cut their global emissions feel. There have to be practical incentives for them to make such cuts, just as there were incentives for the poorer nations of the EU to become part of the Single Market and (in many cases) the single currency. There is no reason why such arrangements could not work just was well in the case of a Global Union, though it is clear that the participation of the European Union itself in such an organisation, given its enormous economic clout, would be an essential precondition.

In June 2008, the European Council, comprising the heads of state and government of the twenty-seven member countries, stated that the European Union will encourage developing countries 'especially to support food security'.[9]

In January 2009, the European Parliament passed the following resolution:

> [The European Parliament] calls for a global food inventory regime and a global system of food stocks and believes that the European

Union should take the lead in devising such a system [...] The European Commission is called upon to ensure food security in Europe and around the world.

The European Union is called upon to recognise [...] that global food security is a question of the utmost urgency for the European Union and calls for immediate and continued action to ensure food security for EU citizens.[10]

McClintock outlines a method through which that food security can be ensured without falling foul of the corrupt or protectionist governments. The 'global system of food stocks' as proposed by the European Parliament can be secured though the EU promoting the launch of a new organisation which seeks to *realise at a global level the successful sovereignty-sharing system on which it is itself based.*

Extending the sharing of sovereignty

If a sovereignty-sharing system is really a desirable one, then it could be expected to extend beyond a particular issue like food security in the future. If it was successful, the Global Food Security Community could expand in years to come (both in terms of its numbers and its range of activities), re-naming itself a Global Union and inviting new members to join. Alternatively, it might over-reach itself and draw back, in order to advance again later. It might, like the Europeans in the 1950s, succeed (the European Coal and Steel Community) and then encounter a setback (with the rejection of the Pleven Plan) before finally succeeding more comprehensively (the Treaty of Rome).

As with the European Union, it may well reach a stage where member-states feel that they have reached the high water mark of supranationalism and wish to keep a range of their activities firmly under their own national control. The argument for a sharing of sovereignty, whether regionally or globally, is *not* an argument for sharing it in all areas. There is no reason why the Commission of a Global Union should have competency in areas where the European Commission lacks it. It is hardly conceivable that the European Union, as a member of that Global Union, would be willing to see such a body sharing sovereignty in any area in which its own member-states are unwilling to share sovereignty with each other.

That said, there are areas in which the member-states of the European Union are already willing to share sovereignty, and which would make a vital difference to the world if it were to be shared at a global level. The environmental area, especially where climate breakdown is concerned, is an obvious example. Chapter 5 has already mentioned the limitations of the UN approach, which (at best) achieves agreements that are not binding. The United Nations Framework Convention on Climate Change (UNFCCC) was an international treaty signed by 189 out of 192 states – practically everyone in the world – in 1992 at the 'Earth Summit' in Rio. States agreed to stabilise emissions to a level that did not damage the world's climate. However, they did not achieve the targets they set themselves. As Scholte points out, it was already clear by the end of the last century that implementation of the Framework Convention had proceeded with 'painful slowness' and that 'half a dozen UN conferences through the 1990s' had yielded 'limited concrete results'.[11] Comprehensiveness (which a Global Union would certainly lack, at least initially) is no guarantee of effectiveness.

McClintock's proposed Global Union would permit the achievement of agreements that were binding and enforceable – at first on nothing like one hundred and eighty-nine states, and in the case of climate change on very few of the 'worst emitters', but with some prospect of being able to enlarge over time after a measure of success has been demonstrated. It is worth reiterating once again why a Global Union can succeed in compelling its members to action in a way that the UN can't. It is, as Part I showed, a combination of carrot and stick. The carrot is hugely significant. Poor countries do not take action to reduce pollution because they feel that they cannot afford to, and that rich countries (whose overall pollution may be greater) are trying to make them even poorer than they already are. A Global Union operating in the manner of the European Union would use its 'own resources' to provide assistance, the sort of structural and cohesion funds that enabled the EU to pressurise its weaker members into accepting the Single European Market in the 1980s, the single currency in the 1990s, or the rough impact of capitalism on the formerly 'protected' communist countries of Central and Eastern Europe during the first decade of the new century.

At the same time, the 'stick' would be there with the carrot. The binding decisions of the Global Union would have to be implemented by member-states, or sanctions would be imposed. There would be a World Court of Justice and a global equivalent of Community law, but before such terms are taken to be more grandiose than they are, it should be emphasised once again that this 'World Court' would only make binding decisions in areas in which the members of the Global Union had agreed to share sovereignty.

Just as Greece could both receive substantial assistance from the European Union in terms of preparing it to join the euro, and at the same time be fined for failing to implement directives on environmental improvements, so a member of the Global Union, however poor, could be fined for failing to implement the directives issued by a World Court of Justice. This would ensure that member-states implemented decisions which had been made.

The EU as a member of a Global Union

The last section argued that a Global Union does not have to begin with any of the global 'big players' involved. However, one 'big player' is essential to it – the EU itself. Yet what are the chances of the EU being willing to act as a member of a sovereignty-sharing Global Union? How likely is it that (in an area of policy which would require the unanimous consent of its member-states) the EU would be willing to take part?

It is easy to see why it might balk at the proposal. Here is an institution which has fought many bloody internal battles over the last two decades (at least), and which is now (probably) at the high water mark of its sovereignty-sharing ambitions. The 'supranationalists' and the 'inter-governmentalists', having fought each other to a stalemate, lie bruised and battered on the floor. Along comes someone while they're stretched out half-dead in the boxing ring and cheerily informs them: 'That was a great attempt to win the European Title: now how about squaring up for a shot at the World Title?' As someone who has not prepared this book without taking up the time of patient EU officials, the author can confirm that some of these 'boxers' look as if they might just be able to summon enough reserves of energy to floor the person asking them such a question.

However, some of them have also been kind enough to regret such instincts upon reflection. Their view becomes more positive when a number of points are made absolutely clear in justifying this proposal for a Global Union.

The first was explained earlier in this chapter. This proposal *will not seek a sharing of sovereignty in any area where it is not already shared within the European Union*. The EU will obviously not wish to re-engage in the bloody battles it has already fought on an even wider stage. Of course even within areas related to food security, environment and (another area where a Global Union might be effective) energy security, there are aspects which are 'shared competency' between the

Commission and the member-states. The presumption must be that this will also be the case in the Global Union. The EU is not going to cede more sovereignty in a Global Union than its member-states already cede within the EU. If the Treaty of Lisbon can achieve some sort of 'closure' on that issue, the Global Union is not going to re-open those wounds.

The second point is financial. The EU is not going to provide more money. Instead, it is going to make better use of the money which it already spends. The EU has a long history of development aid, a natural concomitant of the fact that many of its members used to be colonial powers. This perspective is easily forgotten. In 1957, when the Treaty of Rome finally healed the wounds of World War Two, France was fighting a brutal colonial war across the Mediterranean, trying to prevent Algerian independence. The Europeans brought peace to Europe while they were still at war elsewhere. Decolonisation developed alongside a range of agreements with former colonial powers, which to some extent represented policies to cover the imperial retreat of the Europeans.

Trade relations had originally proceeded along familiar lines of imperial preference and exchanges between industrialised European countries and their (sometimes forcibly de-industrialised) former colonies. Now they had to be reworked in terms of encouraging developing nations in a post-colonial world. Development aid began with the Yaoundé Convention between the EC and eighteen African states in 1963. In 1975 the Lomé Convention expanded the programme to forty-six ACP (Africa, the Caribbean and Pacific) states. By 2000, when the Cotonou Agreement was reached, the number of states involved had risen to over seventy.

There is no doubt that relatively large amounts of money are involved. The EU spends more on overseas development assistance than the United States – on some estimates (problems of definition make it hard to quantify) it amounts to half the total spent worldwide, though there have been considerable implementation problems.

The Cotonou Agreement was distinctive because it introduced an element of 'political conditionality' into aid provision, emphasising 'respect for human rights, democratic principles, the rule of law and good governance'.[12] But it was equally distinctive for the European Union's declaration that after the twenty years during which Cotonou is to apply it will end all EU-specific trade protection – with the exception of the least developed countries. In other words, the approach which seeks to maintain privileged partnerships with specific ex-colonies in the name of solidarity (and to some extent expiation) will have been replaced by a system that focuses on the eradication of poverty at international level. What happened between Lomé and Cotonou is that as it grew in size from involving an initial eighteen to involving more than a third of the world's countries, the policy has been forced to think in terms of dealing with global problems of poverty and not just helping a few particular countries who have suffered from colonial exploitation by specific European nations.

The proposal for a Global Food Security Programme managed at supranational level is consistent both with the emphasis upon 'political conditionality' and the way in which the EU is widening its consideration to global problems of development, rather than simply those that are tied to its colonial past. But it is certainly not going to require 'more money'. As said, the EU already spends something like half of worldwide spending on overseas development assistance (with the reservations concerning quantification and implementation that always have to be made). A substantial contribution to the 'own resources' of a Global Food Security Community would simply form a part of this existing budget. Since even the emergency aid supplied by the EU under ECHO (European Community Humanitarian Office) runs to well over half a billion euros, the figures for overseas development assistance as a whole clearly run to billions. A slice of this would have a substantial impact on the funds of any Global Union.

Moreover, it would be money better spent. A supranational mechanism would provide a way of delivering the considerable amount of aid which the rich nations have at their disposal in a manner that requires firm institutional mechanisms for its proper management and delivery. A sovereignty-sharing arrangement is the only effective answer to the charge that so much aid disappears into the pockets of corrupt government leaders and officials in developing countries. In this sense supranational arrangements would be far from reflecting the sort of naïve idealism of which anyone who talks of a 'Global Union' is too easily accused. It is more accurate to say that it is a hard-nosed way of ensuring that money is either put to good use or is not given (and the EU has already become hard-nosed enough to talk about 'political conditionality' since the Cotonou agreement). The opportunities for waste and corruption would be severely curtailed. At the same time the offer of support and investment, including assistance in developing the institutions to manage a global equivalent of the *acquis*, would make it less likely that there would be a blanket refusal to cooperate on grounds of interference with national sovereignty. That has not been the case with countries – even those recently engaged in wars based on bitter differences between national and ethnic groups – that have been offered membership of the European Union.

However, these are 'negative' points – reasons why the EU would not find itself politically compromised or financially burdened by such a proposal. It is important to emphasise that there are also important 'positive' reasons why a Global Union would be attractive to the European Union.

The first was pointed out at length in the last chapter. A Global Union will release Europe from its sense that it cannot enlarge indefinitely and the tendency as a consequence to relapse into a 'Fortress Europe' mentality. On the one hand it wishes to influence its neighbours; on the other hand it cannot continue to do so by making them members, arguably the one effective form of influence that it has shown itself capable of exercising so far. From this perspective participating in a Global Union, rather than adding to the EU's burdens, provides a means of easing them. The North African countries, for instance, would be invited to join the EU within a Global Union which shares sovereignty initially an area vital to many of them (food security). This would be a far better approach than offering them 'privileged' or 'strategic' partnerships which simply confirm their 'second-class status'. More controversially, the same approach could be adopted towards countries whose presence in two continents makes it difficult to place them in either.

Secondly, a Global Union would open up the possibility of a real world presence for a European Union that has so far only tried to lose itself in the pack or accept whatever role other global institutions are prepared to give it. There is no doubt that the EU is in something of a quandary where its efforts at developing a role in the world are concerned.[13] Anand Menon claims that 'the EU suffers from our inability to cope with its uniqueness'.[14] Arguably, however, the EU suffers from *its own* inability to cope with its uniqueness. Endless discussion takes place as to how the European Union, given all the resources it possesses, can transform itself into a 'global actor', but little appears to come of these deliberations. What its leaders and officials never seem capable of doing is use the uniqueness of their own form of government in order to encourage something new. Instead they try to hide themselves in the crowd, like nervous schoolchildren in a dangerous playground.

Conclusion

This chapter has introduced McClintock's idea of a Global Union. It has pointed out two aspects that would need further discussion, namely the mechanism whereby the EU operates as a 'single member' of the putative GU and the process whereby regional unions spring up at the same time as a Global Union. However, it has also pointed to important ways in which McClintock's proposal provides the sort of mechanism that can allow for effective and binding decisions – the sort of mechanism that has proved so effective in Europe itself.

In the second section it addressed the specific issue of Food Security as McClintock's suggestion for the Global Union's equivalent of Coal and Steel. It argued that a system involving the sharing of sovereignty was the only one which would effectively control price hikes and provide the sort of stable market environment which would encourage agriculture to develop – precisely the aim behind the decision of the G8 Summit in July 2009 to earmark twenty billion dollars in order to encourage agricultural development in developing countries (although a clear method of doing so has yet to be determined, and addressing such problems is never a matter of money alone). A contrast was drawn between the system operated by the UN's World Food Programme, inadequate and occasionally counter-productive, and that which a Global Union of sovereignty-sharing states would administer.

There are of course a number of other areas within which a Global Union could share sovereignty, and a number of issues, like energy security and climate breakdown, that are at least as pressing as that of Food Security. A relatively defined area has been chosen deliberately, however, both in order to demonstrate how a 'supranationalist' approach could more effectively deal with the problems involved and in order to reflect the fact that it would build on success in one area in order to move into others – though without moving into any area that is not already part of the sovereignty-sharing arrangements of the European Union itself.

The chapter went on to argue that though the initial membership of a Global Union would be small, it could only happen if the EU was prepared to play a leading role in its creation. Will it do so? There are 'negative' reasons which might not dissuade it from doing so. It requires no further concessions of sovereignty or a re-opening of wounds in the endless battle between 'supranationalists' and 'intergovernmentalists'. It requires no injections of capital that are not already earmarked for development aid, besides which that aid itself is increasingly being seen as part of a programme to deal with poverty on a global scale and to attach 'conditionality' to any assistance given, both of which would make it easier to tailor the EU's aid and development programme to the demands of a sovereignty-sharing global body dealing with food security.

But there are also 'positive' reasons encouraging the EU to participate. It may be shell-shocked over Lisbon and looking for 'closure', but the issue of enlargement will not go away. The EU is on the horns of a dilemma between a reluctance to enlarge indefinitely and awareness of the fact that only the prospect of EU membership for its neighbours enables it to exercise real influence over its 'near abroad'. A Global Union provides a possible way round that dilemma.

More generally, it offers the EU a way out of its current malaise. Arguably a successful ratification of the Treaty of Lisbon will enable it to look outwards more confidently. It may be able to appreciate the virtues of its own institutional structures once they are no longer the subject of such intense and bitter internal wrangling. This in turn might lead to a more serious appraisal of an approach which argues that the sharing of sovereignty has merits as an arrangement on a global scale. It could develop more effectively what Keukeleire calls a 'structural foreign policy',[15] though the structures would be determined in the first place by *its own institutional format*. Rather than simply insinuate itself into existing structures, it would be bold enough to support the potential implicit in the mechanics of its own uniquely designed organisation. This is the 'Copernican Revolution' which it needs to undertake.

10
The Copernican Revolution

Introduction

According to Andrew Linklater:

> The success the EU has had in blurring the contrast between domestic and international politics invites philosophical reflections about what the EU should aim to achieve as a normative power committed to promoting community in international relations.[1]

Drawing heavily upon Norbert Elias, Linklater talks about a 'European civilising process' and writes that 'many visions of the EU have looked beyond the nation-state to new forms of political community which are more internationalist'.[2] But has the EU yet found the best way in which to give practical expression to these visions in its external policies? If Ulrich Beck is right to say that 'Europe has become a laboratory experiment in inclusive sovereignty', then there comes a time when 'inclusive sovereignty' has to be taken out of the European laboratory and applied to the world outside.[3]

Robert Kagan is looking for the 'transmission of the European miracle to the rest of the world' as Europe's 'new *mission civilisatrice*'.[4] But if there really is such a 'European miracle', would it not be more appropriate for the EU to attempt to set up some new organisation which might be able to embody the 'miracle' on a global scale, rather than limit itself to mere 'partnerships' and multilateral relationships with existing organisations? What is needed is a Copernican Revolution in the thinking of the EU.

In his book entitled *What's Wrong With the United Nations and How to Fix It*,[5] Thomas Weiss claims to be following the analysis in Thomas

Kuhn's famous *The Structure of Scientific Revolutions*.[6] Examining how the Copernican revolution came about, Kuhn emphasised how the old Ptolemaic model had remained in being long after its weaknesses had been understood and after it had been sustained by an ever more complex series of rationalisations of planetary behaviour; the rationalisations were always harder to sustain intellectually, but more comfortable psychologically, than a 'leap' into a new system (what Kuhn called a 'paradigm shift'). But then there came a tipping point, when the failures of the old system proved too much and the risk of an entirely new approach was found to be inevitable. 'By not imagining a fundamentally different system, we make the continuation of the current lacklustre one all the more inevitable', says Weiss.[7]

Precisely – but for that very reason the answer is not to 'fix' the UN, the endless attempts to reform which represent precisely the sort of ever more complex attempts to 'fix' the Ptolemaic system that always end in failure. The answer is to launch an entirely new global institution based on the sharing of sovereignty.

Some two centuries ago the defeat of Napoleon left Europe struggling to rebuild itself on more secure foundations. A Congress assembled at Vienna, as a century later one was to assemble at Versailles. The French writer Saint-Simon observed that:

> The aim of this congress is to re-establish peace between the powers of Europe, by adjusting the claims of each and conciliating the interests of all. Can one hope that this aim will be achieved?

Saint-Simon's answer to his own question was pessimistic and a prescient anticipation of the fate of the 'Concert' system of regular meetings between the Great Powers, which began to break down within a few years of the end of the Napoleonic Wars (although nations continued to meet when a crisis occurred). It is worth quoting once again:

> Assemble congress after congress, multiply treaties, conventions, compromises, everything you do will lead only to war; you will not abolish it, the most you can do is to shift the scene of it.[8]

It is difficult not to feel a similar sense of frustration in the twenty-first century, when groups of leaders meet and make pronouncements on the global breakdown, whether financial or climatic. Whatever format they choose – G8, G20, UN, IMF or some bespoke backdrop specially tailored for their latest piece of summiteering – the outcome is a pious statement of intent, a declaration of some 'target' without a mechanism for reaching it, or (at best) a firm outline of commitments which they then fail to live up to.

Between Saint-Simon and our own century lie two centuries of war, the second arguably more destructive than the first. There has been evidence of a 'civilising' process within states, in terms for instance of growing opposition to public executions and floggings. Sociologists like Norbert Elias saw this as evidence of changing sensibilities towards violence. Such changing sensibilities, however, only seemed to apply to relations *within* states, not to relations *between* them. States were and are capable of proclaiming their opposition to violence at home while imposing it with ruthless brutality on those outside their national borders.

Elias recognised the importance of developing institutions which would overcome this dichotomy, and he wrote very shrewdly about it. 'We may be entering an era', he wrote, 'in which it will no longer be individual states but unions of states which will serve mankind as the dominant social unit'.[9] Note that he talks of 'unions of states', not of a single world state. Indeed the fact that we had not learned how to curb wars convinced him that 'modern times' represented less a late stage of human development than the era of 'late barbarianism', as human beings learned to sweep away cruel and violent behaviour from the one area in which was still permitted (and even encouraged and glorified). This is where we are now, late barbarians who have learned (up to a point) to be civilised in one area of our lives while still able to indulge our barbarian tastes in another. We take pride in the fact that the Colosseum, where perhaps half a million people and countless animals were slaughtered for the delectation of the 'civilised' Roman Empire, is now a scene of concerts and exhibitions, and even that it has become part of a campaign to abolish capital punishment. But such sensitivity is of little value if thousands are still being slaughtered in war.

This book has sought to outline how the 'civilising process' which Elias wrote about might be extended into the international arena without this entailing the end of the nation-state, the rock on which so many earlier attempts to do this have foundered. This is the 'Copernican Revolution' by which the 'domestic analogy' can at last be taken further, and Hobbes' warnings about a state of nature applied to the relations between states and not simply between individuals. Of course the appropriateness of the 'domestic analogy' has been questioned, but the argument of this book is that it has been questioned largely because of a presumption that it must entail a single world state. Presume that it means the end of the nation-state (or its significant downgrading) and you are likely to conclude that the arrangement is hardly practical when people have a natural and often fierce sense of patriotism. The choice then seems to lie between accepting the anarchy of nations and wondering idealistically with John Lennon whether we can 'imagine' a 'brotherhood of man' without countries.

But this is not the only choice. As a 'normative power' the European Union should seek to make its own sovereignty-sharing arrangements a global norm. This is not an attempt to 'Europeanise' the world; it is an attempt to apply globally a system that has done so much to heal the wounds of Europe. It does not represent a belittling, still less the obliteration, of nation-states, but a way of binding them to observe community decisions in those areas where they consent to share sovereignty.

They may, of course, refuse such an arrangement or even join and then leave it. That is always possible. Even a single 'world state' might experience a breakaway by a discontented 'region'. But as the chapters on the development of the EU tried to show, there are reasons to expect that nation-states, even proud and powerful ones like France and Britain, will choose to remain part of such a system. If they have much to lose materially by leaving, then they will think twice about doing so. De Gaulle wanted the passing dalliance with a maiden that he identified as a treaty arrangement; but instead he had a tempestuous marriage which lasted despite frequent rows. The UK was more like the confirmed bachelor who finds himself somehow landed on the aisle against his will, a Macmillan marching step by step towards the Senate house of the University of Cambridge accompanied by a crafty Monnet. Monnet knew that the British, unable to be persuaded by theoretical discussions of the benefits of supranationalism, might let themselves be carried into the community by 'events, dear boy, events', Macmillan's own explanation of how things so quickly change in politics. Some of the British liked to pun about Monnet as 'the root of all evil', but the country made its application to join all the same.

Doubtless the current global 'big players', China, Russia and the US, will be reluctant to share sovereignty even in a limited area, but real progress in 'global governance' requires a measure of ambition. There is a financial, economic and environmental world crisis. People are sick of endless summiteering leading nowhere. There is an opportunity for an organisation both more modest and more ambitious than those that provide endless rounds of meetings for leaders with 'dialogue commitments'. Moreover, the Global Union does not have to begin with any of these 'big players' involved; it can show itself to be effective without them before it draws them in.

A Union to serve the nation-state

An extension of sovereignty-sharing at global level will require the consent of the individual nation-states themselves, who will have to recognise such a move as in their national interests. However, as Chapter 8 has sought to make clear in the context of the EU's relations with its 'Near Abroad', there is every indication that states will find a limited sharing of sovereignty acceptable if by so doing they become part of a more secure and prosperous environment. The very fact that the European Union has been so successful at attracting the countries on its borders indicates that other countries might be prepared to enter into a sovereignty-sharing arrangement at global level.

This has remained the case throughout the whole history of what became the EU through successive waves of enlargement. Former military and communist dictatorships have turned into democracies with functioning market economies. When there has been a move towards market liberalisation, as in the 1980s, or towards a single currency in the 1990s, the poorer nations have insisted upon support through the structural and cohesion funds. The EU has always maintained a sense of the need to make capitalism acceptable to its poorer member-states. The combination of carrot and stick has meant that when these states agreed to be bound by Community law, they also recognised that they would receive help in being able to abide by its rules. This is arguably the sort of approach that might make poorer countries of Africa or Asia willing to join a Global Union. They will be asked to do something that they can see to be in their interests as nation-states.

From its origins in a six-member Coal and Steel Community, what became the European Union has swept through Europe, leaving almost no country behind in its wake. Greenland, unable to make its application independently of Denmark, chose to leave; Iceland remained outside, though the recent financial crisis has led to talk of joining; Norway twice voted narrowly to stay outside; only Switzerland has failed to come close to joining. Something like half a billion people went in, while ten million stayed outside. Moreover, those like Norway who stayed outside nevertheless adopted much of the *acquis communautaire* in order to maintain close economic ties with the Community. Norway, Iceland and Switzerland are part of the Schengen agreement that opens up the Community internally to visa-free travel.

Though there are 'euro-sceptics' in every member-state as well as outside them, it is fair to say that the European Union overall has proved immensely attractive.

To some extent this point has been lost in the ferment of the European Union's own internal tensions concerning the Constitutional and now the Lisbon Treaty. These tensions have produced an arguably exaggerated degree of speculation concerning the future of the EU as an organisation. In reality, the structures of the European Union, though complex, are solidly based. There is no chance of them either collapsing into a collection of sovereign states or a single European superstate. The principles of 'inter-governmentalism' and 'supranationalism' are too firmly embedded for either to be removed. Those who say that the 'high water mark' of 'supranational' development has been reached with the Treaty of Lisbon are probably right; as a result the EU will settle into an equilibrium where it is recognised that certain things are done best at the level of the Community and others at the level of the nation-state. For, to repeat the point made all along in this book, the Community has the attraction that it does have because it can be seen to serve the interests of the many nation-states who form its members.

At the moment there is still a certain degree of speculation about 'where the EU is going' in terms of its metamorphosis into a single state or its disintegration into nothing more than a treaty arrangement between separate sovereign states. However, the EU has evolved far enough for neither to be a realistic possibility. Whether the result is seen as a desirable institutional pattern or an unwelcome stalemate, it is clear that neither side any longer has a hope of checkmating the other.

The 'stalemate' or 'equilibrium' is obscured by the fact that language is often used in order to present two camps as far apart when they are in reality much closer to each other than either cares to make out. The 'realists' and 'inter-governmentalists', who stress that sovereign states remain key actors in all EU activities and who emphasise that the EU was developed precisely as a means of upholding or even rescuing the nation-state, are not adopting a position which is incompatible with supranationalism. Too many of those who simply oppose the 'functionalist' to the 'inter-governmentalist', or the 'realist' to the 'idealist', forget that supranational arrangements only work when nation-states recognise them to be in their individual interests.

Much of the literature becomes unnecessarily complicated as it tries to stake out positions around particular terms or phrases in order to promote a particular view of the institutional make-up of the European

Union.[10] Though it is clear that there is constant friction between – and a constant jostling for power between – the various institutions, it is equally clear that none of them is going to succeed in wresting control from the others.

All of which means that the European Union has a chance of being taken for the hybrid that it is, within an institutional framework that may eventually acquire a settled character. The more it is recognised as an established sovereignty-sharing organisation binding together the nations of Europe, the less foolish the idea of a global sovereignty-sharing organisation will seem.

The sharing of sovereignty and the domestic analogy

Given the terrible wars of the twentieth century, it is unsurprising that people have constantly asked themselves why the destructive behaviour of nations cannot be brought under the sort of control that is applied to the destructive behaviour of individuals. It needed the optimism and self-confidence of the nineteenth century to believe that coercion was not needed in the international sphere as much as the domestic sphere. The First World War brought such naivety to an end.

Two crucial developments made this issue one of overwhelming importance. One was rapid technological change culminating in the development of weapons of mass destruction. The other was the integration of whole populations into the mechanism of the nation-state, which made the exploitation of nationalist sentiment both tempting and effective for government elites.

Yet despite the huge loss of life in two world wars, the means of coercion in the international sphere remains highly unsatisfactory. The reason advanced here is that it has always been seen to entail the creation of a single world state. Saint-Simon lamented the constant round of congresses and summits leading nowhere, but American peace advocate William Jay had the answer to those concerns about an unstable post-Napoleonic world:

> It is obvious that war might instantly be banished from Europe, would its nations regard themselves as members of one great society, and, by mutual consent, erect a court for the trial and decision of their respective differences.[11]

'One great society' was essentially a federal state like Jay's own United States. The idea was always of a world based upon a single state, albeit one with substantial internal devolution like the US, the Swiss Confederation or the United Provinces (the last two were frequently-cited examples a century earlier, when Abbot Saint-Pierre wrote his *Project for settling an everlasting peace in Europe* as the Treaty of Utrecht brought another period of conflict in Europe to an end in 1714). If the Peace of Westphalia in 1648 had established the nation-state as the basic unit of international relations, then subsequent outbreaks of war led to a presumption that an international system to guarantee world peace must also be based upon the nation-state.

There was therefore nothing new about the urgent debates that followed the huge loss of life in the First World War. Another century, another terrible European war. Utrecht, Vienna and now Versailles. There was acceptance of the failure of the Hague conferences, a latter-day Congress system, though some like Walter Schücking, Professor of International Law at the University of Marburg, believed that more lasting institutions like a World Parliament could somehow be tacked onto them.[12] Like the others who speculated about methods of international coercion, his recommendation was for a 'world federal state'.

Those who struggled with the creation of a better international order after World War One were so convinced that a single world state was the only possible means of enforcing international law that they were determined to avoid mentioning the domestic analogy. The 'League to Enforce Peace' made sure that that they never spoke of it. They knew the dilemma they were in: what they believed was the most effective method of global governance was simply taboo in a world of strong patriotic instincts. The League of Nations chose its language carefully. It had a 'Covenant' and not a 'Constitution' (the EU might have learned the advantages of avoiding the latter word as it struggled with what was turned into the 'Constitutional Treaty' until it was finally defeated by referenda in France and the Netherlands). It was a 'League' of Nations, not a 'Union' of Nations. It had an 'Assembly', not a Body of Delegates. After World War Two the same concerns led Roosevelt to reject Soviet suggestions of a 'World Union' in favour of the 'United Nations'.

Yet however careful they were in the language they used, the domestic analogy inevitably crept in. When Robert Cecil, Head of the League of Nations section of the Foreign Office, argued for the establishment of a permanent Court of Justice after the First World War, the analogy he drew was with the institution of the Star Chamber under Henry VII, the first of the Tudor monarchs in England and the one who brought to an end a generation of effective Civil War between the rival houses of York and Lancaster, the so-called Wars of the Roses.

Such an analogy was once again drawn from the process of building a strong and centralised state (if not the nation-state in the sense it was to acquire in the nineteenth century through mass engagement). As the Second World War drew to a close the same trend could be seen in the thinking of US President Roosevelt. His idea of the US, Britain, the Soviet Union and China, the four victorious powers, acting as the world's 'Four Policemen', was essentially an idea built on the analogy with domestic law enforcement. Roosevelt pointed out that a policeman who had to go to the Town Hall and convene a meeting before he arrested a felon could not act very effectively, a prescient enough anticipation of the sort of problems which were to arise under a system of five veto-wielding powers in the new Security Council of the UN. He complained to Soviet Ambassador Gromyko that when a husband and wife fell out and took their case before a judge, they did not consider themselves entitled to have a vote in the case. But these analogies from domestic law cut no ice with the Soviet Union, just as they were to cut no ice with the US itself. Each country used its veto when its own interests were at stake. The domestic analogy proved as inappropriate as it was unavoidable.[13]

There needed to be another way. Apart from the rather vague notions of the so-called WOMP (World Order Models Project) associated with writers like Richard Falk and Myres McDougal, who believed that some sort of 'central guidance mechanism' should replace the present system of nation-states,[14] the only clue for an alternative approach came from those who recognised that binding international arrangements could be introduced *without* introducing a single world state. Arguably Kant recognised this with his call for a 'union of states'. As Suganami points out, there were a number of thinkers such as Leonard Woolf, Hersch Lauterpacht, a Cambridge Professor and judge at the International court of Justice during the inter-war years, and C.A.W. Manning, for whom 'the problem of world order could be handled within the framework of the sovereign states system if the system could be equipped with those institutions derived by analogy from the domestic sphere'.[15]

But how could the problem be handled *effectively* within such a framework? On this even writers like Kant and Woolf were unclear. The problem was that once realism about human patriotism drove you into an acceptance of the continuation of the sovereign states system, you were forced to concede a system that was bound to make the domestic analogy inapplicable. The sovereign states would always get in the way, whether they were under a system like that of the League of Nations or the United Nations.

It is precisely this dilemma, this book argues, from which a system of shared sovereignty allows some escape. The point cannot be put more strongly than this, since the system (like all the others) is not foolproof. However, the sharing of sovereignty, even though it is reasonable to assume that it will be in some but not all of the areas in which nation-states interact with one another, has a binding power in the sense that enough of a nation's self-interest is entrenched in the workings of the system to which it is committed that it is unlikely to withdraw.

The book has argued that this has been one of the greatest successes of what became the European Union, not only through the way in which the UK was drawn in[16] but also through the way in which Gaullist France stayed in. Two proud and independent nations, whose identity could never be compromised by any successful arrangement of member-states within the European Union, have remained committed to its working. They have been willing to implement Community law and even accept the sanctions that follow from infringements of that Law. It is true that both nations have those who would like to leave the Union; at the same time, if it is true that the high-water mark of shared sovereignty has been reached and that the Treaty of Lisbon will mark that high tide, then there is reason to think that euro-scepticism will not be so strong in years to come.

As for smaller countries, they have in almost all cases been more than willing to join a Union which offers them a degree of security. Even countries with a distant prospect of membership have been willing to attempt to meet the requirements for entry. This is where the EU has proved most successful at exercising 'soft power' in the world, though it should always be remembered that 'soft power' is in fact quite hard. If a country doesn't have enough resources, the consequences for its citizens are not slight.

It is not unthinkable for a Global Union to grow up in the same way. For smaller countries it will offer security; larger ones will be more resistant, but if their self-interest is sufficiently enmeshed in the system in those areas where they prove willing to share sovereignty, then they may also be willing to take part.

The principle of a Global Union is that it is better to start small, both in terms of countries and areas of shared sovereignty, and work up. Organisations that begin by giving everyone a seat round the table, such as the UN, the African Union and UNASUR, find that there is nothing effective they can do. One hundred and eighty countries will sign up to a deal to cut their global emissions, and only a handful will actually do so. It is strange to think that those who advocate a Global Union are often accused of being too 'idealistic'; running throughout this book has been a degree of pessimism about organisations like the UN which will make many readers feel uncomfortable. At the same time, the belief that a Global Union will be effective is based not on a naïve confidence in the ideals of its members but the way it can be constructed in such a manner as to serve the interests even of its larger members.

The 'domestic analogy' has meant that those advocating an effective form of global governance have vexed themselves with the question of how independent sovereign states could ever allow an effective method of enforcement at global level. They have found no answer to this. Either they have to clear away the sovereign states and create a single world state to enforce the law, or they have to accept that the law will not be enforced if the most powerful states do not want to see this happen. Veto-wielding powers, like those in the UN's Security Council, will refuse even to be bound by the International Court of Justice. A far better approach is to encourage nations to submit to a higher authority *in those areas where they are prepared to do so*. Even a limited sharing of sovereignty has a chance of making the organisation sufficiently compelling that even its more powerful members will stay in. Moreover (and here the 'functionalists' have a point) cooperation in the supranational sphere will make cooperation in the inter-governmental sphere more effective, even though it will not lead to supranational arrangements in thorny areas such as foreign policy and defence.

As said, there is nothing particularly 'idealistic' about advocating this way forward towards effective global governance. If there is a tendency towards naïve idealism, it lies with those who think that other organisations, particularly the UN, can be turned inside out and made effective. There is a need to see through this idea, as Monnet and Schuman saw through the 'Council of Europe' sixty years ago and realised that something altogether different was required. There is a need to be realistic, in other words, when offering world governance proposals. It is important to avoid both the optimism that thinks a bit of tampering with some favoured existing institution will do the trick, and the over-ambition which thinks that the sharing of sovereignty can proceed in any other manner than through carefully managed stages.

The EU and its malaise

In an essay of 1989, *The End of History?*, later written up in into a book in 1992, Francis Fukuyama anticipated that with the end of the Cold

War we might have reached 'the end point of mankind's ideological evolution and the universalisation of Western liberal democracy as the final form of human growth'.[17] That judgement now looks naïve. Indeed a number of recent books have suggested a much more dangerous scenario, a return to the sort of destructive great power rivalry that built up in the nineteenth century and then exploded in the early twentieth. Robert Kagan's recent book, *The Return of History and the End of Dreams*,[18] its title deliberately challenging Fukuyama's idea of history as having somehow gone away, warns of just such a scenario. Even Fukuyama himself, who famously remarked that the European Union with its partial sharing of sovereignty behaved like ex-smokers who wanted everyone else to experience the symptoms of their withdrawal from sovereignty, remarked more recently in the Guardian's 'Commentisfree' section[19] that 'I believe that the European Union more accurately reflects what the world will look like at the end of history than the contemporary United States.' Perhaps he recognised that his own imagery was more positive than he'd intended; if the EU is a community of ex-addicts who have come to realise the dangerous consequences of untrammelled sovereign states, then there is plenty about the EU to represent the sort of 'healthy lifestyle' that eventually makes ex-addicts forget their former addiction and simply enjoy the better world they now live in.

But if Fukuyama came to recognise some of the merits of the European Union, the same can hardly be said of the viewpoint inside the EU itself. Jean Monnet's biographer François Duchêne, towards the end of his book, remarked that 'European Union is *inter alia* a way of exploring a new world'.[20] Fifty years on, there is less exploration of new worlds than a profound malaise, both at 'eurocratic' level and among academics themselves, including the hundreds of John Monnet professors who, rather than exploring any new world, prefer to wade laboriously through the old one. Approval of the EU comes in the form of a plodding analysis of its complex and ever-changing workings, while those who rightly perceive weaknesses in the body couch their criticisms in apocalyptic terms.

Oxford Professor of Politics Jan Zielonka's work on the EU, for instance, is by no means that of an arch euro-sceptic, but you have to read the books in order to discover this. The titles – *Europe as Empire, Europe Unbound, Explaining Euro-Paralysis*[21] – are all clearly designed to suggest the familiar and contradictory nightmares concerning the European Union, lusting for imperial power but also unable to act effectively or to manage its borders. The current malaise runs so deep that every analysis has to be presented as an attack – perhaps it is assumed that that is the only sort of analysis anyone will read.

This book argues that there is another, much more positive, self-confident approach that could be taken both by and towards the European Union, an approach that is frequently more apparent to those who view the EU from the outside, measuring it against their own experiences of regional cooperation. It is an approach which seeks not only to defend the supranational arrangements which are at the heart of the European Union, but to argue for their application at global level.

Can the EU manage a Copernican revolution?

This book has tried to show the merits of a sovereignty-sharing arrangement, and to argue that what has been successful at European level should be attempted at global level. However, this can only happen if the EU is prepared to play a leading role in its creation. Is there really any chance of it doing so? This was the difficult question considered at the end of the last chapter, where both negative and positive reasons were given for believing that it might be prepared to do so.

There are three reasons why the EU might prove more ambitious than might be expected at present. The first is the international situation. No international situation can be called 'uniquely volatile' – volatility is the stuff of politics – but the current climate of financial failure and environmental threat has increased the concern about finding effective forms of trans-national organisation. What all sides of the debate agree about is the huge level of contemporary interest in 'global governance'. There is an awareness that mechanisms have to found for dealing with world problems that threaten to be overwhelming. The necessity of change provides an opportunity for new thinking.

The second reason for thinking that the EU might consider a Global Union more seriously is the fact that with the ratification of the Treaty of Lisbon finally complete, this successful outcome is likely to end at least two decades of tinkering with its treaty basis that has forced the EU to look inwards and occupy itself with its own workings, like a patient who can do nothing but retire to bed and groan. A deep consciousness of its own vulnerability as an institution has made it unwilling to project itself in any original manner beyond itself. Thus the malaise mentioned in the last section, which seems to affect everything said within or written about the EU – save when it is written by those who are outside the organisation and its deeply dispiriting ethos altogether. Though the ratification of the Lisbon Treaty will not end the demands for institutional changes, and will leave many problems outstanding like that of enlargement which this book has already discussed, there is a chance that the EU may feel confident enough in its workings to act more ambitiously towards the outside world. For as this book has made clear, there is in fact no way in which the EU could either develop into a 'superstate' or scale itself down to a mere treaty arrangement between states. The supranationalist and inter-governmental elements are too firmly embedded for one to prevail over the other. The EU is what it is – and a broad acceptance of that fact would allow it to look beyond Brussels.

Thirdly, there is the question already discussed of whether the twenty-seven members of the EU could ever reach a unanimous decision to participate in such a Global Union. Obviously there is no certain answer to that. As the previous chapter sought to bring out, concern over whether the EU could do anything effective in external relations has limited the scope of its activity so far.

The argument of this book is that the automatic presumption of natural affinity between the EU and the UN is completely inappropriate – a modern-day equivalent of Schuman and Monnet trying to create an outpost of the Council of Europe rather than strike out with their own sovereignty-sharing project. The EU stays closely attached to the UN not because they are really 'natural partners' – they are more chalk and cheese than horse and carriage – but because it thinks that this is a context in which twenty-seven member-states will work together in the sensitive area of foreign policy, including that of military force.

But is it so clear that those states would not be prepared to consider working together towards the formation of a Global Union? As the last chapter argued, it would not involve any more sharing of sovereignty than already applied within the EU. A Global Union would not threaten the interests of any member-states or tread on the toes of national sensitivities. Indeed the more euro-sceptic nations like the UK, which often sees itself as having sacrificed a world role for a merely continental one, might feel that this was something that provided credibility at the global level and overcame the 'Fortress Europe' mentality which, fairly or unfairly, does much to make the EU unpopular. On the whole the euro-sceptic nations tend to be the more outward-looking ones, concerned with the wider impact of EU policies on the rest of the world and suspicious of programmes like the Common Agricultural Policy (CAP) which they see as a protective mechanism to keep Europe rich and the rest of the world poor. Whether or not this is a fair judgement, it illustrates the political advantage of an EU initiative which is quite clearly directed towards bringing global benefits, and the area of agricultural development might be considered an appropriate starting-point. Indeed, some of the EU's own research provides the basis for a positive judgement concerning a bolder approach to its relations with the rest of the world.[22]

Participation in a Global Union might therefore help to stabilise internal relationships within the European Union. Those who have convinced themselves that there is a single European state in the making would now have to consider whether there was a single world state in the making. This would be even less plausible than the notion of a single European state. The fact that a high authority was being created to manage the sharing of sovereignty between a limited number of states in a particular area like food security would hardly suggest 'a world state in embryo'. The 'globo-sceptics' would be more likely to concede that this was an effective manner of binding nations to respect the laws they have chosen to hold in common, not a surreptitious plan to eliminate nations altogether.

European 'presumption'

A Global Union would demonstrate that the sharing of sovereignty is not something that can only be managed by Europeans. Europeans show a mixture of modesty and arrogance in this respect; modesty, because they don't like to suggest that their 'system' is the best, and arrogance, because they think that such a system can only really apply to a 'sophisticated continent' like their own. Behind this mixture of attitudes is a failure to appreciate the significance of the system itself. Precisely because Europeans fail to claim enough for the system imperfectly recognised within their Union, they look for an explanation of their relative success since the war in terms of 'Europeanness', 'European values' or 'the European way', curious phrases to emerge within a continent with such a long history of warfare and bloodshed. They may even call the extension of the system to others 'Europeanisation', an approach full of neo-imperialist overtones. This is not to argue that supranationalism was parachuted into Europe from above irrespective of particular historical and cultural circumstances; earlier chapters of this book have argued strongly against such a notion. However, recommending a supranational arrangement to others does not mean asking them to 'become European', any more than South Africans and Indians, when they go to the polls using an electoral system largely developed from their former imperial masters, have to see themselves as 'being British'. It is therefore not 'presumptuous' to think that a system that applies to Europe can be taken to the rest of the world; what is 'presumptuous' is the idea that it could only work in Europe.

There are certainly those who dislike the idea of 'forcing western concepts of democracy' upon other parts of the world.[23] On the other hand, most people's willingness to embrace cultural relativity has its limits; should female circumcision or child marriage or the self-immolation of widows be tolerated on such a basis? Even the UN has a requirement, in Article 4 of its Charter, that states which become members must be 'peace-loving'. It is true that discussions in San Francisco in 1945 over whether conditions for membership should include reference to specific forms of government decided against doing so. Nevertheless, the UN has not agonised much about the cultural difficulties involved in assessing what counts as 'a love of peace'.

Moreover, the European Union does not seem to have been troubled about what it calls 'conditionality' in its relations with other countries and regional groups. As was pointed out in Chapter 8, when in 2003 the twenty-year Cotonou arrangement superseded the Lomé conventions with over seventy developing nations, it was accepted that this was an agreement 'that imposes political conditionality, emphasising respect for human rights, democratic principles, the rule of law and good governance'.[24] Sometimes there have been objections to such 'conditionality'. For instance, when human rights and good governance issues were raised by the EU in discussions with ASEAN it provoked hostility concerning culturally loaded definitions and a debate on the meaning of 'Asian values'.[25] However, the EU continued to introduce such requirements into its discussions with groups like ASEAN and MERCOSUR.

Nor has the European Union been troubled by the idea that the Copenhagen criteria represent a culturally-loaded demand upon potential member-states. Nor have the candidate countries themselves seen them as such, even when there are bitter differences over the past, as in the issue of Turkey and Armenia. In practical terms, they get on with trying to comply with the terms of the *acquis communautaire*. This is not least because the *acquis* is a very practical collection of requirements, ensuring that a potential member acquires the administrative capacity to manage a supranational arrangement and is capable of functioning as a market economy within the single market. A great deal of what is required as a condition of membership concerns the ability to cope with the managerial demands of being part of the organisation.

Even if it is true that many of the more political concerns outlined in the Copenhagen criteria, such as the treatment of minorities, do represent a set of cultural values, there is no reason to see these as 'European' values. As Garton Ash points out in the article mentioned above, Canadians have these values in abundance (and they are hardly the same values as those brought by various groups of settlers a couple of centuries ago). The argument from cultural relativity is another form of the argument that supposes there is a huge divide between 'European values' and those of the rest of the world. Reality is more complex than that. Such an approach both underestimates the differences in culture and values between member-states within Europe (Albanians and Swedes arguably have significant differences in values) and overestimates the differences between Europe and the rest of the world. The EU has always insisted upon certain political principles being adhered to by member-states, and indeed is often criticised for failing to do so strongly enough (for instance by letting Bulgaria and Romania join prematurely, or by being too 'soft' on Turkey). It could be expected to make the same insistence as a member of a Global Union.

The need for a trigger

Part I focused upon the particular historical circumstances that gave rise to the European Coal and Steel Community. It agreed with the general consensus that the particular conditions created by the Second World War were crucial to its formation. The dilemma of requiring German recovery for European economic renewal, while fearing the consequences of such a recovery in terms of a political and military revival, was resolved through a decision to bring that recovery under a degree of supranational control. How far, however, do such circumstances apply elsewhere in the world?

There is no doubt that, as Menon says, 'states need strong incentives to engage in institutionalised cooperation',[26] but they do not always have to be the *same* incentives. This book has tried to put the development of supranational institutions in Europe into historical context. This context helps to explain why there was an initial sharing of sovereignty over coal and steel, just as it helps to explain why a French plan to share sovereignty in the area of national defence failed (managing German recovery supranationally in this field was rendered unnecessary by the development of NATO and the confirmation it gave of a continuing US military presence in Europe). Historical circumstances have impeded as well as encouraged moves in a 'supranational' direction.

It is true that in other parts of the world political and cultural circumstances are very different to those in post-war Europe, as the chapter on regional organisations sought to point out. The experience of colonisation in Africa, or the huge cultural, religious and social differences between the ASEAN countries, mean that these are not regional organisations 'in the same position' as Europe after World War Two. It is also true that Europe has a large number of small, compact nations – as the famous Czech writer Karel Čapek remarked, 'The Creator of Europe made her small and even split her up into little parts, so that our hearts could find joy not in size but in plurality'.[27] This has encouraged a degree of interdependence from a very early time. There are also important cultural similarities between countries, although few parts of the world (despite the importance of their indigenous peoples) could match South America for cultural homogeneity as an area dominated by Catholic Christianity and two mutually comprehensible (just about) languages.

At the same time, however, there are new forces that apply today and which encourage the sharing of sovereignty. In the twenty-first century there are factors which may be driving states towards supranational arrangements in ways that were largely unthinkable sixty years ago – for instance under the impact of globalisation which has inevitably shaved away some of the competences which were previously in the hands of nation-states alone. People might not want to go as far as Scholte in claiming that 'contemporary large-scale globalization has contradicted and subverted sovereign statehood',[28] but it has certainly had a considerable limiting effect upon autonomy at state level, as writers like Anne-Marie Slaughter (discussed in Chapter 6) have brought out very clearly. Ulrich Beck writes:

> Against the mental block of the national political monopoly, and against the nightmare vision of an imperial world state whose claim on power could never be escaped, this reformulation and reformation of international political space is intended to facilitate a complex architecture of sovereignty and identity.[29]

Beck's 'reformulation and reformation' in the form of the 'transnational state' is not the same as McClintock's GU (Global Union). Nevertheless, what is interesting is the fact that it shows a determination to develop new forms of global governance born not (or not simply) out of idealist concerns about the behaviour of nation-states, but out of a practical concern to come to terms with an inevitable loss of control in certain areas at state level. Beck and Scholte see globalisation as a process that forces a rethink upon those committed to the so-called 'Westphalian model' of state sovereignty, whether they like it or not.

It is impossible to prescribe exactly what historical conditions are necessary for supranational institutions to emerge at global level. Clearly there were specific circumstances that were highly relevant to Europe's decision after World War Two and which are no longer an imperative today. However, what this section has tried to do is point to factors prompting such moves today which were not present then. The catalyst for a supranational arrangement available to Europe in the 1940s in the aftermath of war may not be present now, but there are other circumstances which could trigger such developments in our own century. The question of food security, discussed in the last chapter, is certainly topical, affects the lives of millions and is crucially linked to problems of climate change and world poverty. But whether it could provide an effective trigger for the formation of a Global Union is inevitably something that cannot be determined in advance.

Conclusion

This book began with the generally accepted point that the world is in the throes of its worst financial crisis since the Great Depression. One of the reactions to this, unsurprising given the way it spread like wildfire among both developed and developing nations, is that 'efforts are being made to refurbish global governance'.[30] Furthermore, the twenty-first century has seen growing recognition of particular problems like international crime (including terrorism) and climate change ('climate breakdown' would be a more appropriate phrase), which cannot be solved at state level alone. The widespread acceptance that dangerous alterations to the climate have taken place, together with the awareness that a 'tipping point' may be approaching beyond which damage is irreversible, makes concerted measures to address the problem essential. Where the disparities between rich and poor are concerned, it is always possible for rich nations to believe (in many ways wrongly) that they can remain largely unaffected by global poverty. This is not an option where global warming is concerned.

Whether or not such dire circumstances are an 'appropriate' trigger for a more widespread attempt to share sovereignty between nations, they certainly require radical action. This book has tried to explain why even a limited sovereignty-sharing exercise, limited in terms of the areas in which it was shared and the number of nations involved, would be much more effective than the other alternatives on offer. It would require, however, a special contribution from the EU, one in which it tried to make global the system that has done so much to curb the destructive tribal instincts of its own member-states.

Meanwhile another book appears in which we read that the EU is a 'provincial norm setter' or that it provides 'a normative basis of global governance'.[31] There are many such phrases doing the rounds in the policy papers and academic articles that circulate endlessly around Brussels, but all these phrases are empty if they have no mechanism for applying this norm. McClintock's book recognises that a serious treatment of the EU as a 'norm setter' requires the construction of a new organisation rather than further tampering with the old ones.

For all the talk of a normative basis of global governance, the 'policy entrepreneurs' of the organisation which Monnet and Schuman founded sixty years ago still fail to see the radical new departure which would be involved if these words were really to have meaning. It is time that the European Union began to recognise the power of its own unique institutional make-up. It is time that, instead of hiding in the shadows of other institutions, it made a determined effort to bring the sharing of sovereignty to the world stage.

Notes

Chapter 1

1. Robert Kagan has been touting the idea of a 'League of Democracies' recently in *The Return of History and the End of Dreams* (New York: Alfred A. Knopf, 2008), a title deliberately designed to challenge Francis Fukuyama's idea of an 'end' to history after the collapse of communism.
2. The 'Concert of Democracies' is proposed by the Princeton Project on National Security report and was discussed in an article by John Ikenberry and Anne-Marie Slaughter in *The Guardian*, Friday, 11th July 2008.
3. Hobbes himself was not enthusiastic about the 'domestic analogy', feeling that whereas a 'state of nature' among individuals was absolutely intolerable, a state of nature among states might be bearable, since individual states could ensure the maintenance of internal peace.
4. They are particularly well set out in Suganami, H. *The Domestic Analogy and World Order Proposals* (Cambridge: Cambridge University Press, 1989).
5. Immanuel Kant, 'Toward Perpetual Peace: A Philosophical Sketch', in Kant, I. *Toward Perpetual Peace and Other Writings on Politics, Peace and History*, ed. Pauline Kleingeld, p. 79 (Yale University Press, 2006).
6. Ibid., p. 80.
7. Ibid., p. 81. There is useful discussion of Kant's position in Habermas, Jürgen *The Inclusion of the Other: Studies in Political Theory* (Cambridge: Polity Press, 1999). See Chapter 7: 'Kant's Idea of Perpetual Peace: At Two Hundred Years' Historical Remove'.
8. Wandering among the ruins could be a harrowing experience. Readers of Tony Judt's *Postwar: A History of Europe since 1945* (London: Penguin, 2005) will note the photograph next to p. 234. A child goes past endless rows of corpses laid alongside a road not far from the former Bergen-Belsen concentration camp. 'Like most adult Germans in the post-war years', Judt comments, 'he averts his gaze'.
9. See Judt, op. cit., pp. 13–41: 'The Legacy of War' for an account of a very different Europe, surrounded by the consequences of its own self-destructive impulses.
10. See Jean Monnet's *Memoirs*, translated R. Mayne (London: Collins, 1978) and published with a useful foreword by former President of the European Commission Roy Jenkins. References to the OEEC and Council of Europe are on pp. 271–3.
11. Menon, Anand *Europe: The State of the Union* (London: Atlantic Books, 2008), p. 112. The quotation is from Francis Fukuyama's famous essay 'The End of History?' published in *The National Interest*, vol. 16, 1989, in the wake of the collapse of communism. Fukuyama has since come to a much more positive view of the European Union. See Chapter 10 below.
12. After violent protests at the summit meeting of the G8 held in Genoa in 2000, a former European Commissioner, Emma Bonino, remarked that the

G8 had 'no treaty and no transparency...Nobody knows what they stand for, which makes them quite different, from the institutional point of view, to the meetings of heads of state and government of the European Union'. Though her view might be challenged where the transparency of European Council meetings is concerned, the general point remains valid where a large number of global organisations are concerned.

13. Anne-Marie Slaughter *A New World Order* (Princeton: Princeton University Press, 2004).
14. Referred to by Peterson and Shackleton as 'new policy-specialised, transgovernmental networks, populated by actors who have more in common with each other than with officials who specialise in other policy areas in their own national states'. See John Peterson and Michael Shackleton (eds) *The Institutions of the European Union*, p. 356 (Oxford: Oxford University Press, 2002).
15. Menon, A. *Europe: The State of the Union*, p. 16 (London: Atlantic Books, 2008).
16. McClintock, John *The Uniting of Nations: An Essay in Global Governance* (Brussels: Peter Lang Press, 3rd edition, 2009).
17. For instance Martin Ortega's *Building the Future: The EU's Contribution to Global Governance*, Chaillot Paper No. 100 (Paris: Institute for Security Studies, 2007), McClintock, John *The Uniting of Nations: An Essay in Global Governance* (Brussels: Peter Lang, 3rd Edition, 2009), Ramseh Thakur and Thomas G. Weiss (eds) *The UN and Global Governance: An Idea and its Prospects* (Tokyo: United Nations University Press, 2007).
18. See Thakur, Ramseh and Weiss, Thomas G., op. cit., p. 245.
19. The phrase is used by Martin Ortega, op. cit., p. 69. Like Ortega, this book believes that institutional mechanisms are very important. For discussion of some of the presumptions behind this, see the useful discussion by John Peterson and Michael Shackleton, the editors of *The Institutions of the European Union* esp. pp. 4–7, 'Why Study Institutions?' (Oxford: Oxford University Press, 2002).
20. The quotation comes from Filippo Andreatta's otherwise useful discussion of terminology in 'Theory and the European Union's International Relations', Chapter 1 of Hill, Christopher and Smith, Michael (eds) *International Relations and the European Union*, p. 30 (Oxford: Oxford University Press, 2005).
21. Taylor, Paul 'The Concept of Community and the European Integration Process', in Hodges, Michael (ed.), *European Integration*, p. 207 (London: Penguin, 1972).
22. Lindberg, Leon and Scheingold, Stuart 'The Failure of the Common Transport Policy: A Comparison with the Success of the Common Agricultural Policy', in Hodges, Michael (ed.), *European Integration*, p. 269 (London: Penguin, 1972).
23. Milward, A. *The European Rescue of the Nation-State*, p. 12 (London: Routledge, 1992).
24. Moravcsik, A. *The Choice for Europe: Social Purpose and State Power from Messina to Maastricht* (Ithaca, New York: Cornell University Press, 1998). Even here it is not clear whether Moravcsik is denying the supranational arrangements within the EU so much as disapproving of them.
25. First coined by Jolyon Howorth in Chaillot Paper No. 43, *European Integration and Defence: The Ultimate Challenge?* (Paris: Institute for Security Studies, 2000).

26. For instance Jean-Marc Ferry's curious contribution, 'European Integration and the Cosmopolitan Way', in Telò, Mario (ed.) *The European Union and Global Governance* (London: Routledge, 2009). Ferry talks of a 'supranational federal state', suggesting that he sees supranationalism leading to a single world state.
27. The document is published by the Council of the European Union. See http://consilium.europa.eu.

Chapter 2

1. Quoted in Davies, Norman, *Europe: A History*, p. 568 (London: Pimlico, 1997).
2. John Osborne's *Luther* was first published in 1961, though it recently enjoyed a revival in London's National Theatre with Rufus Sewell as Luther. The quotation comes from Act 2 Scene 4.
3. Davies, Norman, op. cit., p. 565.
4. Hobbes' *Leviathan* was originally written in 1651. Quotations here come from the version abridged and edited by J. Plamenatz (London: Collins, 1962).
5. Suganami, H. *The Domestic Analogy and World Order Proposals*, p. 12 (Cambridge: Cambridge University Press, 1989).
6. *De jure belli et pacis* was originally written in 1625. See the English translation by F.W. Kelsey (Oxford: Clarendon Press, 1925).
7. May, Larry *Crimes against Humanity: A Normative Account*, p. 9 (Cambridge: Cambridge University Press, 2005).
8. Quoted in Phillips, W.A. *The Confederation of Europe*, p. 183 (New York: Fertig, 1966).
9. Thomson, David *England in the Nineteenth Century*, p. 27 (London: Penguin, 1991).
10. Taylor, A.J.P. *The Struggle for Mastery in Europe 1848–1918* (Oxford: Clarendon Press, 1971).
11. Hobsbawm, E.J. *Nations and Nationalism since 1780* (Cambridge: Cambridge University Press, 1990).
12. Hobsbawm, E.J. 'Mass-producing traditions: Europe 1870–1914', Chapter 7 of Ranger, T. and Hobsbawm, E. (eds) *The Invention of Tradition* (Cambridge: Cambridge University Press, 1992).
13. See John Breuilly's introduction to Ernest Gellner's *Nations and Nationalism*, p. xxv (Oxford: Blackwell, 2006).
14. Ranger, T. and Hobsbawm, E.J. (eds), op. cit., p. 271.
15. Ibid., p. 280.
16. 'Waving Flags: Nations and Nationalism', Chapter 6 of E.J. Hobsbawm's *The Age of Empire* (London: Abacus, 1994). The quotation is from p. 148.
17. Hobsbawm, E.J. *Nations and Nationalism since 1780*, p. 38 (Cambridge: Cambridge University Press, 1990).
18. Suganami, Hidemi *The Domestic Analogy and World Order Proposals*, p. 84 (Cambridge: Cambridge University Press, 1989).
19. Clark, G. and Sohn, L.B. *World Peace through World Law* 3rd edition (Cambridge Massachusetts: Harvard University Press, 1966).

20. Schuman, F.L. *The Commonwealth of Man: An Inquiry into Power Politics and World Government* (London: Robert Hale, 1954); Schiffer, W. *The Legal Community of Mankind* (New York: Columbia University Press, 1954).
21. Schuman, op. cit., p. 494. See also Suganami, Hidemi *The Domestic Analogy and World Order Proposals*, p. 133 (Cambridge: Cambridge University Press, 1989).
22. Elias, Norbert *The Civilising Process* (Oxford: Blackwell, 2000 – Revised Edition). The book was first published in 1936 – shortly before World War Two.
23. Ibid., p. 373.
24. Ibid., p. 375.
25. Ibid., p. 423.
26. Ibid., p. 445.
27. Elias, Norbert *The Society of Individuals*, p. 164 (London: Continuum Press, 2001).
28. Robert Cooper, *The Breaking of Nations*, p. 58 (New York: Atlantic Monthly Press, 2003).
29. Duchêne, François *Jean Monnet: The First Statesman of Interdependence*, p. 409 (New York: W.W. Norton & Co., 1994).
30. Linklater, Andrew 'A European Civilising Process?', Chapter 17 of Hill, Christopher and Smith, Michael, *International Relations and the European Union* (Oxford: Oxford University Press, 2005). The quotation is on p. 370.

Chapter 3

1. See Dinan, Desmond *Europe Recast: A History of European Union* (Basingstoke: Palgrave Macmillan, 2004) for a survey of the main historical developments in the formation of the European Union.
2. See John Peterson and Michael Shackleton (eds) *The Institutions of the European Union* (Oxford: Oxford University Press, 2002) for a description of the different institutions.
3. This is not to say that other international organisations are necessarily 'tidier'. The UN, for instance, has a large, sprawling administration with unclear lines of command.
4. See Alex May, *Britain and Europe since 1945*, p. 16 (Harlow: Longman, 1999).
5. See François Duchêne's biography of Monnet, *Jean Monnet: The First Statesman of Interdependence*, p. 183 (New York: W.W. Norton, 1994).
6. Alasdair Blair's *The European Union since 1945* (Harlow: Pearson Education Limited, 2005) contains a useful appendix of key documents. The quotations in the text are taken from Document 9, 'The Schuman Declaration' on p. 98.
7. Stephen Martin points to what he calls the 'rosy' assessment of Jacques Delors, who talks about the strengths which the High Authority derived from 'its collegiate system and from the independence of its members in discharging its supranational responsibility'. He contrasts this with the 'more sombre' conclusion of Alan Milward, who described the High Authority as 'a powerful international committee within which separate national representatives argued for separate national policies' See his 'Building on Coal and Steel: European Integration in the 1950s and the 1960s', Chapter 6 of Desmond Dinan (ed.), *Origins and Evolution of the European Union* (Oxford: Oxford University Press, 2006). The reference to Delors and Milward is on p. 136.

8. Gillingham, John R. 'The German Problem and European Integration', in Dinan, Desmond (ed.) *Origins and Evolution of the European Union*, p. 77 (Oxford: Oxford University Press, 2006).
9. See Alan Bullock's biography of Bevin *Ernest Bevin, Foreign Secretary*, p. 659 (London: Heinemann, 1983).
10. See Judt, Tony *Postwar: A History of Europe since 1945*, p. 160 (London: Penguin, 2005).
11. See Messenger, David 'Dividing Europe: The Cold War and European Integration', in Dinan, Desmond (ed.) *Origins and Evolution of the European Union*, pp. 38–40 (Oxford: Oxford University Press, 2006).
12. See Young, Hugo *This Blessed Plot: Britain and Europe from Churchill to Blair* (Woodstock: Overlook Press, 1999).
13. Milward, Alan *The Reconstruction of Western Europe 1945–51* (London: Methuen, 1984); *The European Rescue of the Nation State* (London: Routledge, 1992).
14. Quoted and discussed by David Weigall's 'British Perceptions of the European Defence Community', in Stirk, P.M.R. and Willis, D. (eds) *Shaping Postwar Europe: European Unity and Diversity 1945–57* (London: Pinter, 1991).
15. Parsons, Craig 'The Triumph of Community Europe', in Dinan, Desmond (ed.) *Origins and Evolution of the European Union*, pp. 107–124 (Oxford: Oxford University Press, 2006). The quotation is on p. 116.
16. Quoted in Duchêne, op. cit., p. 273. Paul-Henri Spaak, the Belgian Foreign Minister, described Beyen's ideas as 'daring'.
17. Quoted in Dinan, Desmond *Europe Recast: A History of European Union*, p. 93 (Basingstoke: Palgrave Macmillan, 2004).
18. It is perhaps no coincidence that the wilder expressions of British euroscepticism have been fed by newspaper tycoons from the former 'dominions', the Australian Rupert Murdoch and the Canadian Conrad Black.
19. See the documents at the back of the study by Alex May, *Britain and Europe since 1945* (Harlow: Longman, 1999). These words of Macmillan's are quoted in Document 6, p. 104.
20. Ibid., Document 7c, p. 106.
21. See Vanke, Jeffrey 'Charles de Gaulle's Uncertain Idea of Europe', Chapter 7 of Dinan, Desmond (ed.) *Origins and Evolution of the European Union*, p. 143 (Oxford: Oxford University Press, 2006).
22. De Gaulle's changing attitudes can be studied from two major works, E. Jouve's *Le Général de Gaulle et la Construction de l'Europe* (Paris: Librairie général de droit et de jurisprudence, 1967), and A. Peyrefitte's three-volume *C'était de Gaulle* (Paris: Fayard, 1994, 1997, 2000).
23. A. Peyrefitte, op. cit., vol. 1, p. 159.
24. Vanke, Jeffrey 'Charles de Gaulle's Uncertain Idea of Europe', Chapter 7 of Dinan, Desmond (ed.) *Origins and Evolution of the European Union*, p. 159 (Oxford: Oxford University Press, 2006).

Chapter 4

1. Quoted from Bradley, Kieran 'The European Court of Justice', in Peterson, John and Shackleton, Michael (eds) *The Institutions of the European Union*, p. 119 (Oxford: Oxford University Press, 2002).

2. Quoted in Menon, Anand *The State of the Union*, p. 45 (London: Atlantic Books, 2008).
3. Quoted in Nugent, Neill *The Government and Politics of the European Union*, p. 291 (Basingstoke: Palgrave Macmillan, 6th edition, 2006).
4. Ludlow gives the example of fireworks. National governments would set the norms for safe fireworks to accord with the specifications of their domestic producers, and then reject fireworks from elsewhere on health and safety grounds. See Ludlow, F. Piers 'From Deadlock to Dynamism: The European community in the 1980s', in Dinan, Desmond *Origins and Evolution of the European Union*, p. 222 (Oxford: Oxford University Press, 2006).
5. The essay containing these words was first published in *The National Interest* in 1989, as initial euphoria in the wake of the end of the Cold War led some to think that a secure liberal world order was in the making. Fukuyama has since revised his opinions.
6. Sbragia, Alberta M. 'European Union and NAFTA', Chapter 7 of Telò, Mario (ed.) *European Union and New Regionalism* (Aldershot: Ashgate Press, 2007). The quotation is on p. 163. See also Alter, Karen J. 'Who are the 'Masters of the Treaty'? European Governments and the ECJ', in *International Organisation*, 52(1), Winter 1998, pp. 121–47.
7. Dinan, Desmond *Europe Recast: A History of European Union*, p. 105 (Basingstoke: Palgrave Macmillan, 2004).
8. It is arguably the mainstream of British Conservatism too. See, for instance, the arguments of Ian Gilmour in *Dancing with Dogma: Britain under Thatcherism* (London: Simon and Schuster, 1992), where he argues that her Conservatism was a radical departure from mainstream Conservatism in Britain, representing more of a return to Victorian Liberalism. He is also quite clear (see Chapters 3 and 4) that her economic policies were unsuccessful. Unfortunately the popularity of the 'iron lady' with Central and Eastern European countries after their liberation in 1989 obscured the failings of her economic policy (as did the armies of highly-paid 'consultants' who arrived in such countries presuming to tell their governments how they could 'learn from Britain'). Even the willingness of New Labour to prolong the Thatcherite experiment in Britain into the twenty-first century has done little to enhance its credibility, as New Labour is now discovering in the world financial crisis.
9. See Judt, Tony *Postwar A History of Europe since 1945*, p. 305 (London: Penguin, 2006). Judt cites a 76% rise in French butter production 1949–56, a 116% increase in cheese production between 1949 and 1957 and a 201% growth in beet sugar production. Barley and maize crops grew by 348% and 815% respectively. These increases represent the consequences of the opening up of markets within the Six, initially through the European Coal and Steel Community. In fact these figures show considerable growth in production preceding the Treaties of Rome and the arrival of the CAP which added the incentive of guaranteed prices.
10. See Richard T. Griffiths 'A Dismal Decade? European Integration in the 1970s', in Desmond Dinan (ed.) *Origins and Evolution of the European Union*, p. 180 (Oxford: Oxford University Press, 2006).
11. Tsoukalis, Loukas 'Managing Interdependence', in Hill, Christopher and Smith, Michael (eds) *International Relations and the European Union*, p. 233 (Oxford: Oxford University Press, 2005).

12. Ibid., p. 243.
13. Margaret Thatcher *The Downing Street Years*, p. 556 (London: HarperCollins, 1993).
14. Later published as a book by Padoa-Schoppa and others, *Efficiency, Stability and Equity: A Strategy for the Evolution of the Economic System of the European Community* (Oxford: Oxford University Press, 1987). As the title conveys, 'equity' was regarded as a route towards economic efficiency, the end that both Thatcher and Delors desired to achieve.
15. Once again it was in Britain that the principle resonated least. As British Conservative minister Norman Tebbit put it approvingly when addressing a party conference in the 1980s, when his father was out of work he got on his bike and went as far as he could to find employment. However, the 'on yer bike' principle of British governments of the 80s and 90s was thought appropriate when it was out-of-work northerners who should be moving south; it was thought less appropriate when it was out-of-work southerners moving north (at least if they were Portuguese or Spanish after accession in 1986).

Chapter 5

1. Lister, Frederick K. *The European Union, the United Nations, and the Revival of Confederal Governance*, p. 130 (Westport: Greenwood Press, 1996).
2. In fact it did join the League later – in 1934 – after Germany and Japan had withdrawn from it. Ironically, the last 'whimper' of the League came in 1941, when the Soviet Union became the only country ever to be thrown out of the body, after its invasion of Finland. By that time war had broken out and the League had ceased to be relevant.
3. See Stephen C. Schlesinger's *Act of Creation: The Founding of the United Nations*, p. 273 (Boulder, Colorado: Westview Press, 2003).
4. White, Nigel D. *The United Nations System: Toward International Justice*, p. 53 (London: Lynne Rienner, 2002).
5. Lister, writing in 1995, declared that 'the present configuration of power relationships in the world is favourable to the kind of system that the charter has provided for' (op. cit., p. 148). More than a decade on, with rising tension between the United States and a resurgent Russia, that looks an overoptimistic viewpoint. Moreover vetoes have continued to be issued and controversial issues avoided because of a particular Great Power's involvement, just as they were before the fall of communism.
6. Lister, Frederick K., op. cit., p. 130.
7. For instance Rajni Kothari in his *Footsteps to the Future* (Amsterdam: North–Holland Publishing, 1974), part of the World Order Models Project organised in the late 1960s by Saul Mendlovitz.
8. Luard, Evan *A History of the United Nations*, vol. 1, p. 38 (London: Macmillan, 1982).
9. White, Nigel D., op. cit., pp. 97–8.
10. Siglitz, Joseph *Globalisation and its Discontents*, p. 13 (New York: W.W. Norton, 2002).
11. Hence the title of Naomi Klein's recent book *The Shock Doctrine* (London: Penguin, 2007). Klein's analysis is controversial, but her argument that the

IMF and the World Bank pursued a very different approach to problems of development in the 1980s than in the 1940s is not. Equally uncontroversial is the view that the different approach was hardly sanctioned by any change of thinking inside ECOSOC or other parts of the UN hierarchy.

12. See Taylor, P. *International Organisations in the Modern World*, p. 115 (London: Pinter, 1993).
13. See White, Nigel D., op. cit., pp. 128–9.
14. Suganami, Hidemi *The Domestic Analogy and World Order Proposals*, p. 126 (Cambridge: Cambridge University Press, 1989).
15. The US showed an interest in supporting the ICC in the dying days of the Clinton administration, but only if the Security Council could 'screen' what went before it. Effectively the US would be able to veto any particular case being heard.
16. White, op. cit., p. 221. See also Alston, P. (ed.) *The United Nations and Human Rights: A Critical Appraisal* (Oxford: Clarendon Press, 1992).
17. Luard, Evan *A History of the United Nations*, vol. 1, p. 54 (London: Macmillan, 1982).
18. Suganami, Hidemi *The Domestic Analogy and World Order Proposals*, p. 117 (Cambridge: Cambridge University Press, 1989).
19. There is a history of UN wariness over the right of nations to use terrorist attacks as a justification for attacking another sovereign nation. In 1985, for instance, the Security Council passed by 14–0 a resolution condemning Israel for bombing the PLO Headquarters in Tunis. Israel argued that Tunis was clearly harbouring dangerous terrorists who had already been responsible for a number of attacks, much as the US argued that Afghanistan was harbouring dangerous terrorists in 2001. But the Security Council was not prepared to legitimise a 'pre-emptive response' by Israel on these grounds. However, such was the scale of the attack on the Twin Towers that it was generally accepted that the UN could no longer maintain this position.
20. Gray, Christine *International Law and the Use of Force*, p. 13 (Oxford: Oxford University Press, 2004).
21. Cooper, Robert *The Postmodern State and the World Order* (London: Demos, 2000).
22. Mark Leonard *Why Europe will run the 21st Century*, p. 141 (London: Fourth Estate, 2005).
23. Glennon 'The Fog of Law: Self-Defence, Inherence and Incoherence in Article 51 of the UN Charter', in the *Harvard Journal of Law and Public Policy* (2002), cited in Gray, Christine, op. cit., p. 171. See also her discussion of 'pre-emptive self-defence' on the same page.
24. White, Nigel D., op. cit., p. 15.
25. Greer, T. *What Roosevelt Thought: The Social and Political Ideas of Frankin D. Roosevelt*, p. 198 (Michigan: Michigan State University Press, 1965).
26. Clark, G. and Sohn, L.B. *World Peace through World Law* (Massachusetts: Harvard University Press, 1966).
27. Kothari, Rajni *Footsteps into the Future: Diagnosis of the Present World and a Design for an Alternative* (Amsterdam: North Holland Press, 1974); Mazrui, A. *A World Federation of Cultures: An African Perspective* (New York: The Free Press, 1976).

28. Quoted in Reynolds, P.A. and Hughes, E.J. *The Historian as Diplomat. Charles Kingsley Webster and the United Nations*, p. 71 (London: Martin Robertson, 1976).
29. Brierly, J.L. *The Outlook for International Law* (Oxford: Clarendon Press, 1944).
30. Giddes, Anthony *Europe in the Global Age*, p. 217 (Cambridge: Polity Press, 2006).
31. Zamora, S. 'Economic Relations and Development', in Schachter and Joyner (eds) *United Nations Legal Order*, p. 503 (Cambridge: Cambridge University Press, 1996).

Chapter 6

1. Baker, Andrew *The Group of Seven: Global Financial Governance*, p. 136 (London: Routledge, 2006).
2. Stiglitz, J. *Globalisation and its Discontents* (London: Penguin, 2002).
3. Woods, N. 'Making the IMF and the World Bank more accountable', in *International Affairs*, Vol. 77, 1 (2000).
4. See Berkman, Steve *The World Bank and the Gods of Lending* (Sterling, Virginia: Kumarian Press, 2008).
5. See Moore, David *The World Bank: Development, Poverty, Hegemony* (Southville, South Africa: University of Kwazulu-Natal Press, 2007).
6. Guzman, Andrew 'Global Governance and the WTO' *Boalt Working Papers in Public Law No 83* (Berkeley: University of California, June 2001).
7. For a slightly more optimistic view of the potential of the WTO, see the book edited by Gary P. Sampson, *The WTO and Global Governance: Future Directions* (Tokyo: United Nations University, 2008).
8. For an assessment of the OECD, see Mahon, Rianne and McBride, Stephen (eds) *The OECD and Transnational Governance* (Seattle: University of Washington Press, 2008).
9. This seems to be the view of a book published by the IDRC (International Development Research Centre) on *The Power of Peer Learning: Networks and Development Cooperation* by Jean-H. Guilmette. Chapter 3 looks at the 'institutional sociology' of the OECD.
10. Baker, Andrew *The Group of Seven: Global Financial Governance*, p. 246 (London: Routledge, 2006).
11. From an address by Karel de Gucht entitled 'NATO and International Security in the 21st Century', delivered to the NATO Defence College in Rome.
12. For a sympathetic study of NATO enlargement, see Asmus, Ronald D., *Opening NATO's Door: How the Alliance Remade Itself for a New Era* (New York: Columbia University Press, 2002).
13. Ivo Daalder and James Goldgeier 'Global NATO', in *Foreign Affairs*, vol. 85, no. 5, Sept/Oct 2006, pp. 105–13.
14. Strictly speaking NATO's assembly is completely independent of the organisation, since there is nothing in the Washington Treaty to support its formation.
15. Balladur, Eduard *Pour une Union Occidentale entre l'Europe et les Etats–Unis* (Paris: Fayard, 2007); ET *For a Union of the West* (Stanford: Hoover Institution Press,

2009). Balladur's call for a 'Union of the West' is seen as interesting given his Gaullist past.
16. Huntley, James R. *Uniting the Democracies: Institutions of the Emerging Atlantic-Pacific System* (New York: New York University Press, 1980).
17. Beitz, C. *Political Theory and International Relations* (Princeton: Princeton University Press, 1979). From the same period see Bull, H. *The Anarchical Society* (London: Macmillan, 1977). Despite the reference to 'anarchy', Bull's argument is that because of these forms of mutual accommodation the anarchy is more apparent than real.
18. See R.J. Barry Jones *The World Turned Upside Down: Globalisation and the Future of the State* (Manchester: Manchester University Press, 2000); Singer, Roger: *One World: The Ethics of Globalisation* (New Haven, Connecticut: Yale University Press, 2004).
19. Anne-Marie Slaughter 'The Real New World Order' *Foreign Affairs*, Sept/Oct 1997, vol. 76, no. 5 pp. 183–97). The quotation is on p. 184.
20. Brown, Chris *Understanding International Relations* (London: Macmillan, 1997). The 'chandelier' reference is on p. 105. A new edition in collaboration with Kirsten Ainley was published in 2009.
21. Slaughter, Anne-Marie *A New World Order* (Princeton: Princeton University Press, 2004).
22. Ibid., p. 22.
23. Ibid., pp. 132–3.
24. See p. 134 for all these quotations.
25. Ibid., pp. 264–5.
26. Scholte, Jan Aart Globalization: A Critical Introduction (London: Macmillan, 2000), Chapter 6, pp. 134–59.
27. A typical enthusiast for such networks is the former UN Secretary-General Kofi Annan. See his *We the Peoples: The Role of the United Nations in the 21st Century* (New York: United Nations, Department of Public Information, 2000).
28. Scholte, Jan Aart, op. cit., p. 151.
29. Weiss, Thomas G. *What's Wrong with the UN and How to Fix it*, p. 227 (Cambridge: Polity Press, 2008).
30. Saint-Simon, Henri Comte de, *The Reorganisation of the European Community*, translated by Markham, F.M.H. *Saint-Simon: Selected Writings*, p. 34 (Oxford: Blackwell, 1952).

Chapter 7

1. See Fredrik Soderbaum, 'African Regionalism and EU-African Interregionalism', in Telò, Mario (ed.) *European Union and New Regionalism*, p. 294 (Aldershot: Ashgate, 2007).
2. Soderbaum is very critical of this tendency, and sees it as a thinly-disguised attempt to make Africa serve the EU's economic interests.
3. Acharya A. and Johnston, Alastair Iain (eds) *Crafting Cooperation: Regional International Institutions in Comparative Perspective*, p. 265 (Cambridge: Cambridge University Press, 2007).
4. Ibid., p. 137. The chapter by Jeffrey Herbst is called 'Crafting regional cooperation in Africa'.

5. Mayall, James 'The Shadow of Empire: The EU and the former Colonial World', Chapter 14 of Hill, Christopher and Smith, Michael (eds) *International Relations and the European Union* (Oxford: Oxford University Press, 2005). The quotation is on p. 294.
6. By way of example, the South African Development Community (SADC) is economically dominated by South Africa (which represents 70% of its GDP and 20% of its population) and the GNP per capita difference between the richest (Mauritius) and poorest (Congo) country is considerable. Overcoming these differences by promoting intra-regional trade and foreign investment has had very little success in the poorer regions. Progress towards economic convergence has been much more noticeable in the smaller SACU (South African Customs Union), a customs union with a common external tariff and a common currency involving South Africa and the small countries around it (Namibia, Lesotho, Swaziland and Botswana). This grouping is even more dominated by South Africa, but the common currency and external tariffs (together with transfers from South Africa) appear to have achieved much more than the less binding economic and financial ties involved in SADC. There is no doubt, then, that economic and financial instruments can have an effect, but they need to be both binding on memberstates and within the administrative capacity of each one to enforce. See Mario Telò, 'Between Trade Regionalisation and Deeper Cooperation', in Telò, Mario (ed.) *European Union and New Regionalism* (Aldershot: Ashgate, 2007). The references to SADC and SACU are on p. 144.
7. See Kjell A. Eliassen and Catherine Borve Arnesen 'Comparison of European and Southeast Asian Integration', in Telò, Mario (ed.) *European Union and New Regionalism*. The quotation comes from p. 220.
8. See Telò, op. cit., p. 133.
9. See Higgott, R. 'Alternative Models of Regional Cooperation? The Limits of Regional Institutionalisation in East Asia', in Telò, op. cit., p. 94.
10. See a very useful chapter by Derek McDougall 'The East Asian Experience of Regionalism', in Murray, Philomena (ed.) *Europe and Asia: Regions in Flux*, pp. 42–60 (Basingstoke: Palgrave Macmillan, 2008).
11. Yeo Lay Hwee 'The Origins and Development of ASEM and EU-East Asia Relations', in Murray, Philomena (ed.) *Europe and Asia: Regions in Flux*, p. 119 (Basingstoke: Palgrave Macmillan, 2008).
12. Yuen Foong Khong and Helen E.S. Nesadurai 'Hanging together, institutional design, and cooperation in Southeast Asia: AFTA and the ARC', in Acharya A. and Johnston, Alastair Iain (eds) *Crafting Cooperation: Regional International Institutions in Comparative Perspective*, p. 69 (Cambridge: Cambridge University Press, 2007).
13. Quoted in Toshiro Tanaka 'Asian (ASEAN Plus Three) Perspectives on European Integration', in Murray, Philomena (ed.) *Europe and Asia: Regions in Flux*, p. 176 (London: Palgrave, 2008).
14. Philippine President Gloria Arroyo, for instance, was disappointed in the Charter signed at the end of 2007 and even suggested that the Philippines might not be prepared to ratify it in 2008.
15. Hobsbawm, Eric *Age of Revolution*, p. 139 (London: Abacus, 1991).
16. Hobsbawm, Eric *Age of Extremes*, pp. 22–3 (London: Abacus, 1994).
17. Ibid., p. 134.

18. See Alvaro Vasconcelos, 'European Union and MERCOSUR', in Telò, Mario (ed.) *European Union and New Regionalism* (Aldershot: Ashgate, 2007). He talks of 'de-legitimating nationalism' on p. 167.
19. Barnett, Michael and Solingen, Etel 'Designed to fail or failure of design? The origins and legacy of the Arab League', in Acharya A. and Johnston, Alastair Iain (eds) *Crafting Cooperation: Regional International Institutions in Comparative Perspective*, pp. 190–1 (Cambridge: Cambridge University Press, 2007).

Chapter 8

1. Statement of the European Commission, 'The European Union and the United Nations: the choice of multilateralism', 10th September 2003, COM (2003) 526 final. See also Geoffrey Edwards account of 'The Pattern of the EU's Global Activity', in Hill, Christopher and Smith, Michael (eds) *International Relations and the European Union* (Oxford: Oxford University Press, 2005). Effective multilateralism, he declares, 'has long been a cornerstone of the EC/EU's external relations' (op. cit., p. 41).
2. The ancient University of Louvain or Leuven was split in 1968 following protests by Dutch-speaking students objecting to the presence of French professors and classes. They managed to break the university up. The central library holdings were divided into two (insofar as they could be) and French speakers founded a new university on a greenfield site at Louvain-la-Neuve in Wallonia. See 'The stateless state: why Belgium matters', in Judt, Tony *Reappraisals: Reflections on the Forgotten Twentieth Century*, pp. 240–1 (New York: Penguin, 2008).
3. Wouters, Jan, Ruys Tom and Hoffmeister, Frank (eds) *The EU and the UN: An Ever Stronger Partnership* (The Hague: T.M.C. Asser Press, 2006).
4. Wouters, Jan *The UN and the EU: Partners in Multilateralism*, an EU Diplomacy Paper (4/2007) produced by the Department of EU International Relations and Diplomacy Studies at the College of Europe, Bruges.
5. Rasch, Maximilian B. *The European Union at the United Nations: The Functioning and Coherence of EU External Representation in a State-Centric Environment* (Leiden: Martinus Nijhoff, 2008).
6. Wouters, Ruys and Hoffmeister, op. cit., p. 14.
7. See Monnet's *Memoirs*, pp. 271–3 (London: Collins, 1978).
8. It is worth examining the relevant European Commission website. See http://ec.europa.eu/education/jean-monnet/doc623_en.htm
9. Regelsberger, E. and de Flers, N.A. 'The EU and Regional Cooperation', in Hill, Christopher and Smith, Michael (eds) *International Relations and the European Union*, p. 324 (Oxford: Oxford University Press, 2005).
10. See Edwards, G. and Regelsberger, E. *Europe's Global Links: The EC and Interregional Cooperation*, p. 13 (New York: St. Martin's Press, 1990).
11. Leonard, Mark *Why Europe will run the 21st Century* (London: Fourth Estate, 2005).
12. Hettne, Björn 'Interregionalism and World Order: The Diverging EU and US models', in Mario Telò (ed.) *European Union and New Regionalism*, p. 107 (Aldershot: Ashgate, 2007).

13. Waltz, K. 'The Emerging Structure of International Politics', *International Security*, vol. 18, no. 2, p. 70.
14. Andeatta, Filippo 'Theory and the European Union's International Relations', Chapter 2 of Hill, Christopher and Smith, Michael (eds) *International Relations and the European Union* (Oxford: Oxford University Press, 2005). The quotation is on p. 25.
15. Hettne, Björn 'Interregionalism and World Order: The Diverging EU and US models', in Mario Telò, op. cit. See the section of the chapter beginning on p. 113 which is entitled 'Interregionalism as world order: Pax Europaea?'.
16. See H. Mahony 'EU of 25 is almost full, says Patten', *EU Observer*, 29th December, 2003.
17. Telò, Mario 'The European Union and the Challenges of the Near Abroad', Chapter 11 of Telò, Mario (ed.) *European Union and New Regionalism* (Aldershot: Ashgate, 2007). The quotation comes from p. 229.
18. 'The EU and the Mediterranean: Open Regionalism or Peripheral Dependence?' Chapter 13 of Telò, op. cit., p. 267.
19. Seidelmann, Reimund 'The EU's neighbourhood policies', in Telò, Mario (ed.) *The European Union and Global Governance*, p. 281, note 10 (London: Routledge, 2009). The footnote modifies considerably the comment in the main text (p. 277) that 'De facto, ENP replaces the old Barcelona Process as well as the past cumulative membership efforts *vis-à-vis* the Central Eastern and South-Eastern European countries.'
20. A case would have to be made on grounds of historical and cultural links to Europe (including those based on former colonial ties with France and Spain). It is arguable that these ties do in certain cases override the 'geographical facts on the ground'. French Guiana and Guadeloupe, as overseas French 'departments', are part of the EU, as are island complexes like the Azores and Madeira (through their connection with Portugal). However, when the connection is less formal, the problems establishing the overriding nature of historical and cultural ties becomes more difficult. It is arguable that in the case of Cyprus such ties meant that there was no serious questioning of its 'European credentials' despite its Eastern location. In this case the geographical considerations occupy the sort of 'grey area' that Turkey occupies, whereas it is clear that the southern seaboard of the Mediterranean is outside anyone's geographical understanding of Europe.
21. See Vasconcelos, 'European Union and MERCOSUR', Chapter 8 of Telò, Mario (ed.) *European Union and New Regionalism* (Aldershot: Ashgate, 2007) where he discussed various types of regionalisation. Vasconcelos admits that 'open regionalism', in his words, 'was – and still is – a vague concept' (p. 165). Unfortunately that is true of a lot of the terms used in this field.
22. Ibid., p. 165.
23. Martinez, Luis 'EU's exportation of democratic norms: the case of North Africa', Chapter 8 of Laidi, Z. (ed.) *EU Foreign Policy in a Globalised World* (London: Routledge, 2008).
24. A study in 2004 had already put illegal migration levels at an annual figure of half a million. See Jandl, M. 'The estimation of illegal migration in Europe', *Migration Studies*, XLI, 153 (March 2004), p. 150.
25. It is true that FDI has fallen during the recession of 2009, but these states would have been affected by worldwide recession in any circumstances.

26. Dallago, Bruno (ed.) *Transformation and European Integration: The Local Dimension* (Basingstoke: Palgrave/Macmillan, 2006).
27. Smith, Karen 'Enlargement and European Order', Chapter 13 of Hill, Christopher and Smith, Michael (eds) *International Relations and the European Union* (Oxford: Oxford University Press, 2005). The quotation is on p. 284.
28. See the 'Analysis' article in the *Financial Times*, Friday, April 3rd, 2009, p. 7.
29. Statement of the European Commission on 'Strengthening the European Neighbourhood Policy', 4th December 2006.
30. Fischer, Sabine (ed.) *Ukraine: Quo vadis?*, Chaillot Paper No. 108 (Paris: Institute for Security Studies). The chapter by Kataryna Wolczuk examines Ukraine's relations with the EU in the context of the European Neighbourhood Policy.
31. 'The New Enhanced Agreement between the Ukraine and the EU: Will it further Democratic consolidation?' by Natalia Shapovalova (Madrid: FRIDE Working Paper No. 62). See www.fride.org.
32. Fischer, Sabine, op. cit., p. 13.
33. See the useful discussion provided by *The Economist* in its special report on the European Union of 17th March 2007 entitled 'Fit at 50?'.
34. Smith, Karen, op. cit., p. 282.
35. Schimmelfennig and Sedelmeier (eds) *The Europeanisation of Central and Eastern Europe* (Ithaca, New York: Cornell University Press, 2005). The term is common in books which approach the EU in terms of social transformation rather than institutions of governance – see Delanty, Gerard and Rumford, Chris *Rethinking Europe: Social Theory and the Implications of Europeanisation* (London: Routledge, 2005) but it is also used by works like Dallago's where the emphasis is very much upon institutional factors. See, for instance, the discussion of 'the Europeanisation of the Balkans' (Dallago, op. cit., p. 206).
36. See the report in the *Financial Times*, Thursday 2nd July 2009, the day that Ivo Sanader resigned, 'Croatian PM quits as bid to join EU stalls'.
37. Rachman, Gideon 'The Death of Enlargement', in Lennon, A.T.J. and Kozlowski, A. (eds) *Global Powers in the 21st Century* (Cambridge, Massachusetts: MIT Press, 2008).

Chapter 9

1. See www.consilium.europa.eu/ueDocs/cms_Data/.../**reports**/104630.pdf.
2. Laatikainen, K. 'Assessing the EU as an actor at the UN: Authority, Cohesion, Recognition and Autonomy', *CFSP Forum*, 2/1, 4–9 The European Foreign Policy Research Unit funded by the European Commission provides the details – see http://www.fornet.info.
3. The assessment of 'dysfunctional multilateralism' between the EU and the UN comes from John van Oudenharen, *Policy Review* No. 117, February 2003. See also Knut Erik Jorgensen's comments which can be found in Laatkainen, K. and Smith, Karen E. (eds) *The EU at the UN: Intersecting Multilateralism*, p. 21 (Basingstoke: Palgrave Macmillan, 2006).
4. *The Guardian*, 29th June 2006.
5. McClintock, John *The Uniting of Nations: An Essay On Global Governance* (Brussels: Peter Lang Press, Brussels, 2009). This is the third edition of the

book, first published in 2007, which updates its approach with specific proposals for a global sharing of sovereignty.
6. Healey, Denis *The Time of my Life*, p. 574 (London: Penguin, 1980).
7. A report in the *Financial Times* of June 12th 2009 declared that 'the cost of commodities such as corn and soyabean has surged this week to levels not seen since late 2007. Wheat and rice prices are not rising as much but remain very high.'
8. 'Funds Crunch Threatens World Food Aid', *Financial Times*, 12th June 2009.
9. See paragraph 36 of the Presidency Conclusions, *European Council* meeting of June 2008.
10. Report by MEP Mairead McGuinness, reference INI/2008/2153. Mairead McGuinness, a member of Ireland's Fine Gael, was re-elected to the European Parlaiament in 2009, where she is a member of the largest party, the EPP (European People's Party).
11. Scholte, Jan Aart *Globalization: A Critical Introduction*, p. 213 (Basingstoke: Macmillan).
12. Vanhoonacker, Sophie 'The Institutional Framework', in Hill, Christopher and Smith, Michael (eds) *International Relations and the European Union*, p. 74 (Oxford: Oxford University Press, 2005).
13. Smith, Michael 'Implementation: Making the EU's International Relations Work', in Hill, Christopher and Smith, Michael (eds) *International Relations and the European Union*, p. 155 (Oxford: Oxford University Press, 2005).
14. Menon, Anand *Europe: The State of the Union*, p. 218 (London: Atlantic Books, 2008).
15. See Keukeleire, S. 'EU Structural Foreign Policy and Structural Conflict Prevention', in Kronenberger, V. and Wouters, J. (eds) *The European Union and Conflict Prevention: Legal and Policy Aspects* (The Hague: T.M.C. Asser, 2004).

Chapter 10

1. Linklater, Andrew 'A European Civilising Process?', in Hill, Christopher and Smith, Michael (eds) *International Relations and the European Union*, p. 370 (Oxford: Oxford University Press, 2005).
2. Ibid., p. 377.
3. Beck, Ulrich *What is Globalization?*, p. 136 (Cambridge: Polity Press, 2000).
4. Kagan, Robert *Paradise and Power: America and Europe in the New World Order*, p. 61 (London: Atlantic Books, 2003).
5. Weiss, Thomas *What's Wrong With the United Nations and How to Fix It* (Cambridge: Polity Press, 2008).
6. Kuhn, Thomas *The Structure of Scientific Revolutions* (Chicago: University of Chicago Press, 1962).
7. Weiss, Thomas G., op. cit., p. 227.
8. Saint-Simon wrote 'The Reorganisation of the European Community' in 1814. It can be found in a collection of his writings by Markham, F.M.H. *Henri Comte de Saint-Simon: Selected Writings* (Oxford: Blackwell, 1952).
9. Elias, Norbert *The Society of Individuals*, p. 164 (London: Continuum Press, 2001).

10. For instance van Apeldoorn, B., Drahokoupil, J. and Horn, L. *Contradictions and Limits of Neoliberal European Governance: From Lisbon to Lisbon* (Basingstoke: Palgrave/Macmillan, 2009).
11. Jay, William *War and Peace: The Evils of the First and a Plan for Preserving the Last*, p. 53 (Oxford: Oxford University Press, 1919). This is the edition by J.B. Scott. Jay's book was originally published in 1842.
12. Schücking, W. *The International Union of the Hague Conferences* (Oxford: Clarendon Press, 1918). This is C.G. Fenwick's translation, published after World War One, but the German original was published before the war in 1912.
13. The opinions of Roosevelt come from the *Memoirs* of Cordell Hull (London: Hodder and Stoughton, 1948). Those of Cecil are from Seymour, E. (ed.) *The Intimate Papers of Colonel House* (London: Ernest Benn, 1926).
14. McDougal, M.S. *Studies in World Public Order* (New Haven: Yale University Press, 1960); Falk, R.A. *Legal Order in a Violent World* (Princeton: Princeton University Press, 1968).
15. Suganami, Hidemi *The Domestic Analogy and World Order Proposals*, p. 96 (Cambridge: Cambridge University Press, 1989).
16. And stayed in when Labour won power in 1974, despite the fact that 'much of the Labour Party still took seriously the old joke that Monnet was the root of all evil.' See Healey, Denis *The Time of My Life*, p. 359 (London: Penguin, 1990).
17. Fukuyama's book was published by the Free Press in 1992; the essay 'The End of History?', in which his main thesis is advanced, was published in 1989 by the international affairs journal *The National Interest*.
18. Kagan, Robert *The Return of History and the End of Dreams* (New York: Alfred A. Knopf, 2008).
19. See the issue of 3rd April 2007.
20. Duchêne, François *Jean Monnet: The First Statesman of Interdependence*, p. 409 (New York: W.W. Norton, 1994).
21. Zielonka, J. *Explaining Euro-paralysis: Why Europe is Unable to Act in International Politics* (Basingstoke: Macmillan, 1998); Zielonka, J. (ed.) *Europe Unbound: Enlarging and Reshaping the Boundaries of the European Union* (London: Routledge, 2002) *Europe as Empire: The Nature of the Enlarged European Union* (Oxford: Oxford University Press, 2006).
22. The European Union produced a White Paper on Governance ('An EU Contribution on Better Governance beyond our Borders') which declared that 'empirical data suggests that when the EU acts on the international stage EU citizens feel the strongest sense of EU identity'. The paper can be read online at: http://ec.europa.eu/governance/areas/group11/report_en.pdf
23. Not all commentators insist that democracy is a 'relative' concept. See Sen, Amartya Kumar *Democracy as a Universal Value*, Journal of Democracy – vol. 10, no. 3, July 1999, pp. 3–17. Sen claims that the rise of democracy is the most important event of the twentieth century.
24. Vanhoonacker, Sophie 'The Institutional Framework' in Hill, Christopher and Smith, Michael (eds) *International Relations and the European Union* (Oxford: Oxford University Press, 2005). The quotation is on p. 74.
25. See Ruland, J. 'ASEAN and the European Union: A Bumpy Interregional Relationship', Discussion Paper C95 produced by the *Bonn Centre for European Integration Studies* in 200121.

Notes   231

26. Menon, Anand *Europe The State of the Union*, p. 33 (London: Atlantic Books, 2008).
27. Wilson, Kevin, Van der Dussen, Jan (eds) *The History of the Idea of Europe*, p. 124 (London: Routledge, 1993).
28. Scholte, Jan Aart *Globalization: A Critical Introduction*, p. 137 (Basingstoke: Macmillan, 2000). See especially Chapter 6, 'Globalization and Governance'.
29. See 'Prospects for a transnational state', part of the chapter 'Contours of World Society', in Ulrich Beck's *What is Globalisation?*, pp. 108–9 (Cambridge: Polity Press, 2000).
30. Quotation from an article by Martin Wolf in *The Financial Times*, 20th May 2009 entitled 'This crisis is a moment, but may not be a defining one'. *The Financial Times*, *The Economist* and *The Guardian* in particular have been running articles throughout 2009 on better ways of organising global institutions.
31. The quotations come from Laidi, Z. (ed.) *EU Foreign Policy in a Globalised World* (London: Routledge, 2008). Europe as 'normative basis of global governance' is on p. 5, while the idea of the EU as a 'provincial norm-setter' is from K. Postel-Vincy's contribution on 'The Historicity of European normative power', p. 44 of the book.

References

Acharya A. and Johnston, Alastair I. (eds) *Crafting Cooperation: Regional International Institutions in Comparative Perspective* (Cambridge: Cambridge University Press, 2007).
Alston, P. (ed.) *The United Nations and Human Rights: A Critical Appraisal* (Oxford: Clarendon Press, 1992).
Annan, Kofi *We the Peoples: The Role of the United Nations in the 21st Century* (New York: United Nations, Department of Public Information, 2000).
van Apeldoorn, B., Drahokoupil, J. and Horn, L. *Contradictions and Limits of Neoliberal European Governance: From Lisbon to Lisbon* (Basingstoke: Palgrave Macmillan, 2009).
Asmus, Ronald D. *Opening NATO's Door: How the Alliance Remade Itself for a New Era* (New York: Columbia University Press, 2002).
Baker, Andrew *The Group of Seven: Global Financial Governance* (London: Routledge, 2006).
Balladur, Eduard *Pour une Union Occidentale entre l'Europe et les Etats-Unis* (Paris: Fayard, 2007); ET *For a Union of the West* (Stanford: Hoover Institution Press, 2009).
Beck, Ulrich *What is Globalisation?* (Cambridge: Polity Press, 2000).
Beitz, C. *Political Theory and International Relations* (Princeton: Princeton University Press, 1979).
Berkman, Steve *The World Bank and the Gods of Lending* (Sterling, Virginia: Kumarian Press, 2008).
Blair, A. *The European Union since 1945* (Harlow: Pearson Education Limited, 2005).
Brierly, J.L. *The Outlook for International Law* (Oxford: Clarendon Press, 1944).
Brown, Chris *Understanding International Relations* (London: Macmillan, 1997).
Bull, H. *The Anarchical Society* (London: Macmillan, 1977).
Bullock, Alan *Ernest Bevin, Foreign Secretary* (London: Heinemann, 1983).
Clark, G. and Sohn, L.B. *World Peace through World Law*, 3rd edition (Cambridge Massachusetts: Harvard University Press, 1966).
Cooper, Robert *The Postmodern State and the World Order* (London: Demos, 2000).
—— *The Breaking of Nations* (New York: Atlantic Monthly Press, 2003).
Dallago, Bruno (ed.) *Transformation and European Integration: The Local Dimension* (Basingstoke: Palgrave Macmillan, 2006).
Davies, Norman *Europe: A History* (London: Pimlico, 1997).
Delanty, Gerard and Rumford, Chris *Rethinking Europe: Social Theory and the Implications of Europeanisation* (London: Routledge, 2005).
Dinan, Desmond *Europe Recast: A History of European Union* (Basingstoke: Palgrave Macmillan, 2004).
—— (ed.) *Origins and Evolution of the European Union* (Oxford: Oxford University Press, 2006).

Duchêne, François *Jean Monnet: The First Statesman of Interdependence* (New York: W.W. Norton, 1994).
Edwards, G. and Regelsberger, E. *Europe's Global Links: The EC and Inter-regional Cooperation* (New York: St. Martin's Press, 1990).
Elias, Norbert *The Civilising Process* (Oxford: Blackwell, 2000 – revised edition).
—— *The Society of Individuals* (London: Continuum Press, 2001).
Falk, R.A. *Legal Order in a Violent World* (Princeton: Princeton University Press, 1968).
Fischer, Sabine (ed.) *Ukraine: Quo vadis?*, Chaillot Paper No. 108 (Paris: Institute for Security Studies).
Giddes, Anthony *Europe in the Global Age* (Cambridge: Polity Press, 2006).
Gilmour, Ian *Dancing with Dogma: Britain under Thatcherism* (London: Simon and Schuster, 1992).
Gray, Christine *International Law and the Use of Force* (Oxford: Oxford University Press, 2004).
Greer, T. *What Roosevelt Thought: The Social and Political Ideas of Frankin D. Roosevelt* (Michigan: Michigan State University Press, 1965).
Grotius, Hugo *De jure belli et pacis* translated F.W. Kelsey (Oxford: Clarendon Press, 1925).
Habermas, Jürgen *The Inclusion of the Other: Studies in Political Theory* (Cambridge: Polity Press, 1999).
Healey, Denis *The Time of my Life* (London: Penguin, 1990).
Hill, Christopher and Smith, Michael (eds) *International Relations and the European Union* (Oxford: Oxford University Press, 2005).
Hobbes, Thomas *Leviathan* edited by J. Plamenatz (London: Collins, 1962).
Hobsbawm, E.J. *Nations and Nationalism since 1780* (Cambridge: Cambridge University Press, 1990).
—— (ed.) *The Invention of Tradition* (Cambridge: Cambridge University Press, 1992).
—— *The Age of Empire* (London: Abacus, 1994).
Hodges, Michael (ed.) *European Integration* (London: Penguin, 1972).
Howorth, J. *European Integration and Defence: The Ultimate Challenge?* Chaillot Paper No. 43 (Paris: Institute for Security Studies, 2000).
Hughes, E.J. and Reynolds, P.A. *The Historian as Diplomat. Charles Kingsley Webster and the United Nations* (London: Martin Robertson, 1976).
Hull, Cordell *Memoirs* (London: Hodder and Stoughton, 1948).
Huntley, James R. *Uniting the Democracies: Institutions of the Emerging Atlantic–Pacific System* (New York: New York University Press, 1980).
Jay, William *War and Peace: The Evils of the First and a Plan for Preserving the Last* (Oxford: Oxford University Press, 1919).
Johnston, Alastair I. and Acharya, A. (eds) *Crafting Cooperation: Regional International Institutions in Comparative Perspective* (Cambridge: Cambridge University Press, 2007).
Jones, R.J.B. *The World Turned Upside Down: Globalisation and the Future of the State* (Manchester: Manchester University Press, 2000).
Jouve, E. *Le Général de Gaulle et la Construction de l'Europe* (Paris: Librairie général de droit et de jurisprudence, 1967).
Joyner, C.C. and Schachter, O. (eds) *United Nations Legal Order* (Cambridge: Cambridge University Press, 1996).

Judt, Tony *Postwar: A History of Europe since 1945* (London: Penguin, 2006).
—— *Reappraisals: Reflections on the Forgotten Twentieth Century* (New York: Penguin, 2008).
Kagan, Robert *Paradise and Power: America and Europe in the New World Order* (London: Atlantic Books, 2003).
—— *The Return of History and the End of Dreams* (New York: Random House, 2008).
Kant, I. *Toward Perpetual Peace and other Writings on Politics, Peace and History*, Pauline Kleingeld (ed.) (Yale University Press, 2006).
Klein, Naomi *The Shock Doctrine* (London: Penguin, 2007).
Kothari, Rajni *Footsteps into the Future: Diagnosis of the Present World and a Design for an Alternative* (Amsterdam: North Holland Press, 1974).
Kronenberger, V. and Wouters, J. (eds) *The European Union and Conflict Prevention: Legal and Policy Aspects* (The Hague: T.M.C. Asser, 2004).
Kuhn, Thomas *The Structure of Scientific Revolutions* (Chicago: University of Chicago Press, 1962).
Laatkainen, K. and Smith, Karen E. (eds) *The EU at the UN: Intersecting Multilateralism* (Basingstoke: Palgrave Macmillan, 2006).
Laidi, Z. (ed.) *EU Foreign Policy in a Globalised World* (London: Routledge, 2008).
Lennon, A.T.J. and Kozlowski, A. (eds) *Global Powers in the 21st Century* (Cambridge, Massachusetts: MIT Press, 2008).
Leonard, Mark *Why Europe Will Run the 21st Century* (London: Fourth Estate, 2005).
Lister, Frederick, K. *The European Union, the United Nations, and the Revival of Confederal Governance* (Westport: Greenwood Press, 1996).
Luard, Evan *A History of the United Nations*, vol. 1 (London: Macmillan, 1982).
McBride, Stephen and Mahon, Rianne (eds) *The OECD and Transnational Governance* (Seattle: University of Washington Press, 2008).
McClintock, John *The Uniting of Nations: An Essay On Global Governance* (Brussels: Peter Lang Press, 3rd edition, 2009).
McDougal, M.S. *Studies in World Public Order* (New Haven: Yale University Press, 1960).
Mahon, Rianne and McBride, Stephen (eds) *The OECD and Transnational Governance* (Seattle: University of Washington Press, 2008).
Markham, F.M.H. *Henri Comte de Saint-Simon: Selected Writings* (Oxford: Blackwell, 1952).
May, Alex *Britain and Europe since 1945* (Harlow: Longman, 1999).
May, Larry *Crimes Against Humanity: A Normative Account* (Cambridge: Cambridge University Press, 2005).
Mazrui, A. *A World Federation of Cultures: An African Perspective* (New York: The Free Press, 1976).
Menon, Anand *Europe: The State of the Union* (London: Atlantic Books, 2008).
Milward, Alan *The Reconstruction of Western Europe 1945–51* (London: Methuen, 1984).
—— *The European Rescue of the Nation State* (London: Routledge, 1992).
Monnet, Jean *Memoirs*, translated by R. Mayne (London: Collins, 1978).
Moore, David *The World Bank: Development, Poverty, Hegemony* (Southville, South Africa: University of Kwazulu-Natal Press, 2007).
Moravcsik, A. *The Choice for Europe: Social Purpose and State Power from Messina to Maastricht* (Ithaca, New York: Cornell University Press, 1998).

Murray, Philomena (ed.) *Europe and Asia: Regions in Flux* (Basingstoke: Palgrave Macmillan, 2008).
Nugent, Neill *The Government and Politics of the European Union* (Basingstoke: Palgrave Macmillan, 6th edition, 2006).
Ortega, Martin *Building the Future: The EU's Contribution to Global Governance*, Chaillot Paper No. 100 (Paris: Institute for Security Studies, 2007).
Osborne, John *Luther* (London: Methuen, 1971).
Padoa-Schioppa, T. (ed.) *Efficiency, Stability and Equity: A Strategy for the Evolution of the Economic System of the European Community* (Oxford: Oxford University Press, 1987).
Peterson, John and Shackleton, Michael (eds) *The Institutions of the European Union* (Oxford: Oxford University Press, 2002).
Peyrefitte, A. *C'était de Gaulle*, 3 vols. (Paris: Fayard, 1994, 1997, 2000).
Phillips, W.A. *The Confederation of Europe* (New York: Fertig, 1966).
Ranger, T. and Hobsbawm, E. (eds) *The Invention of Tradition* (Cambridge: Cambridge University Press, 1992).
Rasch, Maximilian B. *The European Union at the United Nations: The Functioning and Coherence of EU External Representation in a State-Centric Environment* (Leiden: Martinus Nijhoff, 2008).
Regelsberger, E. and Edwards, G. *Europe's Global Links: The EC and Inter-regional Cooperation* (New York: St. Martin's Press, 1990).
Reynolds, P.A. and Hughes, E.J. *The Historian as Diplomat: Charles Kingsley Webster and the United Nations* (London: Martin Robertson, 1976).
Rumford, Chris and Delanty, Gerard *Rethinking Europe: Social Theory and the Implications of Europeanisation* (London: Routledge, 2005).
Sampson, Gary P. *The WTO and Global Governance: Future Directions* (Tokyo: United Nations University, 2008).
Mahon, Rianne and McBride, Stephen (eds) *The OECD and Transnational Governance* (Seattle: University of Washington Press, 2008).
Schachter, O. and Joyner, C.C. (eds) *United Nations Legal Order* (Cambridge: Cambridge University Press, 1996).
Schiffer, W. *The Legal Community of Mankind* (New York: Columbia University Press, 1954).
Schimmelfennig, F. and Sedelmeier (eds) *The Europeanisation of Central and Eastern Europe* (Ithaca, New York: Cornell University Press, 2005).
Schlesinger, S.C. *Act of Creation: The Founding of the United Nations* (Boulder, Colorado: Westview Press, 2003).
Scholte, Jan Aart *Globalization: A Critical Introduction* (Basingstoke: Macmillan, 2000).
Schücking, W. *The International Union of the Hague Conferences* (Oxford: Clarendon Press, 1918).
Schuman, F.L. *The Commonwealth of Man: An Inquiry into Power Politics and World Government* (London: Robert Hale, 1954).
Seymour, E. (ed.) *The Intimate Papers of Colonel House* (London: Ernest Benn, 1926).
Shackleton, Michael and Peterson, John (eds) *The Institutions of the European Union* (Oxford: Oxford University Press, 2002).
Shapovalova, Natalia *The New Enhanced Agreement between the Ukraine and the EU: Will it Further Democratic Consolidation?* (Madrid: FRIDE Working Paper No. 62; www.fride.org).

Singer, Roger *One World: The Ethics of Globalisation* (New Haven, Connecticut: Yale University Press, 2004).
Slaughter, Anne-Marie *A New World Order* (Princeton: Princeton University Press, 2004).
Smith, Karen E. and Laatkainen, K. (eds) *The EU at the UN: Intersecting Multilateralism* (Basingstoke: Palgrave Macmillan, 2006).
Smith, Michael and Hill, Christopher (eds) *International Relations and the European Union* (Oxford: Oxford University Press, 2005).
Sohn, L.B. and Clark, G. *World Peace through World Law* 3rd edition (Cambridge Massachusetts: Harvard University Press, 1966).
Stiglitz, Joseph *Globalisation and its Discontents* (New York: W.W. Norton, 2002).
Stirk, P.M.R. and Willis, D. (eds) *Shaping Postwar Europe: European Unity and Diversity 1945–57* (London: Pinter, 1991).
Suganami, Hidemi *The Domestic Analogy and World Order Proposals* (Cambridge: Cambridge University Press, 1989).
Taylor, A.J.P. *The Struggle for Mastery in Europe 1848–1918* (Oxford: Clarendon Press, 1971).
Taylor, P. *International Organisations in the Modern World* (London: Pinter, 1993).
Telò, M. (ed.) *European Union and New Regionalism* (Aldershot: Ashgate, 2007).
—— (ed.) *The European Union and Global Governance* (London: Routledge, 2009).
Thakur, R. and Thomas G. Weiss (eds) *The UN and Global Governance: An Idea and its Prospects* (Tokyo: United Nations University Press, 2007).
Thatcher, Margaret *The Downing Street Years* (London: HarperCollins, 1993).
Thomson, David *England in the Nineteenth Century* (London: Penguin, 1991).
Weiss, Thomas and Thakur, R. (eds) *The UN and Global Governance: An Idea and its Prospects* (Tokyo: United Nations University Press, 2007).
Weiss, Thomas *What's Wrong With the United Nations and How to Fix It* (Cambridge: Polity Press, 2008).
White, Nigel D. *The United Nations System: Toward International Justice* (London: Lynne Rienner, 2002).
Willis, D. and Stirk, P.M.R. (eds) *Shaping Postwar Europe: European Unity and Diversity 1945–57* (London: Pinter, 1991).
Wilson, Kevin, Van der Dussen, Jan (eds) *The History of the Idea of Europe* (London: Routledge, 1993).
Woolf, Leonard *The War for Peace* (London: Routledge, 1940).
Wouters, Jan, Ruys Tom and Hoffmeister, Frank (eds) *The EU and the UN: An Ever Stronger Partnership* (The Hague: T.M.C. Asser Press, 2006).
Wouters, Jan *The UN and the EU: Partners in Multilateralism* (Bruges: EU Diplomacy Paper 4, 2007).
Young, Hugo *This Blessed Plot: Britain and Europe from Churchill to Blair* (Woodstock: Overlook Press, 1999).
Zielonka, J. *Explaining Euro-paralysis: Why Europe is Unable to Act in International Politics* (Basingstoke: Macmillan, 1998).
—— (ed.) *Europe Unbound: Enlarging and Reshaping the Boundaries of the European Union* (London: Routledge, 2002).
—— *Europe as Empire: The Nature of the Enlarged European Union* (Oxford: Oxford University Press, 2006).

Index

Acharya, Amitav 134
acquis atlantique 123–4
acquis communautaire 72, 124, 147, 160, 164, 166, 171, 191, 199, 210
  and African Union 135
  and UNASUR 146
Adenauer, Konrad (German Chancellor) 53
Afghanistan
  intervention in 92, 117–18
African, Caribbean and Pacific (ACP) countries
  'strategic partnership' with EU 154
  see also Cotonou Agreement; Lomé Convention
African Regional Bodies 130
African Union (AU) 9, 130–6, 155, 204
  administrative weaknesses 134–5
  and Arab League 139, 147
  colonial past 133–4
  and EU 131–2, 135, 147–8, 154–5
  and UNASUR 145
Allende, Salvador (Chilean President) 143
al-Qaeda 92
Andean Community 144–5, 147
  and EU 145
Andreatta, Filippo 156, 216
Anglicanism 18
Annan, Kofi (UN Secretary-General) 81, 91, 93, 224
Arab League 139, 146–7
  and African Union 139, 147
  Charter 146
Argentine
  and Brazil 143–4
  military government of 143
Arnesen, Catherine B. 137
Arroyo, Gloria (President of Philippines) 148, 225
Asia-Europe Meeting (ASEM) 138

Asia-Pacific Economic Cooperation (APEC) 123, 127, 137
  and Japan 137
  and US 137
Asian Free Trade Association (AFTA) 136, 138–9
Association of South-East Asian Nations (ASEAN) 9, 123, 130, 136–41, 146–8, 212
  ASEAN + 3 137
  ASEAN Charter 140–1
  ASEAN Free Trade Area 136
  ASEAN Regional Forum 137
  ASEAN and EU 136–7, 139–41, 155, 210
  'informal' integration approach 137–9, 141, 146
  ASEAN and US 138
  ASEAN and UN 140
Atlanticism 123
Attlee, Clement (British Prime Minister) 41
Augsburg, Peace of (1555) 17, 32
Austria
  and the Far Right 162

Baker, Andrew 103, 105, 112–13
Balance of power 125
Balkans, war in 132
Balkan states and the EU 135, 147, 157, 161–5, 171
Balladur, Eduard (French Prime Minister) 102, 122, 124, 129, 223–4
Baltic states
  and NATO 117
Bandeira, Moniz 146
Barcelona process 157, 159–60
Barnett, Michael 146
Basle Committee on Banking Supervision 126
Batista, Fulgencio (President of Cuba) 142

Beck, Ulrich   195, 212–13
Beitz, Charles   124
Belarus
   and EU membership   165
Belgium
   divisions   226
Benelux
   from customs union to EEC   46
Bevin, Ernest (British Foreign
      Secretary)   37, 41
Beyen, Johan Willem (Dutch Minister
      for Foreign Affairs)   46
Bidault, George   44
Bigman, Nicholas   166
Bilateral trade deals   138, 144,
   146, 159
Black, Conrad   219
Blair, Alasdair   218
Bolivar, Simon   142
   and Bolivia   142
   and a United States of South
      America   142
Bonino, Emma   215–16
Brazil
   and Argentine   143–4
   part of G20   101
   relations with MERCOSUR and
      UNASUR   145
   military government   143
   independence from Portugal   141
   dispute with US at WTO   108
Bretherton, Russell   47
Bretton Woods Agreement   103,
   105–7, 112
Briand, Aristide (French Prime
      Minister)   5
Brierly, J.L.   98
Britain
   and the Commonwealth   114–16
   and the Congress system   22
   and the EEC   44, 48–50, 60, 66,
      198, 230
   and EU enlargement   123
   and the European Coal and Steel
      Community   40–2
   and European Free Trade Area
      (EFTA)   48–9, 136
   and European Regional
      Development Fund   65–7, 71
   and German recovery after
      World War II   37–8
   and a Global Union   208
   and the League of Nations   80
   and the Messina Conference   47
   and migration   221
   and monarchy   25–6
   and sharing sovereignty   6–7,
      40–2, 45, 172, 198
   and the single currency   70
   and the Single European Act   67–9
   and structural funds   70
   and Thatcherism   62, 68, 220
British Commonwealth *see*
   Commonwealth
Brown, Chris   125
Brussels, Treaty of   44
Bulgaria
   admitted to EU   147, 162

Cajetan, Cardinal   17–18
Canada
   relations with the Commonwealth
      and the IFO   116
   as member of EU   176
   as member of Global Union   178
Canning, George   22
Čapek, Karel   212
Cardoso, Fernando Henrique
      (President of Brazil)   144
Cassis de Dijon   57
Castro, Fidel (President of
      Cuba)   142
Catholicism   20–1
Cavell, Edith   2–4
Cecil, Robert   202
Charles I (King of England)   18
Chavez, Hugo (President of
      Venezuela)   143, 145
Che Guevara   143
Cheysson, Claude (French Foreign
      Minister)   155
Chicago School of Economics   86
Chile
   and Global Union   178
   and MERCOSUR   144
China
   and ASEAN   136
   and Global Union   100, 198

and IMF 104
and International Criminal Court 90
and Southern Mediterranean 160
Christendom 17–19, 169
Churchill, Winston (British Prime Minister) 34, 41, 44
Clark, Grenville 28
Climate change 100, 188, 213
Cohesion policy 61, 67–71
  and structural funds 164, 167, 171, 184, 199
Cold War 28, 38, 82, 118, 121, 133, 205–6
  and Helsinki Process 121
Colonialism 190–1, 212
  and African Union 133–4
  and South America 141–3
  and Southern Mediterranean 159
Common Agricultural Policy (CAP) 51, 59–60, 63–4, 166, 171, 184–5, 208, 220
  background to 62–3, 185, 220
Common Foreign and Security Policy 162–3, 173
Common Market *see* European Economic Community
Commonwealth, British 49, 102, 114–16, 128
Community Assistance for Reconstruction, Development and Stabilisation (CARDS) 163
'concentric circles' approach 158, 170
Concert of Democracies 2, 215
Concert of Powers
  compared to UN 98
Confederation, idea of 4
Conference on Security and Cooperation in Europe (CSCE) 121
Congress system 21–2, 196, 202
Cooper, Robert 93
Copenhagen criteria 71, 118, 120, 157, 160, 163, 165, 169, 176, 210–11
Copernican Revolution of the EU, Chapter 10, passim
Costa v. ENEL 56

Cotonou Agreement 190–1, 210
Council of Europe x, 5, 7, 36–7, 39, 42, 51, 78, 99, 154, 208
Court of International Justice (after World War One) 28, 202
'credit crisis' 103, 111–13, 126, 128, 220
  need for new institutions to deal with it 111–13
Crimean War 22
Cromwell, Oliver (Lord Protector of England) 3, 19
Cultural relativism 209–11, 230
Cyprus
  unification of 169–70
Czech Republic
  and Copenhagen criteria 90
  and NATO 117

Dallago, Bruno 161
Darwin, Charles 22, 63
D'Azeglio, Massimo (Italian statesman) 24
Da Silva, Luiz (President of Brazil) 145–6, 148
De Gaulle, Charles (French President) 7, 38, 44–6, 50–4, 59–60, 109, 123, 198
  Gaullism 123, 223–4
De Gucht, Karel (Belgian Foreign Minister) 117, 119–20
Delors, Jacques (President of the European Commission) 68–70, 218, 221
Depression, Great 213
D'Estaing, Giscard (French President) 112
'dialogue commitments' 138, 155, 198
Dinan, Desmond 218
Dinh, Luong 139, 148
Disraeli, Benjamin (British Prime Minister) 25
Doha Development Round *see* World Trade Organisation (WTO)
Domestic analogy 3–4, 6, 7, 20–1, 28, 33, 197–8, 200, 202–3, 205, 215
Duchêne, François 33, 206

East Asian Economic Group   137
Eccles, David   49
Eden, Anthony (British Prime Minister)   44, 49
Elias, Norbert   x, 29–32, 195, 197
Eliassen, Kjell A.   137
Empty Chair Crisis   51, 60
Erdogan, Recep   169
Europe
  in the nineteenth century   21–3
  in the seventeenth century   18
  at war   4–5
EU (European Union)
  Basic structure and development
    cohesion policy   61, 67–71
    enlargement of   66–72, 157, 168, 192, 194, 199
    formation and nature of   5–7, 38, 54–9, 208
    later development of   65–73
    own resources   59–61, 173
    regional development   65–7
    sharing sovereignty   7, 13–14, 33, 53, 171–2, 189–94
    structural funds   164, 167, 171, 184, 199
    supporting vulnerable economic sectors   62–5
  As model for global governance
    EU agencies compared to UN 'agencies'   87–8
    model for a Global Union   73, 148, 156, 189–94, 198
    one of several 'Great Powers'   156
    model for other regional unions   147–8
    reluctance to believe in its own form of government   13–14, 155–6, 175–6, 189, 192, 200, 205–7, 214
    EU resources compared to UN resources   94–5, 173
    tensions from the beginning   48
    uniqueness of   148, 156, 177, 192
    and a world state   13, 200
  Policy areas
    bilateral trade deals   159
    development aid   190–1
    foreign policy   9–10
    military resources   173–4
    approach to its 'near abroad'   9, 102, 157–61, 170, 192, 194, 199, 227
  Relation to other bodies
    African Union   131–2
    ASEAN   136–7
    Council of Europe   78
    double representation on global bodies   113
    MERCOSUR and UNASUR   143–6
    NATO   120
    UN   x, 83–4, 95, 98–9, 151–4, 174–5
    Union of the West   123–4
    WTO   179
  Terminology
    'concentric circles'   158, 170
    'dialogue commitments'   155
    'inter-regionalism'   155–6, 171
    'multilateralism'   152, 156–7, 171, 174–5
    'privileged partnership'   170, 190–1
    'ring of friends'   157
    'strategic partnership'   9, 154–6, 158, 171
    'variable geometry'   124, 158
    'vertical government networks'   127
European Aeronautic, Space and Defence Company (EADS)   174
European Atomic Energy Agency (EURATOM)   46–7
European Coal and Steel Community (ECSC)   6–7, 10, 12, 35, 38, 43, 46–7, 55, 78, 96, 133, 143, 177, 187, 193, 199, 211, 220
  and Franco-German engine of EU   133
  and MERCOSUR   143
European Commission   35, 39, 166–7, 187
  compared to African Union Commission   131

European Community Humanitarian Office (ECHO) 191
European Community Law 7, 13, 35, 54–9, 199
  compared to Andean Community 145
  compared to ASEAN 140
  compared to Global Union 184, 188
  and national law 56–7, 220
  sanctions to enforce 57–8
  compared to UN 98
European Council of Ministers 35, 57, 186
  compared to Assembly of the African Union 131
European Court of Human Rights 36
European Court of Justice 35, 55–7
  compared to African Court of Justice 132
  compared to International Court of Justice 83
  Court of First Instance 55
European Defence Community (EDC) 43–5, 50
European Economic Community (EEC) 7–8, 12, 47–51, 56, 123
European Free Trade Association (EFTA) 7, 48–9
  compared to Asean Free Trade Area (AFTA) 136, 139
European Integration 39, 58
European Investment Bank 164
European Law *see* European Community Law
European Monetary Union (EMU) *see* Single Currency
European Neighbourhood Policy (ENP) 157, 166–8, 227
European Parliament 35, 86, 186
  compared to pan-African Parliament 131–2
European Regional Development Fund 65–7
European Security Strategy 14
European Security and Defence Policy 174

European values 5, 168, 176, 209, 211
'Europeanisation' 228

Falk, Richard 203
Federation 4–5
Federalism *see* Federation
Ferrero-Waldner, Benito (EU External Affairs Commissioner) 153
Ferry, Jean-Marc 217
Financial Crimes Enforcement Network (FINCEN) 126
First World War 2, 5, 13, 22, 27–8, 33, 37, 201–2
Fontainebleau Summit 60, 67
Food security 10
Fouchet Plan 51
France
  Attitude towards sharing of sovereignty 6–7, 35–6, 42–5, 172, 198
  and Bastille Day 25
  and the CAP (Common Agricultural Policy) 63
  and the EDC (European Defence Community) 43–5, 211
  fined by the European Court of Justice 58
  and German recovery after WWII 34, 37–8
  and the International Francophone Association (IFO) 115–16
  and the League of Nations 80
  efforts to promote a Mediterranean Union 157
  meeting of G6 at Rambouillet 112
  and the Suez Crisis 47
  and the Treaties of Rome 46–7, 50–2
Freud, Sigmund 29
Friedman, Milton 86, 103–4
Fukuyama, Francis 7, 57, 205–6, 215, 220
'functionalism' 10–12, 39, 65, 177, 200, 205

G7 (Group of 7 nations) 101, 111–13, 125–6

G8 (Group of 8 nations) 101, 111–12, 125, 215–16
  and food security 182, 185, 193
G20 (Group of 20 nations) 101, 111–14
G200 (Group of 200 nations) 101, 112, 114
Gaddafi, Muammar (President of Libya) 133
Gaitskell, Hugh (leader of British Labour Party) 50
Galileo Galilei 19
Garton Ash, Timothy 14, 176, 211
General Agreement on Tariffs and Trade (GATT) 106–7
Geneva Convention 22
Genscher, Hans-Dietrich, (German foreign minister) 155
George IV, (British monarch) 25
Germany
  Africa has no 'German' problem 133
  and the *Cassis de Dijon* case 57
  finds money for Jacques Delors' plans 68–70
  managing German recovery after WWII 37–8, 132, 211
  and NATO 117
  and the Treaties of Rome 46–7, 63
  Weimar Germany 85–6
Giddes, Anthony 98
Gillingham, John 39
Gilmour, Ian 220
Gladstone, William (British Prime Minister) 26
Global Competition Network 127
Global Food Security Programme 181–6, 191, 213
Global Union x, 7, 53–4, 73, 113, 151, 172, 176–94, 196–214
  basic structure
    binding laws 58–9, 72, 178–9
    enlargement of 187
    EU a single member of 9, 113, 177, 189–92
    need to start small 204
    own resources 61–2, 184, 188
    support for vulnerable economic sectors 65, 72, 184
  relation to other bodies
    European Coal and Steel Community (ECSC) 59, 96, 184
    EU enlargement 192
    regional unions 178, 180
    the UN 96, 100
  tasks of
    food security 10, 59, 62, 65, 96, 181–7
    need for a Copernican Revolution 196–214
Globalisation 8, 102–3, 113, 124, 128, 212, 224
González, Felipe 70
Governance, Global
  definition of 10–11
  'effective multilateralism' and 151–5
  and a Global Union x, 99–100, 180, 198, 205, 207
  and globalisation 8, 102, 124, 128
  'Governance' and 'Government' 10, 125
  Models for 1, 8–9, Chapter Six passim, 202
    EU as model for 53, 189–94
    UN as model for x, 99–100
  see also Sovereignty, Sharing
Grand Colombia 142
Gray, Professor Christine 93, 222
Great Power rivalry, danger of 156, 206
Greece
  fined by the European Court of Justice 58
  measures to help it adjust to single market 68–9
Greenland
  left EU 176
Greer, Thomas 97
Gromyko, Andrei (Soviet Foreign Minister) 203
Grotius, Hugo 20
Guatemala
  reform movement in 142

Gurria, Angel (Director-General of OECD) 111
Guzman, Andrew 107–9

Haas, Ernst 12
Habermas, Jürgen 215
Hague Peace Conferences 22, 202
Hague Congress (1948) 39
Hague, William 115
Hallstein, Walther (President of European Commission) 51, 59–60
Hardy, Thomas 26
Hayek, von Friedrich 86
Healey, Denis (British Chancellor of the Exchequer) 178, 230
Henry VII, (King of England) 202
Herbst, Jeffrey 134
Herriot, Edouard (French Prime Minister) 6
Hettne, Björn 155–6
Higgott, Richard 137–8
High Authority 35, 39–40
Hobbes, Thomas 2, 18–21, 27–9, 109, 124, 198, 215
Hobsbawm, Eric 23, 142–3
Hoffmeister, Frank 152–4
Howorth, Jolyon 13
Hungary
  joins NATO 117
Huntley, James R. 122
Hwee, Yeo Lay 138

Iceland
  applying to EU 176, 199
Imperialism 26, 142–3, 159, 209
India
  part of G20 101
  and OECD and 110
Innocent X, Pope 17
'institutionalist' approach 157
inter-governmentalism 11–12, 36, 200
  absence of binding law from 54–9
  and Britain 52
  and the Council of Europe 37
  and the EU 200
  and France 51
  and NATO 119–20

compared to supranationalism 11, 13, 35–6, 48, 55–6, 125, 200
  and the UN 83
inter-regionalism 155–6
International Bank for Reconstruction and Development (IBRD) 105–6
International Court of Justice
  see United Nations
International Criminal Court 90–1, 98
International Criminal Tribunals
  see UN
International Development Association 105
International Francophone Association (IFO) 114–16, 128
International Fund for Agriculture Development (IFAD) 94
International Labour Organisation (ILO) 111
International Law 3–4, 20–1, 28, 31, 202
  and the ASEAN Charter 140
  and European Community Law 56
  and the International Court of Justice 88
  and the UN 89, 92–4, 97–8
International Monetary Fund (IMF) 1, 85–7, 91, 101–7, 109–10, 113, 126, 128, 152, 155, 159, 222
  relationship to UN 84–5, 99, 103, 105
International Trade Organisation (ITO) 107
Iran
  and Arab League 146
Iraq
  intervention in during the 1990s 96
  intervention in after 2003 127
Ireland
  and structural funds 71–2
Israel
  and OECD 111
  relationship to UN 82–3

Italy
  and the *Costa v. ENEL* case 56
  and Italian 24–5
  attempt to regulate pasta products 57
  unification of 24

Japan
  and Asia-Pacific Economic Cooperation (APEC) 137
Jay, William 201
Jenkins, Roy (European Commission President) 215
Joffe, George H. 157
Johnston, Alastair I 134
Jorgensen, Knud E. 175
Jouve, E 51, 219
Judt, Tony 41, 215, 220
Just war 21

Kagan, Robert 2, 195, 206, 215
Kant, Immanuel 3–4, 11, 203, 215
Kennedy, John (US President) 50
Keukeleire, Stephan 194
Keynes, John Maynard 85–7, 103
  Keynesianism 85–6, 103
Khong, Foong 138
Ki-Moon, Ban (UN Secretary-General) 182
Klein, Naomi 221–2
Kohl, Helmut, (German Chancellor) 68, 70
Korean War 43–4, 117
Kosovo,
  1999 intervention in 91
Kothari, Rajni 98
Kuchma, Leonid (President of Ukraine) 168
Kuhn, Thomas 196
Kuijper, Pieter-Jan 153–4

Lauterpacht, Hersch 203
Lavrov, Sergei, (Russian Foreign Minister) 165
Law of the seas 21
  Law of the Sea Convention 1982 89

League of Democracies 1–2, 102, 122
  compared to 'democracy caucus' at UN 122
League to Enforce Peace 28, 202
League of Nations 28, 79, 202–3, 221
  compared to UN 79–80, 88–9
Lennon, John 198
Leonard, Mark 93, 155
'liberal intergovernmentalism' 13
'liberalism' 11
Lindberg, Leon 12
Linklater, Andrew 195
Lippmann, Walter 118
Lisbon, Treaty of 14, 72, 165, 194, 200
Lister, Frederick 78, 83, 221
Lockerbie Case 88–9
Lomé Convention 190, 210
Luard, Evan 84, 92
Ludlow, F.P. 220
Luther, Martin 17–18
Luxembourg Compromise 51

McCain, John (US Senator) 1–2, 102, 122, 129
McClintock, John x, 9–10, 59, 62, 176–88, 193–4, 212, 214
Maastricht, Treaty of 48, 57, 70, 146
Macmillan, Harold (British Prime Minister) 49–50, 198
Major, John (British Prime Minister) 70
Manning, C.A.W. 203
Marshall Plan 41, 109
Martin, Stephen 218
Martinez, Luis 159
Mauriac, François 38
Maxwell, Robert 166
May, Alex 21, 37
Mayall, James 134
Mazrui, A. 98
McDougal, Myres 203
Mediterranean Union 157
Menon, Anand 7, 9, 192, 215–16
MERCOSUR (South American Common Market) 9, 130, 141–7
  compared to EU 144
  origins compared to ECSC 143

response to attempted coup in Paraguay   143
'strategic partnership' with EU   154–5
Merkel, Angela (German Chancellor)   111, 170
Messina Conference   46–7
Milward, Alan   12, 43, 218
Mitterand, François (French President)   69
Monarchy, as institution   25
Monnet, Jean   x, 5–6 , 33–4, 39, 45–6, 49, 154, 198, 205, 208, 214–15
  heirs to Jean Monnet   154
Monostatism   19
Monroe Doctrine   142
Moravcsik, Andrew   13, 216
Morocco
  applies to join European Community   158, 227
Morrison, Herbert (British Deputy Prime Minister)   40
'multilateralism'   14, 100, 151–4, 156–7, 180, 226, 228
'multipolarity'   11, 178
Murdoch, Rupert   219
Mutual recognition, principle of   57

Napoleon   44, 196
  Napoleonic Wars   21, 196
Nation *see* nation-state
Nation-state   Chapter Two, passim
  in Christendom   17–19
  as a 'civilising force'   29–31
  within the EU   6–7, 13–14, 200–1
  within a Global Union   197–8
  and globalisation   124–8, 212
  in Hobbes   18–20, 27
  managing relations between nation-states   2–3, 6, 92–3, 203
  in modern Europe   4–7, 41
  the nation becomes the nation-state   22–7, 31–2, 200
  and the sharing of sovereignty   43, 54
  see also Global Governance

Nationalism   4, 6, 24–5, 143–4, 162, 201
  need to 'de-legitimate' nationalism   143
  nationalism and supranationalism   162
NATO (North Atlantic Treaty Organisation)   1, 42, 45, 96, 101, 116–23, 128, 132, 169, 211, 223
  after the Cold War   117–19
  Global NATO   118, 120–1
  as an inter-governmental body   119
  compared to OSCE   121–2
neo-functionalism   12, 177
neo-realism   11, 156
Nesadurai, Helen   138
Netherlands, The
  approach to European Coal and Steel Community   42
  and the *Van Gend en Loos* case   56
Nicaragua   88, 143
Nice, Treaty of   55
Non-governmental organisations (NGOs)
  and globalisation   124
  and the IMF   104
North American Free Trade Association (NAFTA)   102, 144, 159
Norway
  and EU membership   158, 166, 199

Obama, Barack (US President)   170
OECD (Organisation for Economic Cooperation and Development)   42, 48, 101–2, 109–11, 128, 155
OEEC (Organisation for European Economic Cooperation)   5, 7, 42, 47–8, 109, 154
OPEC (Organisation of Petroleum Exporting Countries)   1
'open regionalism'   158–61, 227
Organisation for African Unity (OAU) *see* African Union
Organisation for Security and Cooperation in Europe (OSCE)   101, 116, 121–2
  compared to NATO   121–2
  relations with UN   121

Ortega, Martin   216
Orviedo, General (Paraguayan politician)   143
Orwell, George   156
Osborne, John   17, 217
Own Resources
  in the EU   59–61
  absence of in the UN   94

Padoa-Schoppa, Tommaso   69, 221
Paris, Treaty of (1951)   39
Parsons, Craig   45
Patriotism   2–3, 6, 31, 36, 198, 203
Patten, Chris (EU Commissioner)   157, 163
Peterson, John   216
Peyrefitte, A.   219
Pleven Plan   43, 45, 187
Poland
  help in meeting Copenhagen criteria   90
  joins NATO   117
Political conditionality   190–1, 193–4, 210
Pompidou, Georges (French President)   60
Portugal
  measures to help it adjust to single market   68–9
  Salazar dictatorship   71

Qualified Majority Voting (QMV)   51, 67

Rachman, Gideon   171
'realism'   11, 200
Rehn, Olli (EU External Relations Commissioner)   163–4
'ring of friends'   9, 157, 165
Romania
  admitted to EU   147, 162
Rome, Treaties of   45–8, 56, 63, 187, 190
Roosevelt, Franklin D. (US President)   41, 97, 202–3
Russia
  and Council of Europe   99
  and G7   112, 114
  and Global Union   100, 198
  and IMF   106
  and NATO   119–21
  and OECD   111
  and Ukraine   165–7
Russian Orthodoxy   21
Ruys, Tom   152

Saint-Simon, Henri de   129, 196–7, 201
Saint-Pierre, Abbot   202
Sanader, Ivo (Prime Minister of Croatia)   171
Sarkozy, Nicholas (French President)   168, 170
Scheingold, Stuart   12
Schengen Agreement   70, 158, 199
Schiffer, Walter   28
Scholte, Jan Aart   128, 188, 212–13
Schücking, Walter   202
Schuman, Frederick   28
Schuman, Robert (French Foreign Minister)   5–6, 34, 37, 44, 154, 205, 208, 214
  Schuman Declaration   42
  Schuman Plan   38, 40, 48, 133
Schwebel, Judge   89
Seattle protests 1999   107
Second World War   5, 28, 79, 103, 109–10, 132, 176–7, 185, 202–3, 213
Security Council *see* UN
Shackleton, Michael   216
Shakespeare, William   23
Single Currency   70
Single European Act   55, 67–9
Single Market   57, 65, 68–70, 145
  compared to 'common' foreign and security policy   173
Slaughter, Anne-Marie   8, 125–7, 129, 212
Slovakia
  and the Meciar government   162
Smith, Karen   162, 169
Social Contract   2, 18–20, 32, 109
Soderbaum, Friedrich   131–2, 224
Sohn, Louis B.   28
Solana, Javier (EU High Representative)   166
Solingen, Etel   146

South African Development Community
  compared to South African Customs Union 225
South America
  colonialism and 141–3
  as a 'global player' 146
  cultural homogeneity 212
South Mediterranean
  and the EU 158–61, 166–7, 170
  and a Global Union 192
  compared to Western Balkans 165
Sovereignty, sharing
  basic nature of
    binding law 35, 53, 129, 184
    effectively managed by the EU 5, 14, 33, 126–7, 147, 155–6
    and European Community Law 56–9
    and the formation of the ECSC 38–9
    institutional demands of 35–6, 96, 134–6, 140–1, 146–8
    and marriage 53
    and the Treaties of Rome 46–8, 53
    key to global governance 2, 5–7, 12, 14, 59, 100, 127, 129, 147–8, 151, 155, 171–2, 175–86, 195–214
  reaction to
    British attitude towards 40–2, 45
    French attitude towards 35–6, 42–5, 50–2
    British and French attitudes compared 45, 50, 52
    Avoided by the UN 80, 98, 203
  relation to organisations apart from the EU
    African Union 132–6
    ASEAN 139–41
    Commonwealth and IFO 116
    Council of Europe 36–7
    G7, G20 113–14
    Global Food Security Community 181, 184, 186, 193–4
    Global Union 187–9, 193–4
    MERCOSUR 144–5, 148
    NATO and 119–20
    OECD 110
    OSCE 121
    UNASUR 145–6
    Union of the West 123–4
    World Trade Organisation (WTO) 108, 129
Soviet Union
  and ASEAN 136
  and Cold War 117
  and European recovery after World War II 38
  relations with the US 41
  and League of Nations 79, 221
  supports UN veto 203
Spaak, Paul-Henri (Belgian Foreign Minister) 46–7, 219
Spain
  and General Franco 71
  measures to help it adjust to Single Market 68–9
  measures to help it meet demands of monetary union 70
  South America and 141
Spanish-American War 142
Spengler, Oswald 122
Stabilisation and Association Process 163
Stalin, Joseph 41, 44
Star Chamber 202
state of nature 18–20, 32, 124, 197
Stiglitz, Joseph 103
Streit, Clarence 118
Structural Foreign Policy 194
Structural Funds *see* Cohesion Policy
Suez Crisis (1956) 47
Suganami, Hidemi 33, 89, 92, 203
Superstate *see* World State
Supranationalism 6, 8, 12, 34–5, 162, 183, 186, 209–11, 217
  definition of 35
  compared to inter-governmentalism 11, 13, 35–6, 48, 55–6, 108, 110, 125
  see also sovereignty, sharing
Switzerland
  and EU membership 158, 166, 199
  Swiss Confederation 202

Taft, William (US President)   28
Tanaka, Toshiro   148
Taylor, P.   86–7
Tebbit, Norman   221
Telò, Mario   137, 157, 162
Thakur, R.   10
Thatcher, Margaret (British Prime Minister)   67–9, 220–1
Thatcherism   62, 220
Thomson, David   22
Torres, Camillo   143
Thirty Years War   18, 20, 32
Trade liberalisation
  and the EU   160
Treaties, the making and unmaking of   33, 35, 53, 109
Treaty of Franco-German friendship   51, 53
Treaty on European Union (TEU)   158
Tsoukalis, Loukas   67
Tudjman, Franjo (President of Croatia)   171
Turkey
  Arab League and,   146
  British policy and   123
  as candidate for EU   158, 161, 169–70, 210
  NATO and   118

Ukraine
  and EU entry   165–70, 228
  and NATO   118–19
  'Orange Revolution'   166, 168
  relations with Russia   119, 165, 167, 170
  joins WTO   168
Ulribe, Alvaro (President of Colombia)   145
UN (United Nations)   Chapter Five, passim
  basic structure of UN
    Administrative Council on Cooperation (ACC)   90
    agencies' of UN   83–7, 89–91, 95, 99, 102, 105, 186
    Charter of UN   78, 80, 92–3, 96–7
    Economic and Social Council (ECOSOC)   84, 87, 90–1, 98, 103, 105, 111, 222
    Emergency Special Session of   82–3
    General Assembly   36, 82–3, 93–4, 98, 104, 114, 154, 175
    International Court of Justice   81–3, 88–91, 93, 98, 143–4, 205
    International Criminal Tribunals created by Security Council   89, 91
    Security Council   8, 78–83, 88–9, 91–4, 96, 98, 120, 127, 148, 175, 203, 205, 222
  organisational problems of UN
    corruption and waste in   95, 186
    'democracy caucus'   122
    food security, handling of   181–7
    funding   94, 99, 129, 184
    inefficiency of   87–91, 95–7, 218
    lacks legal basis for its activities   83, 91–4, 97–8
    military organisation of   96–7
    'pre-emptive self-defence'   93, 222
    reform of   28, 81–2, 90, 97–8
    'Responsibility to Protect' (R2P)   31, 91–2
    Uniting for Peace procedure   82
    veto power within   80, 92, 120, 203, 205, 221
  relations with other bodies
    African Union   134–6
    ASEAN   140
    EU   x, 83–4, 87–8, 94–5, 98–9, 148, 151–5, 169–70, 174–5, 183–4, 204
    other global organisations   84, 89–91, 97–100, 105
    Global Union   78, 99
    League of Nations   79–80, 88–9
    OSCE   121
    UNASUR   145, 148
UNASUR (Union of South American Nations)   141, 145–6, 204
  and African Union   145

and EU 145–6
and UN 145
UNESCO 98, 152
Union of the West (*Union occidentale*) 102, 122
  and a 'Gaullist' approach 123
  and the sharing of sovereignty 123
'Unipolar' world 156
United Kingdom *see* Britain
United Nations Conference on Trade and Development (UNCTAD) 94
United Nations Development Programme (UNDP) 94
United Nations Framework Convention on Climate Change (UNFCCCC) 100, 188
United Nations Industrial Development Organ (UNIDO) 94
United Provinces 202
US (United States)
  relations with economic organisations
    APEC 137
    East Asian Economic Group 137
    International Monetary Fund (IMF) 104–5
    International Trade Organisation (ITO) 107
    OEEC 48
    World Bank 106
    WTO 108
  relations with other organisations
    ASEAN 136–8
    Global Union 198
    International Court of Justice 88, 143
    International Criminal Court 90, 222
    League of Nations 79
    Middle East Partnership Initiative 161
    NATO 121–2
    OSCE 121–2
  relations with other parts of the world
    Afghanistan 92
    South America 142–3, 146
    the Soviet Union after WWII 41, 43
    the 'west' 123
  other issues concerning the US
    bilateral trade deals 146
    European recovery after WW2 38, 41–2, 211
    federalism 201–2
    UN veto 203
Utrecht, Treaty of 202

Van Gend en Loos 70
Vancke, Jeffrey 50–1, 219
Vandenberg, Arthur (US Senator) 80
Vasconcelos, Alvaro 143, 158
Venezuela
  and Hugo Chavez 143
  dispute with US at WTO 108
Versailles, Treaty of 79
Victoria, (British Queen) 25
Vienna declaration on human rights (1993) 90
Vinde, Pierre 110

Wagner, Allan 145
Waltz, K. 156
'war on terror' 92
Warsaw Pact 117, 169
Washington, Treaty of (1949) 116–19
Weber, Eugen 24
Webster, C.K. 98
Weiss, Thomas G. 10, 128, 195–6
'West', concept of 122–3
Western European Union (WEU) 45
Westphalia, Treaty of (1648) 17–18, 32, 202
  Westphalian system 21, 32, 155, 213
  Post-Westphalian age 92–4
White, Nigel D. 80, 85, 90, 97
Wilson, Harold (British Prime Minister) 50
Wolczuk, Kataryna 168, 228
Woods, N. 104
Woolf, Leonard 203
World Bank 85–7, 91, 95, 101–2, 105–7, 109–10, 128, 152, 222

World Court 28, 188
World Economic Council 111
World Food Programme 94, 182–4, 193
World Health Organisation (WHO) 152
World Order Models Project (WOMP) 203, 221
World Parliament 202
World state 13, 28, 31, 33, 197, 201–2, 209, 217
World Trade Organisation (WTO) 1, 85, 101–2, 106–10, 129, 167, 179, 223
  Dispute settlement procedure 89, 107–9, 129
  Doha Development Round 108, 129
  and EU 179
  and UN 89
Wouters, Jan 152–3

Yanukovich, Viktor (President of Ukraine) 167
Yaoundé Convention 190
Young, Hugo 42
Yuschenko, Viktor (President of Ukraine) 166–7
Yugoslavia
  conflict in the 1990s 5, 89, 162–3

Zamora, N.A. 99
Zielonka, Jan 206–7